FOUR YEARS ON THE
GREAT LAKES, 1813–1816

FOUR YEARS ON THE GREAT LAKES, 1813–1816

The Journal of Lieutenant David Wingfield, Royal Navy

Don Bamford & Paul Carroll

Foreword by Barry Gough

NATURAL HERITAGE BOOKS
A MEMBER OF THE DUNDURN GROUP
TORONTO

Edited by Jane Gibson
Copy-edited by Allison Hirst
Proofread by Jason Karp
Designed by Erin Mallory
Printed and bound in Canada by Webcom

Library and Archives Canada Cataloguing in Publication

Wingfield, David, ca. 1789-1863
    Four years on the Great Lakes, 1813-1816 : the journal of Lieutenant
David Wingfield, Royal Navy / by Don Bamford and Paul Carroll.

Includes bibliographical references and index.
ISBN 978-1-55488-393-6

    1. Wingfield, David, ca. 1789-1863--Diaries. 2. Canada--History--War of
1812--Personal narratives, British. 3. Canada--History--War of 1812--Naval
operations. 4. Ontario, Lake (N.Y. and Ont.)--History, Naval--19th century.
5. Sailors--Great Britain--Diaries. I. Bamford, Don II. Carroll, Paul, 1944-
III. Title.

FC443.W55A3 2009   971.03'4092   C2009-900300-7

1 2 3 4 5   13 12 11 10 09

Conseil des Arts du Canada   Canada Council for the Arts   Canadä   ONTARIO ARTS COUNCIL / CONSEIL DES ARTS DE L'ONTARIO

We acknowledge the support of the **Canada Council for the Arts** and the **Ontario Arts Council** for our publishing program. We also acknowledge the financial support of the **Government of Canada** through the **Book Publishing Industry Development Program** and **The Association for the Export of Canadian Books**, and the **Government of Ontario** through the **Ontario Book Publishers Tax Credit** program, and the **Ontario Media Development Corporation**.

Care has been taken to trace the ownership of copyright material used in this book. The author and the publisher welcome any information enabling them to rectify any references or credits in subsequent editions.

J. Kirk Howard, President

www.dundurn.com
Published by Natural Heritage Books
A Member of The Dundurn Group

Front cover: On October 14, 1814, lightning struck the HMS *St. Lawrence* while she sailed on a shakedown cruise. There was significant, but repairable damage, and several crewmembers were killed. Painting by Peter Rindlisbacher. Reprinted with the permission of the artist. Back cover: An aerial view of Wingfield Basin. Courtesy of Telfer Wegg.

Dundurn Press	Gazelle Book Services Limited	Dundurn Press
3 Church Street, Suite 500	White Cross Mills	2250 Military Road
Toronto, Ontario, Canada	High Town, Lancaster, England	Tonawanda, NY
M5E 1M2	LA1 4XS	U.S.A. 14150

We humbly dedicate this work to those soldiers, seamen, and militia of both sides of the conflict in the War of 1812–14, who served King or Commander-in-Chief and country, in a foreign and somewhat hostile land. Many of these men received very little credit for their efforts and sacrifices.

Both sides produced men of high levels of bravery and excellent leadership. Major-General Sir Isaac Brock, K.B. and Captain Oliver Hazard Perry, USN, were honoured by outstanding monuments erected in memory of their battles. Others were remembered in the history books with only a few lines, or at most, a few pages.

The experiences of David Wingfield, away from the battle scenes, are unique in several respects. We hope this work will properly honour him and his compatriots.

CONTENTS

MAPS

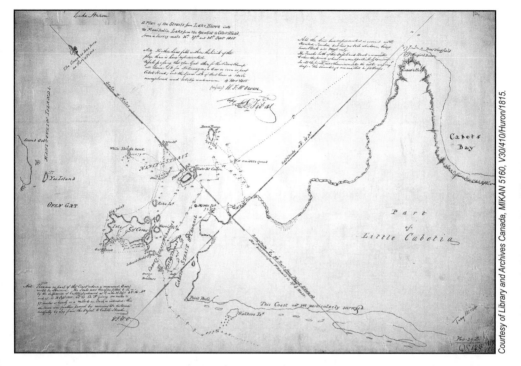

Map 1: *A Plan of the Straits of Lake Huron into the Manitoolin Lake from the Open Gat to Cabot's Head from a Survey made 26th, 27th, and 28th Sept. 1815* by W.F.W. Owen. This sketch map, drawn on linen, is the first map depicted of the entrance to Georgian Bay and the passage across to Wingfield Basin at Cabot Head. It is noteworthy that many of the original names given to islands and landmarks have remained to this day, yet several others have been lost, altered slightly, or completely changed. Isle of Coves is now Cove Island, Point Hurd is Cape Hurd, Walkers Island is Baptist Island, and Nancy Strait is not named in any way on today's nautical charts. The Bruce Peninsula was called Little Cabotia by Owen and his company of assistant surveyors in 1815.

ACKNOWLEDGEMENTS

In their usual fashion, staff at the Royal Ontario Museum, the Art Gallery of Ontario, the New York Public Library, London (Ontario) Public Library, and the D.B. Weldon Library at the University of Western Ontario, have all made resources available as requested. The Great Lakes Cruising Club and The New York State Canal Corporation, through Carmella R. Mantello, have provided helpful clarifications. Research material has been accessed through the Maritime Museum of the Atlantic. The various websites for the General Register Office for the United Kingdom and www.Ancestry.com have been accessed numerous times for the confirmation of genealogical data.

We are indebted to the staff at Library and Archives Canada, particularly G. Déry, librarian, and T. Dubé, military archivist, for helping us track down more information about the source of the Wingfield journal. The Archives of Ontario has also been used as a resource. Paul Adamthwaite, of the Archives and Collections Society, Picton, Ontario, has provided resource assistance several times.

Barry M. Gough is a well-known and acclaimed Canadian historian, writer, and sailor, well acquainted with the life and times of the early nineteenth century. He is a former professor of history and university research professor at Wilfrid Laurier University, 1972 to 2004, after which he retired to the area of his native Victoria, British Columbia. He has spent many summers cruising the Georgian Bay and Lake Huron area on his 32-foot sloop, *Danserye*, based out of Penetanguishene. His sailing experiences and his historical research led to the completion of two books on the War of 1812: *Fighting Sail on Lake Huron and Georgian Bay, The War of 1812 and Its Aftermath* and *Through Water, Ice and Fire: Schooner* Nancy *of the War of 1812*. Gough's informed perspectives have provided valuable reference points for our own research, and for consultation, as this work on David Wingfield has evolved. We have cited his contributions in our bibliography and in a number of endnotes — and want to acknowledge especially his support in finalizing this document. His long-standing career as a professor at the university level, his contributions to esteemed international historical societies, and his legacy of written history in his numerous books and other publications are commendable. We especially appreciate his time and effort in preparing a foreword for this book.

We are indebted to Patrick Folkes, Tara, esteemed Bruce County historian, who first provided contact information for the Wingfield Family Society, and for providing reference sources for original maps, photographs, and an historical description of the Georgian Bay coast along Cape Hurd. Whenever needed, he was but a phone call or an email away!

While the reference cited as the Wingfield Family Society can be acknowledged rather anonymously as a helpful resource, we feel that we must name, in particular, Jocelyn Wingfield, a key historian within the Society, along with Lee Preston, Bob Wingfield, and Wally Goodman. *Wingfield Family Society Newsletter* editor, Zella Morrow, must be recognized for her assistance in creating an electronic format for the David Wingfield Family Tree shown as Appendix A to this volume. Mick Heath, search room assistant at the St. Martin Parish of the Church of England in Horsley, should also be noted for his efforts in trying to find the burial information for our David Wingfield. Colonel Peter Trustram Eve must be acknowledged for his on-site efforts at Horsley to search the churchyard, albeit unsuccessfully, for the actual tombstone. The inscriptions on many of the nineteenth-century markers have been eroded beyond recognition.

Special mention is required for Merilyn Hywel-Jones, who, at the last minute, uncovered important new information about David Wingfield's service record and some of his activities over the years of his retirement on half pay. Without this information, we would have lost the flavour of Wingfield's final years, the sadness, and the somewhat tragic end to an otherwise esteemed career and fine set of accomplishments in the Lake Service for the Royal Navy. Merilyn is a military, naval, and graveyards researcher "of the very top grade," according to Jocelyn Wingfield, through whom we were able to acquire her research services in the United Kingdom.

Ina Toxopeus, current chair of the Friends of Cabot Head, provided information for Appendix F on that topic. John Tozer assisted in the search for appropriate illustrative material from the Wingfield Basin area. Ann Method Green, public relations chair, DeTour Reef Light Preservation Society, and Brian S. Jaeschke, registrar for Mackinac State Historic Parks, assisted in the search for contemporary photographs for that area west of Manitoulin Island.

Heidi Hoffman, artist, who contributed to Don Bamford's last book, *Freshwater Heritage*, has once again produced a number of drawings and maps to illustrate the text. It is also appropriate to acknowledge the fine artwork of Don Bamford's distinguished friend, the internationally acclaimed maritime artist Charles L. "Chick" Peterson, who provided original paintings for *Freshwater Heritage*, one of which, *The* Nancy *Under Sail* is included here. Tribute must also be paid to the late O.K. "Ozzie" Schenk for his majestic painting of the HMS *St. Lawrence* under full press of canvas. Neither can we omit recognition for the wonderful images of Peter Rindlisbacher of the Canadian Society of Marine Artists, for his dramatic painting of the cover image showing the mighty *St. Lawrence* at the moment she is struck by lightning on her maiden voyage and for his images in the colour plates section.

Finally, our acknowledgements would be incomplete without the mention of copy editor Allison Hirst of Dundurn Press, and editor Jane Gibson and publisher Barry Penhale of Natural Heritage Books, now a Member of the Dundurn Group, for ongoing guidance and inspiration to complete this work. Jane, especially, must be acknowledged for her relentless penchant for detail as the editing process was completed. She is truly a driving force.

And Mary Carroll, Paul's wife, has assisted with proofreading and checking the sense of the language on numerous occasions as both Don and Paul have exchanged countless email notes as this new adventure in long distance, mostly electronic, collaboration has unfolded.

A NOTE ABOUT
THE TITLE OF THE JOURNAL

The diary held by Library and Archives Canada was originally described as the *Com. David Wingfield Papers*. Wingfield was a little more verbose with his actual title: *Four Years on the Lakes of Canada in 1813, 1814, 1815 and 1816 by a Naval Officer Under the Command of the Late Sir James Lucas Yeo, K^t., Commodore and Commander-in-Chief of H.M. Ships and Vessels of War Employed on the Lakes*. Wingfield added: *Also Nine Months as Prisoner of War in the United States of America*. The Library and Archives Canada reference number is MG24F18.

FOREWORD
BY BARRY GOUGH

About four decades ago I began a personal odyssey to examine the maritime roots of Canada's history. I am not the first to launch forth on this great chart of the Canadian experience though I have already probably outlived all who have gone before in this enterprise — and I am by no means near the end of the saga. The seas and waters of Canada are complex in their geographical features, and an historian such as myself learns in the course of day-to-day work that the Arctic is much different from the Pacific Coast just as the Great Lakes are different from the Atlantic shore. Environments dictate the forms of human activity. Yet the seas bind Canada together, and our great cities, with one or two exceptions, are portals on salt and fresh water. Although Canada fronts on the United States along our southern boundary and juts up against Alaska on our far northwestern limit, we Canadians are a maritime people. We may not proclaim this fact but it lies in our past and in our present occupations. We depend on water communication for much of our trade, and in times past the command of the oceans was a vital determinant in what would transpire on the battlefields of Upper and Lower Canada. To all of these themes and sub themes I have been drawn, and the experience has been refreshing and rewarding. So it is with the authors who have brought David Wingfield's writings into print — at last and for all to enjoy.

The War of 1812 occurred at a time in world affairs when all was topsy-turvy. Napoleon and his revolutionary army had not been beaten, and was fighting its Russian campaign. The United States, which had fought off the British in its Revolutionary War, was still seething with objections and complaints concerning what American politicians, statesmen, and journalists regarded as the overbearing attitude of the British, particularly as expressed in measures to seize British seamen sailing in American ships. But there was another reason the Americans were sore: in the continental interior, Canadian fur traders and British military personnel, who ran the Indian Department, had been successful in winning the Native nations over to the British imperial cause. It was this last theme that brought, and required, the British to send military power into the heartland.

Every cannon, every hank of rope, every pound of ammunition had to be brought via the St. Lawrence River system. From Quebec to Montreal, then to Kingston and York, then to Fort Erie to Detroit, then to Michilimackinac, Sault Ste. Marie and beyond, the power of the British was expressed in one long line characterized by its precarious nature and exposure to the enemy on its flanks. Lieutenant Wingfield was but one naval officer sent to the Lakes theatre, but what sets him aside from so many others of the Royal Navy in the Lakes command was that he kept a journal. Others may also have done so, but it is Wingfield's that has survived, and a very fine journal it is, too — not the crabbed and brittle statements that have characterized so many such attempts at good literary form. It is clear from this text that Wingfield was not only well educated; he was a perceptive and sensible recorder of the many experiences that naval service, including his being for a time a prisoner of war in American hands, had brought his way.

The War of 1812 was fought over three years. The campaigning began in the spring and concluded by the fall, and then the preparations would begin anew. We are given in this text a view of the wild state of the north country of Canada and, at the same time, a portrait of the much more developed towns and farms of the American interior. The difference in the states of development is striking. For this reason, and others, Wingfield's text is an important document in the social and urban history of Upper Canada and the northeastern United States.

Don Bamford and Paul Carroll, partners in this historical enterprise, are to be lauded for making a work of this sort accessible to the reading public. It would have been so easy to let the original sit at National Archives Canada, where serious researchers might consult it. But, by making it accessible to the general readership, our authors have crossed the boundary between the professionals and the generalists. It is clear that they possess a passion for things historical, especially those things marine in nature. They know full well that it is from firm knowledge of what happens in the local spheres that a broader understanding can develop of national and even international history. Much harping has been done about Canadians not studying or knowing their history, but is this really so? They know that their history is different from that of the United States, Mexico, or the United Kingdom, and they know that our institutions are different. What may be missing in the Canadian historical psyche is a form of déjà vu — that the same old stories have been told time and time again. We need fresh voices. We need new interpretations. We need new heroes and new heroines, and we could use a few more anti-heroes and anti-heroines as well (for they are there, too, in our past).

David Wingfield is one of the new level of personalities that need to be brought into our historical discussions and knowledge. He is like

Courtesy of the Canadian Coast Guard.

Cabot Head Light Station and portion of Wingfield Basin, *circa* 1970s. This aerial shot is taken from the collection of lighthouse records compiled by Ron Walker, Department of Fisheries and Oceans, Canadian Coast Guard, Parry Sound, Ontario.

Lieutenant Miller Worsley of the ill-fated schooner *Nancy*, a figure who deserves to be better known. Today Lieutenant Wingfield is commemorated in various place names of Ontario, notably Wingfield Basin, east of Tobermory and just west of Cabot Head. I have anchored there many times, safe from wind and surf outside. It is a lovely basin, a haven for boaters and birdwatchers. Its narrow entrance leads to a large basin that is formed on its west and south sides by limestone ramparts. That it is named for a famed young British naval officer of the War of 1812 adds to its charm and reminds us, as this book does, that those who served King and Country answered a higher calling, one whose legacies still endure.

Wingfield Basin is atypical of Great Lakes harbours, for it seems to be a giant sink formed by a collapse of limestone bluffs east of Tobermory. The harbour provides safe anchorage for small vessels and is a superb yachtsman's retreat, secure as it is from raging wind and surf that comes with stiff northers. It is a tight entrance and exit, and can only be safely navigated by lining up two illuminated range markers and keeping on that line. In earlier days, Wingfield Basin was a place for squared timbers to be gathered in large rafts for outward shipment. Later it became a fishermen's night refuge harbour. Nowadays it is a recreational haven, heritage site of note, and an excellent birdwatchers' paradise. A small dock has been placed by the Friends of Cabot Head to permit easy shore access to the restored lighthouse, museum, and trails areas.

— Barry Gough

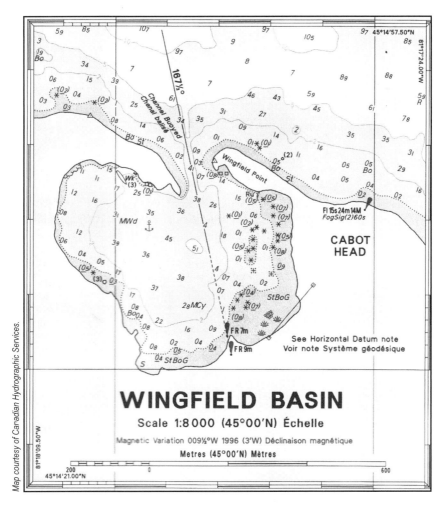

Map courtesy of Canadian Hydrographic Services.

Map 2: Canadian Hydrographic Service (CHS) chart for Wingfield Basin. Wingfield Basin lies almost directly west of Cabot Head lighthouse, Georgian Bay, where the forested ramparts of the Bruce Peninsula extend south to the bottom of the bay. This small, circular harbour was surveyed by William Fitz William Owen, RN, and named for his fellow officer, Lieutenant David Wingfield, who assisted with part of the survey work in 1815. The results of these expeditions appeared in British Admiralty and later CHS charts down to the present day. The plan of Wingfield Basin comes from the 1996 edition Owen Sound to Cabot Head. (Caption by Barry Gough.)

PREFACE
BY PAUL CARROLL

Collaborating on a second book with Don Bamford has been an edifying experience. It has further expanded my knowledge and understanding of Canadian history as well as provided me with another opportunity to share a passion for maritime heritage with a knowledgeable, thoughtful, and studious mariner who has been a sailing mentor and a good friend for more than three decades. It is an honour to pool resources in such a project designed to bring one more aspect of Canadian history to the attention of the general reader who shares more than a passing interest in our intricate heritage.

The first project with Don was to assist with the completion of the manuscript for *Freshwater Heritage: A History of Sail on the Great Lakes, 1670–1918* and to research visuals and supplementary materials for the text. Its publication was a highly successful venture and supported Don's effort to bring a comprehensive history of sailing on the Great Lakes to the attention of a popular readership. Prior to that partnership, I assisted Robert C. Lee with additional research, visuals, and technical and promotional support for his book *The Canada Company and the Huron Tract, 1826–1853*, as published by Natural Heritage Books in 2004.

My first contact with Natural Heritage came almost two decades ago, around 1990, when I acted as editor for the re-publication of a book by local author and raconteur, Gavin Green. The *Old Log School* has been a popular title with those who want to recall the way of life in pioneer times in rural areas of Ontario similar to Huron County.

My earlier efforts in writing Canadian history have been limited to the publication of short articles in local history and the authoring, editing, and publication of several successive volumes of the annual

Historical Notes, as part of the Huron County Historical Society, of which I am a life member. I have also written much about the marine history of the local community along the shores of eastern Lake Huron and have gathered major research information, as yet unpublished, about the ship-wreck *Wexford*, one of the long-lost vessels that fell victim to the Great Storm of November 1913. Its wreckage was only discovered in the year 2000, offshore, near Bayfield, in some twenty-five metres of water, while I was part of an underwater search and survey team with David L. Trotter, the well-known Great Lakes shipwreck aficionado, who has discovered more Great Lakes shipwrecks than any other person.

"The David Wingfield Diary," as it is described by Library and Archives Canada, has rested — the original out of circulation because of its fragile nature — in our national archives for the better part of a century, since it was first donated to be held there by a descendant of the junior officer, in late 1932. The journal notes have been consulted by historians from time to time, mainly for their contributions to our understanding of certain events in the War of 1812. To the best of our knowledge, this is the first time the complete journal has been transcribed, and that any effort has been undertaken, on a broader scale, to learn more about the author and his contributions to this era in our history.

Don Bamford acquired a photocopy of the sixty-eight-page, handwrit-ten notes in 1972. He has painstakingly transcribed the entire set of pages, preserving as much as has been practicable the authenticity of the original documentation, with only a few technical changes designed for the ease of the modern-day reader, as noted elsewhere. My own contribution to that transcribing task has been nominal and more technical in nature. Because of my own experience with the transliteration of documents related to land acquisition and leases in Upper Canada, in the same era, I hope I have been able to reduce the number of undecipherables in the journal to a minimum, thus supporting the ease of reading for our audience of current day heritage enthusiasts. I have also assisted Don with the expansion of his text and historical notes, and have compiled the biographical informa-tion about Wingfield himself. Finally, given Don's ripeness at age 89, I have been able to provide technical and literary support throughout, to supplant tired eyes, failing keyboard fingers, and other needs when necessary.

Let it be understood though, that Don, in spite of advancing years and failing health, is as sharp as the proverbial tack when it comes to the need for analysis and consideration of the best way to express a necessary point. Sometimes, he is unnecessarily intimidated by the reputation of the professional historians with whom, at times, he may offer a different opinion or set out an alternate interpretation of certain events or their locations. I have always encouraged that he speak out based on his own meticulous review of the evidence. Where we have chosen to speculate, beyond the availability of facts, we have both tried to indicate our shortcomings.

Don believes strongly that Canadian history should be presented in a manner that makes it as widely available as possible to the "common man," as he calls us. Further, it is his hope as an amateur historian, and my own wish as a retired educator, that such volumes can also find their way into the hands of students at the elementary and secondary school level. Such an introduction, it is hoped, will lead students forward to a more formal study of our history through the contributions of well-known professionals such as the Malcomsons and authors such as Barry Gough, and others listed in our bibliography for this text.

We have tried, not only to present an accurate rendition of Wingfield's writings, but also to amplify with extensive notes, the political and military situation of the time. Wingfield's writings convey, quite well, his perceptions of the social and cultural nature of the times in the northeastern United States. His observations offer a candid perception of life and survival techniques in the more isolated areas of Upper Canada during his postings on the Georgian Bay and Mackinac Island areas of northern Lake Huron.

With the assistance of key members of the Wingfield Family Society, we have been able to glean much information about David Wingfield's family, and have been able to speculate a little about his life in England during his post-service retirement years. There are a number of questions yet to be answered, but the current exercise has shed some additional light on a little-known Canadian historic figure for whom more attention is warranted. Information about the Wingfield Family Society is included in Appendix B.

If you were to visit the Cabot Head area of the northern Bruce Peninsula in Ontario, you would come across a point of land and a small, protected basin carrying Wingfield's name from 1816. Wingfield Basin, guarded by Wingfield Point and the Cabot Head Lighthouse, *circa* 1896, is nurtured by a small and enthusiastic group called Friends of Cabot

Head, where this story and other tales from the immediate area are celebrated. Wingfield Basin remains a popular small boat anchorage, visited annually by countless yachters who often use this secluded harbour as a stopping point while transiting Georgian Bay. A piece about the Friends group and its work is also included as Appendix F.

Painting by Paul Carroll.

Cabot Head Light, circa 1896. A watercolour painting with ink, showing the light station as it appeared when it was new.

Four Years on the Great Lakes, 1813–1816: The Journal of Lieutenant David Wingfield, Royal Navy is an easy but informative read. It is one way to get a glimpse of life and attitudes as seen by a young, enthusiastic junior naval officer, serving in the Great Lakes naval service at a time when our country was at loggerheads with our southern neighbour, where he had an opportunity to consider the perspectives from both sides of the border during his tenure in Upper Canada, including time as a well-treated prisoner of war. Wingfield was present here from May 15, 1813, until September 30, 1816.

As a final note, the concluding major edit of this manuscript took place while I travelled on board a small sailboat, plying those same waters surrounding Manitoulin Island as travelled by David Wingfield on his voyages in this same area. I have searched out the ruins of old Fort La Cloche, an isolated north shore outpost, similar to those established at the time of Wingfield and earlier, as supply depots and trading posts for those who ventured further beyond into the wilderness areas. It has been an inspirational and memorable experience — especially as I have swatted the descendants of those same pesky and oversized mosquitoes as described in Wingfield's own words in the pages of his journal.

— Paul Carroll

INTRODUCTION

The Source of the David Wingfield Journal

David Wingfield claims to have been born at Windsor, in Berkshire County, England. The date is most likely 1792.[1]

He entered the navy in 1806, at the age of fourteen, but the official details of his early years there are particularly sparse. His service period with the Royal Navy included his time in the Lake Service in Upper Canada in the midst of the hostilities of the War of 1812, where his role and that of his colleagues was to protect that colony from aggressive attacks by the American neighbours.

Our story about David Wingfield has been developed from a thorough review of his journal of notes, made following his time in Canada, during his early retirement years back in Stroud, in Gloucester, in southwest England. He wrote his memoirs in 1828. His recollections are vivid, and are detailed and complete. He has obviously worked from field notes of some sort, probably kept as a form of diary during his time with the Lake Service.

We would not have been able to tell most of his story in the absence of his journal. David Wingfield would largely have disappeared from accounts of Canadian history if it had not been for the thoughtful consideration of one of his descendants. A certain Miss Wingfield determined that a relic document in her possession, carefully retained and passed along by her antecedents, should be placed in the then Public Archives of Canada collection in Ottawa. She contacted the Canadian Government Trade Commissioner in Bristol, Douglas S. Cole, whose office arranged the transfer of the document. A December 28, 1932, note that accompanied the handwritten journal, reported that Miss Wingfield had delivered the diary that day to Cole, and that "Miss Wingfield is the daughter of the late Commander David Wingfield."[2] The original manuscript was stamped as received in Canada, January 19, 1933. Over the years several requests have been made to publish the diary, according to Timothy Dubé, Military Archivist, Library and Archives Canada, but he has never seen a finished work. He, along with Bruce County historian Patrick Folkes indicate that an extract was published in the *Dalhousie Review* as "David Wingfield and Sacketts Harbour."[3]

According to Jocelyn Wingfield, a key family historian: "The Wingfield Family Society has a pencil pedigree of this Stroud & Painswick, Gloucester Branch made up mainly from information gathered about thirty years ago and from that recently derived from Lee Preston, another family genealogist."[4] Jocelyn suggests that Miss Wingfield would have been a spinster who had inherited the David Wingfield diary, by 1932 was not expecting to marry, and would be the last Wingfield of her immediate line. He offered two possible theories about how the diary came to Ottawa. The first he has discarded as unlikely, but both versions are presented as a matter of interest:

"I further postulate," he says, in the first and now discounted instance, "that David Wingfield, RN, likely left his precious diary, not to his eldest son John, Tailor & Draper (1832–75), or to Thomas, Fireman, but to son number three, Henry Eggleton Wingfield, Fleet Engineer, Royal Navy."[5] He continues:

> It is possible that he may have held Henry's naval position in higher esteem than the sons in the merchant naval service. Henry was surely dead by 1933 and his son Arthur Eggleton Wingfield, (1887–92) predeceased him. This left several daughters: Gladys (b. ca. 1889, m. 1908, living or lived, admittedly, in London (Wandsworth), but no longer 'Miss Wingfield', and Amelia Bradley Wingfield (b.1895) who lived in Bristol. This leaves Edith Maude Wingfield (b.1892) and Dorothy Seymour Wingfield (b.1894). In 1932, Edith Maude would have been 40 and Dorothy Seymour — both spinsters — would have been 38.[6]

Edith and Dorothy were both born, incidentally, at Portsea, according to Wingfield Family Society records, on Portsmouth Harbour's edge, a big naval base. If either were still alive in 1932, one would need to know the Christian name, but in those days the senior, elderly spinster of the family would have been called "Miss Wingfield" by all and sundry; no first name would be used.

In 1932, at the time of the donation of the diary, had they survived, David Wingfield's daughters would have reached the ages of: Sarah, 97; Emma Lawson, 96; Louisa Ann, 91; Ellen Jane, 87; and Christiana (Christina/Christa) Mary, 78.

"There was a Norman Edward Wingfield in the RAF, born in 1899 at Stonehouse or Stroud, but he died in 1918, so possibly he had no descendants. If, however, he is the same line as Edward Wingfield one might be able to proceed further," suggests Jocelyn.[7]

Without further detail about the elusive Miss Wingfield, her exact status and relationship as a descendant of David remain uncertain.

However, with further research, and consideration of more genealogical evidence, Jocelyn Wingfield has revised his declarations about the arrival of the journal notes in Ottawa. He writes, "In Kelly's 1902 Directory of Bristol, on page 328, a Miss C.M. and a Miss S.W. Wingfield were listed as mistresses/teachers at the Ladies School at 6 Belgrave Place, Bristol."[8]

Jocelyn purports that they simply have to be Sarah W. Wingfield (b.1836, d.1903), and her sister Christiana (Christina/Christa) Mary Wingfield (b.1855). In the 1901 Census they were living together in Bristol. In the June quarter of 1902, Christiana Mary was married in Stroud, Gloucester. Since Sarah Wingfield of Bristol died in 1903, the mystery inheritor of the diary and its donor to Canada simply has to be Christiana Wingfield, David's youngest daughter. He suggests:

> Maybe — if it is worked through — one will see that the daughters kept returning to David's old home where they were raised in Stroud in the 1840s–60s when David was alive. Sarah, and her sister, Ellen Jane W. (d.1885) both died in Winchcombe, to the north of Stroud, where their sister Louisa Ann Shill lived, they presumably lodged

with the Shills, or at least died at their house. Such
speculation might be able to be confirmed by combing
through the census records in some additional detail.[9]

Looking down one of the steep streets of Stroud.

Courtesy of Jocelyn Wingfield.

Looking Down One of the Steep Streets of Stroud, sketch by Hugh Thomson,
1919. This would be one area surely frequented by David Wingfield and his
family members during their residence there. From *Highways and Byways in
Gloucestershire*, by Edward Hutton. London: Macmillan & Co. Ltd., 1932.

When David Wingfield died in 1864, sons John and Thomas had already fled the nest. Living at the old family home in Stroud would be David's second wife, Penelope, presumably all the daughters, and Henry, born 1850, the future fleet engineer, RN, according to Jocelyn. Strange the diary was not actually left to Henry in view of the naval connection, and, regardless of the ownership route or location of the diary, Jocelyn Wingfield currently concludes, "I presume Henry was dead before 1933."

One final wrinkle in this mystery is the existence of other family descendants with the first name Christiana or known as Christa. Christiana, David's granddaughter, daughter of eldest son John, or even one of his second son Thomas's children might have been our Miss Wingfield. David's daughter would have been seventy-eight, and John's Christiana, sixty-seven, in 1932. Perhaps it could have been either. The pencilled note on the actual document, by Trade Commissioner Cole, however, suggests that the donor of the actual document was indeed the daughter of David Wingfield.

Unless additional information is forthcoming about the acquisition of the original artifact, the correct transmission route will never be known with absolute certainty.

Leaving for Canada

In any event, according to his journal, David Wingfield sailed on the *Woolwich*, out of Plymouth, on March 31, 1813. He arrived at Quebec on the evening of May 5. On board with him were Commodore Sir James Lucas Yeo, four Royal Navy captains, eight lieutenants, twenty other warrant officers, and 450 seamen. He returned to England from Canada three years later, on September 30, 1816. We know little about his life after that date. However, his journal provides a vivid documentary of his adventures in that three-year period.

The original hand-written manuscript and our additional notes cover five periods in history and his life:

1. The early years, 1792 to March 31, 1813.
2. His service at Kingston from his arrival on May 16, 1813, to his capture by the Americans on October 5, 1813.
3. His experiences as a prisoner of war until he returned to Kingston in July of 1814.
4. His service at Kingston and adventures in Upper Canada until September 30, 1816.
5. The latter years, following his return to England.

What happened afterwards? As noted, we really know very little of his life after leaving Canada. One can only speculate about some of his activity, as we have done in the section on his biography.

David Wingfield: The Man

A review of his own writing tells us much about David Wingfield, the man, his values, his attitudes, and some of his beliefs.

Wingfield was a descriptive writer. It is apparent that he had obtained a reasonably good education and possessed a good command of the English language. His writing style was typical of the period with much of the sentence structure being conversational. The journal itself shows the flourish of an artistic hand, replete with the then-common overuse of upper case letters and inconsistent punctuation. Judged according to today's conventions, he had much to learn. Yet compared to other more official documents written in the same time period, his approach was at least as good as those who prepared such papers for the Crown in Upper Canada. The style and the structure of the 1835 lease for Goderich Harbour, for example, between the Canada Company and the Crown, compare closely to that used by Wingfield. These characteristics are also apparent in numerous Crown Patents as archived in their original handwritten form in the Public Archives of Ontario or those held by the Ontario Ministry of Natural Resources at their archives and records facility in Peterborough.

On the other hand, as to his general character, his willingness to accept responsibility, and his leadership abilities, it is easier to derive such interpretations from the content of his writings. Apparently, even though we have only his own words as evidence on the subject, he stepped forward with great courage, even for a military man. He showed an ongoing willingness to take on any assigned task and to see it through to completion. Wingfield worked quite independently at times and showed good leadership. It appears that he never had to discipline any of the men under his control. He got along well with his fellow officers and seemed to be at ease when in conversation with the American commander and officers, and with dignitaries he encountered during his stay in America.

Never did he hesitate to offer his own opinions about battle strategy. In his writing he did not show any indecision in suggesting the strengths and shortcomings of his superiors or their antagonists in the military setting. It is apparent that he could see beyond the limited horizons of his own position. Wingfield demonstrated a kind of global vision that would suggest he had the potential for promotion to a higher rank with broader responsibilities of leadership and decision-making. His commentary about battle strategies seemed to show that he could see the larger picture clearly and could consider alternative approaches that might have been more successful.

His brief expression of momentary despair and his display of deeper emotion when taken prisoner by the Americans can be forgiven. He saw all chance of promotion and the prospects for his future naval career radically altered to encompass the bleak prospect of incarceration and long-term confinement in a foreign land. He seemed temporarily, at least, to be taken quite aback. On the other hand, his apparent absence of overt emotional reaction is portrayed in his reviews of several rather gruesome, quite bloody events and battle encounters, all written in a quite matter-of-fact fashion. He seemed able to distance himself from the carnage in a particularly rational fashion.

It is obvious that he was not required to learn the modern day niceties of expressing some of his attitudes in a politically correct fashion. Witness his rather blunt observations about the Natives he encountered in the earlier days of his travels in the Lake Ontario areas. Such descriptions were not atypical of other writers of the time and reflect the blatant prejudices directed at a culture that differed from the conventional mores of a European society. Stories exaggerating the actions of Native warriors in battle were a major propaganda tool of the time, used by both sides. And seemingly he was not to recognize the destabilizing impact of European contact on the Native culture. However, given his much more analytical observations about the aboriginal peoples, as expressed later during his visits to the Manitoulin Island and Mackinac Island areas, it is clear that he was not restricted to a prejudiced and oftentimes stereotypical view. It is interesting that Wingfield ascribes negative changes that occurred in the demeanour and lifestyle of the Natives as happening only after their contacts and engagements with the Europeans who interacted with them. It is also noteworthy that he felt highly enough about one Native youngster that he arranged passage home with him at the end of his Lake Service, and placed the young lad in an English school for a period of time.

It would have been very interesting to learn about his activities when he found himself "on the beach"[10] once back in England. Did he farm or pursue any trade? Was he active in civic affairs in his community? Did he keep any other form of diary? Did he write for other purposes? Did he monitor the marine traffic and the naval activity in the nearby Gloucester harbour lands? Certain information, addressed later, indicates that he had great difficulty making ends meet. He attempted to supplement his modest naval pension income as a shopkeeper, but in what goods we have no information. At this stage, we know nothing more about his labours or his recreational pursuits. We can only speculate about what he might have done either to maintain his financial solvency or to amuse himself.

David Wingfield: The Naval Officer

Likewise, we are puzzled about whether he actually remained at the rank of lieutenant throughout these years. According to military archivist Timothy Dubé of Library and Archives Canada, "William R. O'Byrne's *A Naval Biographical Dictionary*, published by John Murray, 1849, lists David Wingfield, upon his 1816 return to England as Lieutenant from 20 March 1815, after which he was placed on half pay." The O'Byrne biography states, "… on his arrival he took up a commission bearing date

20 March 1815 ..."[11] apparently backdated to the time just following his appointment as an acting lieutenant in the field.

While earlier references to his rank in the Wingfield journal are to master's mate or lower, we accept that he was appointed to be acting lieutenant on February 15, 1815, at the time he was named as master of the *Surprise*, as he notes, just in passing, in his journal. His rank would have to be confirmed officially by the Admiralty at some time. We know from his service record that he received his official commission as lieutenant when he was discharged at half pay. It was not uncommon for a junior officer to have his rank confirmed at retirement, or even, at times, to be promoted. In Wingfield's case, the official *Officers Services*[12] record book shows the following: "Recommended for confirmation of Acting Order by Captain W.F.W. Owen, Senior Officer on the Lakes of Canada, inclosing parole of honour as an hostage for security of Seamen claimed by England as deserters, taken on American War Ships; and for conduct which appeared to meet his approbation on Lake Huron," dated February 26, 1816. The same record first shows him listed as lieutenant from March 21, 1815. While there are minor discrepancies in the dates used by various secondary sources, the official record book seems to be the best reference for documentation.

Was he ever actually promoted to the rank of commander? We have not been able to document the answer to this question. We know from the records, that as late as 1860, he was still listed as a lieutenant, just four years prior to his death.

One consideration is that, simply with the passage of time, as senior officers died off, according to Merilyn Hywel-Jones, a knowledgeable United Kingdom archives researcher, Wingfield would automatically inherit the rank of commander at some juncture. However, in 1861, in the census records for that year, he was still shown as a lieutenant. Did he receive a promotion then, in the last three years of his life? To date the question remains open as supporting documentation is yet to be discovered.

Further, his death certificate describes him as a "Greenwich Pensioner." Our knowledge indicates that some retired naval personnel, injured, ill, or otherwise disabled, entered special care at a hospital called Greenwich, some distance downstream and east of London, at the prime meridian, in the well-known village of that same name. The mandate of the hospital, as expressed in its founding charter of October 25, 1694, stated the hospital's purpose as, "the reliefe and support of Seamen serving on board the Ships and Vessells belonging to the Navy Royall... who by reason of Age, Wounds or other disabilities shall be uncapable of further service...and unable to maintain themselves."[13]

According to the Internet site for the National Maritime Museum,[14] the full name of the hospital was The Royal Hospital for Seamen, Greenwich: A Refuge for All. It has a remarkable history worth pursuing.

These naval retirees became known as Greenwich Pensioners. We are not aware of any system of ranks that were maintained within that group, although it is apparent that a committee or council of commissioners may have governed them. A posting on the website for Ancestry.com notes that there were also "out" patients on the Greenwich Pensioner list: "A Greenwich Hospital pensioner was a Royal Navy sailor who had been found to be suitable to be granted an army pension through disability or having completed full-service. He would subsequently be placed upon the Royal Hospital, Greenwich Board. The term therefore indicated that the man was a military pensioner as opposed to a civilian one. An out pensioner was one who lived at home and received his pension through an Admiralty agent. An in-pensioner was one actually resident at Greenwich."[15]

Also noted elsewhere, you will read that Wingfield's death certificate records him as "Commander" at half pay. A pencilled note on the front page of the journal copy from Library and Archives Canada also reads "Com.," perhaps a short form for the same term. (The normal abbreviation is "Cdr.") We do not know why this notation was added. We do have records to confirm that the Miss Wingfield who delivered the journal ascribed it to Commander David Wingfield, her ancestor — we believe, her father. It is possible that the title "Commander" was used simply as a term of endearment, worth more to an elderly sailor than an actual promotion from Admiralty House. To further confuse the issue, in the 1975 *Union List of Manuscripts in Canadian Repositories,*[16] he is noted, surely in error, as "Commodore Wingfield." Even after consideration of these matters, Wingfield's status as Greenwich Pensioner is still unresolved.

Wingfield may have been sick or injured in his last years. As such, he possibly could have been convalescing in Greenwich Hospital, which was the base hospice for these pensioners, or was an outpatient who stayed at home. He could have been referred to as the commander there too, at the stage when respect mattered more than official titles. If so, his rank, "Commander," most likely would be added to his death certificate.

We can make assumptions, but at this stage, there is no documentation to verify any of these speculations.

The Lake Service in Canada[17]

Why were David Wingfield and the other almost five hundred seamen and officers sent to Canada in 1813?

America had declared war on Britain and Canada on June 18, 1812. The British Army, Canadian Militia, and Provincial Marine desperately needed help to hold off the attackers. Britain started to gather trained officers, soldiers, and seamen from European, Caribbean, and other service theatres, and to transport them to Canada as quickly as possible.

Why did America declare war? Literally hundreds of books and articles have been published about the war. The authors have posited many reasons for its declaration.

To simplify a still contentious subject, the reasons frequently given are:

1. Britain's harassment of American shipping, to prevent supplies getting to Napoleon's forces, and to ensure that adequate supplies reached British forces. Great Britain had been fighting, at times almost single-handedly, against Napoleon's forces since 1792.[18]
2. Britain's habit of taking British seamen forcibly, from neutral vessels, and impressing them into the British navy.
3. British fur-trading activity in the areas northwest of what America claimed as its own, e.g. Ohio, Illinois, Mississippi, Wisconsin, Michigan, and even further west.
4. The presence of several British forts in these states, primarily to protect its fur trading activity, as well as to deal with and to influence the Native people.

The first two reasons were summed up by the War Hawks, primarily from Kentucky and the South with their oft-touted slogan, "Free Trade and Sailors' Rights."[19] The latter two reasons were largely suppressed or ignored as irrelevant by some in the Congress and other officials of Washington who promoted the war. The New England states were generally unenthusiastic about the war. They were heavily involved in trade and shipping with nations considered to be the enemy, and a war would cut into their livelihood. Some of these states even refused to supply militia forces, which Washington demanded. Some of the reluctant states even refused to contribute to the war loans sought by Washington to support and strengthen the war effort.

Other states, particularly in the South, were much more eager to support the war. They wanted new land for settlement and development. From their perspective, the fur trade profits should line their own pockets rather than those of the British. According to some, the British and the Native people, whom some called "sojourners on our land,"[20] must be driven out so American expansion could proceed unfettered.

It is worth mentioning that in this text we have retained the name "Indian" as it was commonly used throughout the nineteenth and twentieth centuries, until the current era. We respect that more contemporary terminology such as First Nations people or aboriginals might be more appropriate, but in the present context, we judge, with respect, that the usual nomenclature is more suitable in this context. It must be pointed out that both sides used the Native warriors as allies throughout the war. They, however, were fighting for what they deemed to be their own land, and would support the side that they felt had the best chance of settling a particular problem to their satisfaction.

There were others who felt that the War of Independence had not been completed satisfactorily and deemed that America had a divine right to control all of North America. They believed that the United States had a "manifest destiny"[21] to capture and hold all of British North America, and that the country to the north was a ripening fruit, just ready for the plucking. In 1810, in a speech to Congress, Henry Clay, Democratic-Republican senator from Kentucky, stated, "The conquest of Canada is in your power. I trust I shall not be deemed presumptuous when I state that I verily believe that the militia of Kentucky are alone competent to place Montreal and Upper Canada at your feet."[22]

The David Wingfield Papers are well known to historians of the War of 1812, on both sides of the border. The 68-page journal has long been available from Library and Archives Canada, in Ottawa.[23] Historians of this war have read his journal up to the point when peace was declared and the fighting ceased in mid-February 1815. After that, the attitude seems to be, "What could he ever do or say that was worth putting into a history book?" Consequently, half of his journal seems to have been mostly ignored.

His actions, both generally and specifically during the winter of 1815–16, however, were outstanding. They alone elevate his stature to rival that of famous adventurers and explorers, such as Sir John Franklin, Martin Frobisher, Robert Falcon Scott, and Henry Hudson.

It is for this reason that we are writing this text to bring that neglected part of his journal to public attention.

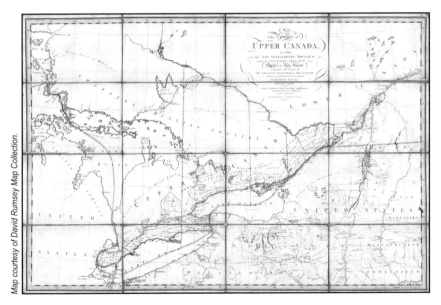

Map courtesy of David Rumsey Map Collection.

Map 3: Map of Upper Canada and Great Lakes Basin, *circa* 1800, compiled by David William Smyth, Esq., at request of Major John G. Simcoe. This map shows Upper Canada and the adjacent waterways as they were recorded in the decade prior to Wingfield's arrival in Canada.

Upper Canada at the Time of Wingfield's Arrival

The situation, in brief, at the time when a war was started between the two nations, neither of which wanted a war, might be described as follows.

At the time, British North America was very sparsely settled, particularly Upper Canada, which covered a large part of present-day Ontario. The total population of Canada was some 300,000, while in the United States of America there were almost eight million persons. The border that really mattered in this war extended from Michilimackinac in the west to Quebec City in the east, some nine hundred miles in total. To defend this border, Sir George Prevost, governor general and commander-in-chief of His Majesty's forces in the Canadas, 1811–15, commanded only around three thousand regular British soldiers and whatever militia he could organize. There were, of course, the Native tribes, as noted before, willing to fight on either side, but generally for their own interests. From the European perspective they were often considered unreliable, and at times a little more eager to kill the enemy than to take prisoners. Used to being independent, rarely could they be persuaded to obey orders given by the military officers. Both sides used the Native warriors, more for their ability to create terror than to fight the more regimented style of European warfare.

Settlement in Canada immediately adjacent to some of the border areas, particularly in the St. Lawrence River Valley and along the shores of Lake Ontario and Lake Erie was somewhat denser than in the Northern States. A large percentage of the population of Upper Canada — some historians estimate as much as 60 percent — were from America. These were settlers in search of land grants or opportunities not open to them south of the border. Except for the United Empire Loyalists, who had come as refugees from the American Revolution, these people had no loyalty to the Crown. The majority just wanted to be left alone, to get on with the heavy work of clearing land, planting and harvesting their crops, and building a sound future for themselves.

On the Great Lakes, the British had a larger fleet of vessels, but principally run by local men with very little naval training and even less experience in fighting. The British also had more ports and shipbuilding facilities along this part of the border. Kingston on Lake Ontario was the principal harbour, but York, the capital of the colony, generally seen as indefensible, and Fort Malden, located on the Detroit River, were also important. Chippawa, at Niagara Falls, was not used as a port until 1815. On the other hand, the United States had no ships functioning on Lake Ontario until war was seen to be imminent, but they did have a small shipyard at Detroit. However, once the war got underway, the yards at Sackets Harbor in New York, near the east end of Lake Ontario, and Presque Isle, along the American shore of Lake Erie, in Pennsylvania, became extremely important. The outcome of the war on the Great Lakes depended largely on which side could build and arm ships the faster.

Both sides made extensive use of the local militia, comprised largely of farmers and tradesmen, who were expected to serve and fight as called upon. Many did not do so, and many settlers on both sides made it clear that they wanted nothing more than to hold to their peaceful civilian life. There were some cases reported where a general and his officers would hold a war council and make plans for an attack to take place the next morning. Come the appointed time, many of their forces had either disappeared or, at times, some refused to obey the order to march. Situations like this happened on both sides. Desertion was not uncommon, even desertion to the enemy. Spying and other forms of disaffection resulted in arrests and, in some cases, sentences to jail, exile, or even to death by hanging.

Since military supplies for the British forces came primarily from England, they were slow to arrive. There were never enough provisions or munitions. Even some of the food for the troops, and fodder for the horses were transported from overseas. The situation was helped somewhat by settlers in New York, Vermont, Ohio, and Michigan providing additional supplies to the British forces. It was the American forces that had a great advantage in the matter of supplies. Almost all of their requirements for shipbuilding, fighting, and general sustenance could come from New York or Boston to Sackets Harbor, or from the Pittsburgh area to Presque Isle, Pennsylvania.

The war had not progressed appreciably up to May 16, 1813, when David Wingfield arrived on the scene at Kingston. There had been some skirmishes on Lake Ontario but nothing of consequence. Shipbuilding rushed on apace at Kingston, Fort Malden, Sackets Harbor, and Presque Isle.[24]

Military activities on land were another matter. On July 12, 1812, the Americans, under General William Hull, invaded Canada at Sandwich, now Windsor, but retreated on August 6 without accomplishing anything of importance. A week later, on July 17, 1812, the British, under Captain Charles Roberts, advancing from his base at Fort St. Joseph, immediately north of Passage de Tour in the St. Marys River, captured Fort Michilimackinac on Mackinac Island. A month later, on August 16, 1812, the British, under Sir Isaac Brock, captured Detroit.

Post at St. Joseph Island, 1804. The watercolour image, by Edward Walsh, illustrates a well-developed settlement on the island, with a number of out-buildings located beside the protective palisade. Daily visits from the Native people would supply needed fresh meat and seasonal fruit. The post was captured and burned by the Americans in 1813.

In the following spring, on April 29, 1813, the American fleet, under Commodore Isaac Chauncey attacked York. Major General Henry Dearborn captured the town, but Brigadier General Zebulon Pike and more than three hundred Americans were killed. The Americans withdrew to Sackets Harbor a few days later. On September 10, 1813, at the Battle of Lake Erie, the American Captain Oliver Hazard Perry defeated the British fleet under Captain Robert Heriot Barclay and captured the entire British fleet. This was the only major sea battle on the Great Lakes during the war.

Courtesy of United States Library of Congress, LC-USZC2-2913.

Perry's Victory on Lake Erie, September 10, 1813. This Currier and Ives print shows the American ships *Lawrence* and *Niagara* fighting various vessels from the British fleet during the Battle of Lake Erie.

Key Figures

The principal actors appearing on the war stage are identified below.

For the Canadian and British side:

Askin, Captain John: A member of a successful trading family based at Sandwich, now part of Windsor, across from Detroit. Askin was the Indian agent at Fort Mackinac on Mackinac Island. Although his title as captain is debatable, he was ranked a captain by the Indian Department of the British Army.

Barclay, Commander Robert Heriot: He joined the Royal Navy in 1797, and was commandant of the British naval forces on Lake Erie in 1813.

Barclay led the British fleet at the Battle of Put-in-Bay, was defeated, and badly injured. He returned to England, where he died in 1837.

Brock, Major General Sir Isaac: Administrator of Upper Canada and commander of the forces there in 1810–12. He led the forces to capture Detroit on August 16, 1812, and led the attack against invading American troops at Queenston Heights on October 13. Although the British were victorious, Brock was mortally wounded and died on the battlefield.

Bulger, Lieutenant Andrew H.: A member of the Royal Newfoundlanders, he served in many parts of Upper Canada, including Fort Mackinac.

Collier, Captain Edward: He joined the Royal Navy in 1796. He commanded a detachment in the Great March (see chapter one, note 1) in January 1813. Collier also served as captain on a number of vessels on Lake Ontario in 1813–14, and later on Lake Huron.

De Watteville, Major General Louis: Along with his regiment of 1,300 men, he was shipped from Spain to Quebec in the spring of 1813. He served in many campaigns.

Downie, Captain George: Commander of the British naval forces, Lake Champlain, 1814.

Drummond, Lieutenant General Sir Gordon: Appointed president of the colonial government and commander of the troops in Upper Canada in 1813. He took Sir George Prevost's place as governor general for a short period in 1815, Prevost having been recalled to explain his conduct of the Plattsburgh campaign of 1814.[25] He oversaw the British relocation, at arm's length, from Fort Mackinac to a site on Drummond Island.

Dunlop, Dr. William "Tiger": Physician, author, woodsman, soldier, politician, and raconteur, was fondly known as "The Warden of the Forests," in his role with the Canada Company.[26]

Le Couteur, Lieutenant John: A member of the 104th Foot, he came to Canada on June 21, 1812, where he served the entire war years and took part personally in the Great March. He was born the same year as Wingfield, but took the army route rather than the naval one for his military career.

Livingston, Robert: Employed by the army, he was a tough and active courier for the Indian Department.

McDouall (also spelled MacDowell), **Lieutenant Colonel Robert:** A member of the Royal Newfoundland Regiment, he was commander at Fort Mackinac in 1814.

McLean, Lieutenant Hector, RN: He was in charge of the *Drummond* (transport) when captured by the Americans at the same time as Wingfield was taken on the *Confiance*.

Mulcaster, Captain Sir William Rowe, RN: He joined the Royal Navy in 1793, at the age of eight, and served with Yeo in other theatres, including the Battle of Cayenne, with the Portuguese in 1809. He came to Canada with Yeo, and was knighted for his bravery at the battle known as the Burlington Races.[27] He was wounded in the attack on Oswego, and was sent to England to recuperate. He died in 1837.

Prevost, Sir George: Governor general and commander-in-chief of His Majesty's forces in the Canadas, 1811–15. He was recalled to England in 1815.

Vincent, Brigadier General John: Commander of the British forces in the Niagara Frontier during 1813.

Worsley, Lieutenant Miller, RN: Master of the *Nancy* at Nottawasaga, who scuttled her rather than let her fall into American hands.[28]

Yeo, Sir James Lucas, RN: Joined the navy in 1793 and was knighted for his success at the Battle of Cayenne, French Guiana, in 1809. He also received a knight's commandery of St. Benito d'Avis from the prince regent of Portugal, being the only Protestant ever so honoured. He was made commander-in-chief of the British naval forces on the Great Lakes in 1813. He served there from May 5, 1813, until March 1815. He continued on active service in the Royal Navy until his death in 1818, at the age of thirty-six.

For the American side:

Armstrong, John: The American secretary of war, 1813–14.

Chauncey, Commodore Isaac, USN: Commander of naval forces on the Great Lakes throughout the war.

Clay, Henry: Speaker of the House of Representatives, 1811.

Dearborn, Major General Henry: Governor of Michigan Territory, commander of the Army of the Northwest from April to August, 1812.

Gregory, Lieutenant Francis, USN: Continued in the navy, reaching the rank of admiral in 1862. He died at age seventy-six.

Harrison, William Henry: Commander of the Army of the Northwest from September 1812.

Macdonough, Commodore Thomas: Led the United States naval forces at Lake Champlain.

Madison, James: President of the United States of America, 1809–17.

Perry, Captain Oliver Hazard:[29] Was in command of naval forces on Lake Erie, 1813. He defeated the British at Put-in-Bay.

Sinclair, Captain Arthur: Commodore Chauncey's flag captain in the battle known as the Burlington Races, September 13, 1813.

Wilkinson, Major General James: Led the Army of the North. He led the American forces from Sackets Harbor down the St. Lawrence River to attack Montreal in October 1813. He suffered defeat at Chrysler's Farm.

Woolsey, Master Commandant Melancthon Taylor: Led American naval forces in several actions on Lake Ontario in 1813. He continued in command of the Lake forces at Sackets Harbor until 1824.

The Early Career of David Wingfield

David Wingfield entered the Royal Navy November 23, 1806, as second-class volunteer on board the *Ruby* (64)[30] with captains John Draper, Robert Hall, and Robert Williams. A year later, he accompanied the *Ruby* expedition of 1807 to Copenhagen during the Napoleonic Wars, and was often in action with the Danish gun-boats in the Little Belt, an area within the sea around Denmark. After serving for a few weeks in the Downs in the *Agincourt* (64), under Captain William Kent, he removed as midshipman[31] in March 1810, to the *Fylla* (20) under Captain Edward Rodney, on the Guernsey station. He was subsequently, in June 1811, present in an unsuccessful boat attack made on two French man-of-war brigs under covering fire from the *Firm* gun-brig; which vessel, after running aground, was burnt by her own crew to avoid her supplies being taken and used by the enemy. While attached next, from August 1811 until March 1813, to the *Diadem* (64) under Captain John Phillimore, Wingfield cruised in the North Sea, visited Lisbon, Portugal, and was actively employed in cooperation with the patriots of the north coast of Spain. On leaving the *Diadem*, he joined the Lake Service of Canada.

This history of Wingfield's early service was gleaned from *A Naval Biographical Dictionary*, published in London in 1894 by John Murray. In addition, his service record, which can be seen in the manuscript room of the British Museum, summarizes his early service as: 1806–10 in the North and Baltic seas; 1810–11 off the French coast; 1811–13 off the north coast of Spain. The record notes that he "Passed, February 1813." The reference "passed" most likely refers to his success with the written examination required to attain the rank of midshipman, which he carried at that time.

More information about Wingfield's early life and family may be found in Part III: The Biography of David Wingfield.

Notes Regarding the Transcription of the Journal

David Wingfield wrote his story in 1828, twelve years after he left Canada, while, we presume, a resident in Gloucester. His manuscript is presented in a fair copperplate hand, not written by quill pen but probably a dip pen, a fairly recent invention, probably manufactured in nearby Birmingham, which had become the world capital of metal-pen nib production by the 1850s. The journal is generally quite legible. In the transcription, where something is illegible, the reader will find brackets around the number of words, which could not be deciphered, e.g. "(four illegible)," or we have substituted "(undecipherable)" when a word, or a portion of a word could not be discerned. In a few cases, we have entered, in square parentheses, what we believe Wingfield intended. The transcription was completed from a photocopy of the fragile original document, which has now been withdrawn from circulation at Library and Archives Canada for conservation reasons.

Don Bamford, commenting about the copying task, says, "My flat-bed scanner gave up in disgust early on. It was just not up to the task of reading the manuscript. My biological-optical scanner and cognitive-recognition equipment was nearly eighty-eight years old before I even touched the keyboard. However, as I worked on, I tried not to put anything into the manuscript or to take anything out of it. There were only two places (as I recall) where Wingfield had repeated himself, and they were obvious. In one instance one word had been repeated, in another case, a phrase had been repeated. I have deleted both." From Don's experience of writing longhand extensively, he knows what happens when one gets tired. At times, Wingfield's handwriting had become quite small and harder to read.

Wingfield frequently used a squiggle followed by the letter *c*. The context suggests that he meant et cetera, thus, given the challenge for the modern day computer to reproduce Wingfield's squiggle, we

Page One from Wingfield's sixty-eight page journal. The handwritten notes have become faded and discoloured, yet are still quite legible. The adventurous spirit and the national pride of the author can be felt in his descriptive phraseology.

have substituted all references with "etc." He also used the letter *p* followed by a word, such as *week*, *diem*, or *cent* meaning "per week," "per diem," and "percent." This usage has been updated in the transcription. These idiosyncrasies added some difficulties to an otherwise easy transliteration. It should also be noted that Wingfield was not consistent with his spelling. *Harbor* and *harbour* are often inter-changed, as are *Surprise* and *Surprize*, and *Sackets* and *Sacketts*, for example. There are other peculiarities as well. On one occasion, he uses the more contemporary spelling *jail* instead of his usual archaic *gaol*. It should further be noted that the spelling *Sackets* has been used in the rest of the manuscript, save for those instances whether other authors or artists are quoted and have used one of the several alternate spellings. In this presentation of Wingfield's journal, intended for the general reader, the general spelling, with the exception of words mentioned in this section, has been updated and made consistent.

The general sentence structure has been preserved and it is noted that writing style, grammar, punctuation, and spelling have evolved a considerable degree in the intervening 179 years. We have made some adjustments to the punctuation throughout the text to help the reader work through Wingfield's long, complex and often convoluted sentence structure. While these peculiarities can add interest to the text, we have replaced the archaic "long s" — usually printed as *fs* — with the customary *ss* as used in contemporary spelling. It is interesting to note the ongoing discussion, especially in genealogical circles, about what to do with the transliteration of the handwritten symbol that looks like the letter *f* without its right-hand cross bar. The symbol does not seem to have a modern-day font equivalent in word processing software. As many of Wingfield's sentences were, by today's standards, very long, a change of topic, usually marked by a colon or semi-colon in the original, is in this version marked by a period with a new sentence following.

Readers of the original document would find inconsistencies with the spellings related to the Mackinac, as pronounced *Mackinaw*, usually in American quarters. The first name, given by the Native people, and taken over by the French was *Missilimackinac*. The fort was located at what is now St. Ignace, but was moved to what is now Mackinaw City. When the British arrived, they changed the name to *Michilimackinac* and moved the fort to the island. The name was too long, so the British or Americans changed the name to *Mackinac*, which is today the name one will find on most contemporary maps. But *Mackinac* is often pronounced *Mackinaw*, as noted — hence, the potential for confusion.

More bewilderment abounds: In the same part of Lake Huron, there is Mackinaw State Forest, Mackinaw City, Colonial Michilimackinac, and of course, the Straits of Mackinac. The common usage today is Mackinac, but in 1813, Michilimackinac was used most often. The spelling *Michilamackinac* has also been seen. Most historians write *Mackinac* in reference to historic times. Wingfield also spells Manitoulin as *Manatoulin*; (it is also seen spelled *Manitoolin* by Wingfield's colleague, Owen.) Wingfield also spelled Nottawasaga as *Nottawaysagua*.

Courtesy of United States Senate Library, Catalogue 33.00014.00. Old Fort Mackinac 1840.

An 1872 oil painting of Fort Mackinac by Seth Eastman.

At times, Wingfield played fast and loose with the use of capital letters. In fact, at times it was difficult to determine whether he intended to use the upper case or lower form. Such was the custom of the time. Other handwritten documents of the era show the same overuse. In those many instances, common usage for today has been applied. If any mistakes have occurred in the transcription, it has been unintentional and the authors apologize. Other historians, amateur or professional, will be able to refer to the typescript knowing it is essentially identical to the manuscript as Wingfield wrote it. All of the authors' notes are shown inside square brackets, not to be confused with Wingfield's words, which are in the regular font.

The * found in the journal manuscript indicates the starting page number in the original hand-written document, which occupies sixty-eight foolscap pages. These, and the numerals for endnotes, along with the alterations as outlined above are the only additions that have been made to the journal. Finally, the names of ships have been italicized in all places to be consistent with contemporary practice. The journal has been divided quite arbitrarily into six sections based on the different locations and the times that Wingfield served in that placement.

While the sixty-eight-page journal has been our main source for this history, countless additional documents have been used to expand and expound upon the matters raised by Wingfield in his writings. We have done our best to document all sources and have written extensive additional notes to supplement the text. Every attempt has been made to be accurate and to acknowledge the multitude of sources for our research. While it is not any excuse that we claim only to be mere amateur historians, for those who would find fault, or, for any errors we have committed, we most humbly apologize for any offence we might have created. Any such errors brought to our attention or the publisher's will be corrected for future editions.

PART ONE

THE JOURNAL OF DAVID WINGFIELD

*Four Years on the Lakes of Canada, in 1813, 1814, 1815
and 1816, By a Naval Officer Under the Command of the
Sir James Lucas Yeo K[t], Commodore and Commander of
H.M. Ships and Vessels of War Employed on the Lakes.
Also Nine Months as Prisoner of War in the United
States of America.*

CHAPTER ONE

JOINING THE LAKE SERVICE
Arrival and Adventures on Lake Ontario

The Lake Service, from the smallness of the scale of the naval operations, created little or no public attention, during the stupendous scenes then acting throughout Europe, in which the military movements under the Duke of Wellington was the Polar Star that attracted all attention, and the navy had sunk into comparative insignificance. But now and then a gallant and daring action forces itself upon public admiration, sufficient to show that supineness was no part of the character of British seamen, but that the harvest had been reaped by the gallant heroes, whose repeated victories over our combined enemies, will be read with admiration in the pages of the history of England's naval warriors — and the gleanings were too trifling in the public estimation to attract any particular notice from their countrymen, though if each engagement was well known it would be found equally deserving of applause with those upon a larger scale.

It is, therefore, no wonder that so little should be known of the Lake Service, or even of the true situation of the Lakes themselves with their importance in an American war. The number of years that have elapsed between the American Revolution and the last war had caused them to be viewed, both by England and America, [as] merely expansive sheets of water, and only useful as a communication and transit of merchandise between the different settlements on their respective borders, as those settlements rose into some importance.

The American war had not been long commenced before a new light seemed to break upon our rulers, which set forth these lakes as necessary to be occupied by a superior naval force to what the enemy had upon them, our naval superiority being absolutely necessary to the keeping of the Upper, and a large portion of, if not the whole, of the Lower Provinces of Canada appended to the British Crown.

This necessity being made obvious, it was immediately acted upon and Sir James Lucas Yeo, with officers, and 500 able seamen was ordered upon the Service: the Americans had been unaccountably inferior in not taking naval occupation of these lakes, as from* [their more readily available] resources they might easily have done; and by so doing have put it out of the power of the British government to regain the advantage, not, at least, without a very great expenditure of blood, and treasure, as the sequel will surely prove.

The vague idea we had of the Service, and the force being commanded by so gallant an officer as Sir James Yeo, made us look back upon it as pregnant with danger; but headed by an officer of our Commodore's known bravery, made us the more anxious to come in contact with the enemy, and the period of our sailing was most ardently desired.

The wished for day arrived on the 31st March 1813, when we sailed from Plymouth in the *Woolwich* store ship, all in as high spirits as the prospect of danger, attended with the hopes of speedy promotion, could make us; and after a tolerable passage we anchored about two miles below Quebec, late in the evening of the 5th May, where the Commodore's party went on shore.[1]

On the return of the boat we heard that the Americans had made an attack upon York, situated on the border of Lake Ontario, and the capital of the province of Upper Canada. They had plundered it of all the public stores, and destroyed the public buildings, among which were the two Houses of Parliament, and also a ship upon the stocks, on board of which Sir James Yeo had designed to hoist his broad pendant. With this news came orders for the officers and seamen to be ready to disembark by daybreak next morning, and to be prepared with three days provisions ready cooked. Every one was now actively employed through the night in securing our chests, and bedding, and getting the provisions cooked, and the men in readiness for disembarkation, [and] before daybreak the *Woolwich* was surrounded by small vessels to convey us to Montreal. By 10 am we were all clear of the ship, divided on board the small craft

---

*Page 2 begins in the original journal.

Quebec Harbour, 1834, by Russell Alexander. Wingfield arrived here May 15, 1813. The harbour and town would not have changed substantially in the period between his arrival and the drawing shown here.

according to their size, and giving and receiving 3 hearty cheers, sailed up the River St. Lawrence with a fair wind.

Everything had taken place so suddenly, that we belonging to the Midshipmen's mess did not think, nor indeed had time, to apportion out our provisions, which were all drawn from the purser, and cooked together in the ship's coppers, being divided among nearly twenty vessels, so that when we aboard the sloop, I and 3 others, began to enquire for something to eat, we found there was no part of the allowance of provisions on board, though some cunning dog had taken care of the grog. One vessel had all the biscuit and another all the beef, which should have been divided among forty-two; the pork, we afterwards learned, had been left on board the *Woolwich*. Our shipmates on board the other vessels were without any provisions; however, the Master of our sloop happened to have plenty of eggs on board which we purchased, and did very well, laughing heartily at those who* could get nothing, when we met them on shore.

On the 8th we arrived at Montreal, but had scarce time to speak to each other, being immediately marched off to Lachine, about 9 or 10

---

*Page 3 begins in the original journal.

miles higher up the river, where the batteaus lay, [these being] flat bottomed boats, peculiarly built, and adapted to the navigation of the St. Lawrence, which, in many places is shallow, and extremely rapid.

After a fatiguing march along a bad road, not being much used to walking on shore, we arrived at our destined place, a village consisting of a few straggling houses. We expected our day's provisions delivered to us immediately, the men having taken no refreshment all day, but we had to wait a considerable time before they could be procured from the commissariat store. In the meantime the seamen had to clean out the coppers, in an old decayed barrack, where they were quartered, which had not been used for years, except casually, and were near an inch thick with filth.

The sailors had plenty of money and were desirous of purchasing some fresh provisions from the inhabitants, not relishing the salt pork issued to them, and after holding a parley amongst themselves, different parties were sent out, unknown to the officers, and in a little more than an hour returned with a plentiful supply of fresh meat, and poultry of almost every description. The salt pork, which had been put into the coppers during the absence of these purveyors, was thrown out, and meat and poultry substituted for it. The sailors paid but little attention to the cutting up of the meat properly, and for the fowls, they were skinned to save the trouble of plucking them.

A party of us Mids formed our mess at the house of an old Scotch woman, from whom we bought a calf, and the men being all employed or intoxicated, we were obliged to kill, and skin it ourselves, which was done after a manner. However, we made a hearty supper, and then lay down before a good fire, for none of us had our bedding, and, for my part I saw nothing of mine until I arrived at Kingston, three weeks after.

We had mustered the seamen into the aforesaid barrack at 8 o'clock, to prevent them from strolling about the country, and a party of soldiers were placed outside, but in the morning, we found a place at the back of the building torn down sufficiently large to admit half a dozen persons. While the sentinel thought all was safe within, Jack was moving about at his pleasure.*

---

*Page 4 begins in the original journal.

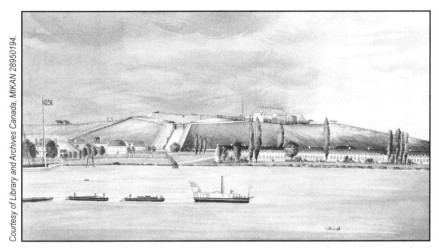

Courtesy of Library and Archives Canada, MIKAN 28950194.

Old Fort Henry, watercolour and ink over pencil by Henry Francis Ainslie, April 1839. Wingfield would not have recognized the enlarged Kingston as the same wilderness village he found "on opening Navy Bay" when approaching by water in 1813.

On the afternoon after our arrival at this place, a sufficient number of boats were collected to convey one Division, and they started up the river with that portion of the baggage, which had arrived from Montreal, at which place an officer with a party of men were stationed to forward it.

Fifty men under a Captain, Lieutenant, and other inferior officers were ordered to take two large gun boats up the river, each of them carrying a 24 pounder carronade. [With] these drawing considerable more water than the flat bottomed boats, and being very unwieldy, it proved a most fatiguing job. On the 11th [of May] about 5 pm we started, for Upper Lachine, a few miles above our halting place, but before the boat I was in joined the other, it was past midnight, as she had the advantage of a pilot well acquainted with the river, while, from our ignorance we frequently lost the eddies and were swept down the stream.

We were about a fortnight on our passage, having to drag the boats up the rapids, and in many places totally to unload them. The men [were] sometimes in the water above their middles for hours together, dragging them through a current running 8 or 9 miles an hour, — and more than once the men and boat [were] swept down the rapids, in consequence of the men not being able to hold their footing, from the foulness of the bottom. In two or three places where the rapids were very strong, the militia was obliged to turn out to assist us; this must be understood as applying only to the particular parts of the river, and well they deserved the name given them.

The Captain commanding the gunboats fell sick when we had got through the most fatiguing part of our job, and returned to England, which made room for the promotion of one Lieutenant, and one Mid, which acted as a good stimulant to others.[2]

On arrival at Quebec where we learned the destruction of our ship at York, which was believed to be the only one on Lake Ontario, we expected to find nothing but large gun boats, but to our surprise, on opening Navy Bay [Kingston], we saw two ships of 23 and 21 guns, a brig of 14 and two schooners of 14 and 12 guns, comprising every sort of calibre, from a 68, to a 4 pounder. But previous to the arrival of Sir James Yeo, [they were] in such a wretched state with respect to discipline and furniture, that they would have reflected disgrace upon a maritime power of the lowest possible grade. They were under the control of the Military Commandant, and officered and manned by provincials, men of no experience whatsoever in naval tactics, while the Americans were amply found in stores, and manned with picked seamen from the sea ports, so that, without this reinforcement our ships would have been unable to put to sea the whole of the* summer.

The arrival of Sir James Yeo at Kingston, with this force, raised the drooping spirits of the inhabitants of that place, and generally of the country at large, who were well aware that the fall of Kingston must necessarily involve the whole country upwards in ruin. It is more than possible that Montreal, itself must soon have fallen into the hands of the Americans, and an attack was daily expected on the former place, but it seems our arrival made them alter their plans.[3]

On overhauling the rigging of the different vessels, we found it very defective, with no naval stores in the place to supply the deficiency, and, nothing but the determined perseverance of Sir James Yeo, and those under his command, could have surmounted the difficulties that hourly present themselves to view. Thus, it can be no wonder that the Americans generally had the superiority upon the Lakes, when it is considered

---

* Page 5 begins in the original journal.

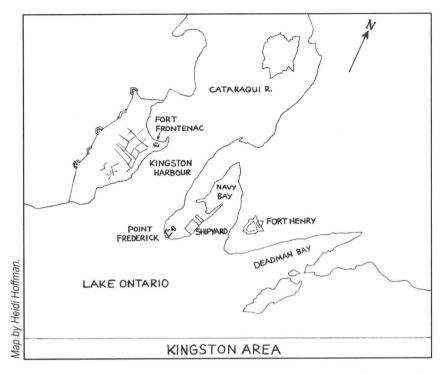

Map 4: Kingston Harbour and Naval Installations. The position of the town site, the old Fort Frontenac, and the newly constructed (1812) Fort Henry are shown.

that the whole of our naval stores had to be sent from England, after being demanded from this place, while the enemy received plentiful supplies from New York, not above 5 or 6 days' journey from their port on Lake Ontario.

Kingston is situated on the border of Lake Ontario, just at the head of River St. Lawrence, and previous to the war, was a place of no great importance. But a large naval establishment being formed, and York having lost its former advantages, principally that of forming a kind of central depot for all kinds of merchandise, to supply the inland settlements, from its lying so open to the incursions of the enemy, all the trade followed to this place, and York was nearly deserted, though [remaining] the seat of government for the Upper Province. Consequently, building became the rage, and at the conclusion of the war Kingston had risen into a large town, with many handsome, and substantial houses, forming several streets. It has a commodious church, likewise a Roman Catholic chapel, but there are few of that persuasion here, also a stone gaol, and council chamber, in which causes are tried.

In Kingston bay are a few wharfs for the convenience of loading and unloading small vessels, but there is not sufficient water for large ships to enter. The harbour for the men of war, called Navy Bay, is about a quarter of a mile from the town, and is formed by a long point of land, called Navy Point, and two small islands, making good shelter, and forming a breakwater to prevent the ice from injuring the ships, when it breaks up in the spring. On Navy Point is our dockyard, none [having been] established previous to our arrival in the country. The port, selected by Sir James Yeo, was ridiculed by the old Provincial naval officers, who deemed it impracticable to lay down ways for building ships, and launching them, particularly on this spot, but those who* openly condemned the whole arrangement lived long enough to see a ship launched, pierced for 98 guns. Their confusion must not have been a little, as they considered the *Wolfe* of 23 guns, quite a prodigy.

The whole is commanded by a high ground, little more than a musquet shot off, upon which is built, since the commencement of the war, a large and strong fort, for that part of the world. It likewise commands the town, and all the outworks, and could, if required, level the whole with the ground.

[In] the latter part of November, or early in December, all navigation ceases on the Lakes, and the ships come into port for the winter, when they are dismantled to their lower masts, the rigging being placed in a loft in the dockyard built for its reception, called the rigging loft, where each ship's furniture is carefully made up, and placed by itself. The hulls of the ships are covered over closely with planks to keep off the snow and preserve the decks; they remain in this situation till March, sometimes till the middle of April, perfectly fixed in ice, six or eight feet thick, and [protected] from the excessive rigour of the season. As no work can be done, the winter is passed in one continuous round of pleasure, which makes it fly away imperceptibly.

In the midst of the amusements, which took place during the first winter, it may be supposed that some real or imaginary offence might create duelling, if only for variety, and so it happened; two officers

---

* Page 6 begins in the original journal.

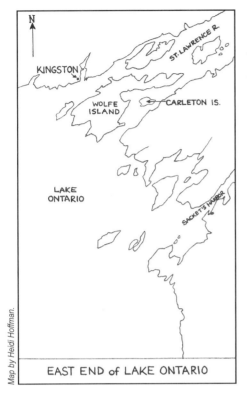

Map by Heidi Hoffman.

N

KINGSTON

ST. LAWRENCE R.

WOLFE ISLAND   CARLETON IS.

LAKE ONTARIO

SACKET'S HARBOR

EAST END of LAKE ONTARIO

Map 5: East end of Lake Ontario, including Sackets Harbor. This area was a significant site during the activities of the War of 1812.

wishing to amuse themselves in this manner. It came to the knowledge of Sir James Yeo; he ordered two watch boxes, which are considerably larger than our sentry boxes in England, to be placed on the ice at about 80 yards distance and immediately facing each other. The belligerents were then supplied with two musquets, and 60 rounds of ball cartridges; [he] ordered them at the same time to take themselves in respective positions, and when they had amused themselves in expending their ammunition, if no mortal wound occurred, they were to send for more. It is almost needless to say that one night, and that passed in jollity with some of their brother officers, was sufficient to reconcile the parties without the loss of powder and ball, which might be applied to better purposes. It is but justice to say that neither of these gentlemen were possessed with that kind of valour which "oozes out of their finger ends" but both behaved gallantly during the war, and were promoted for their brave conduct. By the judicious conduct of Sir James Yeo, in placing duelling in so ludicrous a light, a complete stop was put on that kind of amusement during his command.

The ships were ready for sea by the latter part of May, and a* strong body of troops were assembled at Kingston to make an attack upon the enemy's works at Sacketts Harbour, which, if once in our possession, would have been an end to the naval war on Lake Ontario and saved

* Page 7 begins in the original journal.

some millions of pounds, and thousands of lives, as the Americans had no other harbour along the coast fit for a naval depot. An excellent opportunity [was] likewise offered for putting the plan into execution, the [American] fleet having sailed about 100 miles up the lake to attack one of our forts on the bank of the River Niagara, and not believing that our ships could be prepared for sea so early, they had left the place nearly defenceless. In the afternoon we weighed and stood out of the harbour, anchoring about six miles off Kingston to await the troops who were embarked in batteaux and gun boats; the latter had 24 pounders mounted in circular platforms. The troops did not join the fleet till late in the evening, when it being quite calm, the boats were made fast to the ships.

British Attack on Sackett's Harbour, 1813.

Courtesy of Library and Archives Canada, C-40598.

At daybreak a light breeze sprung up and we got under way, the boats occasionally laying on their oars to keep company. Having but light breezes and frequent calms we made but little progress. About noon, on rounding a point, we came in full view of the enemy about 10 miles distant, who, immediately they perceived us, commenced firing alarm guns to call in the surrounding militia, [and] at 2 pm we were totally becalmed within six miles of the town of Sacketts. Sir James Yeo had gone in shore in his gig some time before to reconnoitre, and perceiving several shots

fired at the boat, a gun vessel was ordered to cover her retreat, if necessary. On her return we received orders to prepare for disembarking the
troops, the ships [were] cleared for action, and nothing was wanting but
a good breeze to take them close enough in shore to cover the landing.
About 6 pm a fresh breeze sprang up dead on the land; the ships bore up
and took in their small sails; the guns were prepared in the gun boats;
and soldiers, who were not employed at the oars, in place of the seamen
who had to fight the gun, had their muskets in their hands, and lay
down at the bottom of the boat to prevent confusion. Every heart now
beat high with eagerness and expectation, but when nearly within gun-
shot of the shore, the ships suddenly hauled their wind and stood out to
sea, making a signal for the boats to follow. As soon as they got a good
offing, they hove to, and the boats assembled round the Commodore's
ship, where we learned that the attack was suspended till the following
morning. This order emanated from the Governor General of the two
Provinces,[4] who was on board the flag ship, and, of course, commander
in chief. The officers being in the Provincial Service, and [its] pay, Sir
James was obliged to* obey, though much against his will. This caused
some altercation between the two Commanders on board, Sir James urging the expediency of an immediate attack, and the Governor alleging the
decline of the day to defer it. This delay, however, put a great damp upon
our spirits, as we plainly saw by our glasses several boats, well manned,
enter the harbour to reinforce the garrison, and well knew they would
be receiving reinforcements all the night, as they kept up an incessant
firing of minute guns. Whereas, if we had made a bold dash at once, it is
most probable but few, if any, guns would have been fired upon us and
the troops would have been landed immediately under their batteries,
and in the town, under cover of the shipping who would have run right
into Sacketts Harbour. We soon after learned that the Americans were
not above 300 strong when we first hove in sight, and had made every
preparation for destroying the public buildings and stores, particularly
a large ship upon the stocks, well knowing it would be the utmost folly
to attempt standing against such a force as they must [have] perceived
we had, independent of the shipping. This day's work ended with ordering the troops on board the ships, and the boats to be made fast to their

---

* Page 8 begins in the original journal.

sterns, except some to row guard along shore during the night; where they captured about 150 of the enemy coming down the lake for Sackets.

When the troops were on board the ships, they made sail further off shore, as the breeze freshened and confirmed blowing dead on the land; at midnight it fell calm and left us about five miles off the town. At dawn of day the hands were turned up, the soldiers embarked the boats, and the ships stood in for the land, but having light baffling winds, they made but little progress and none came within gun shot except a schooner of 10 guns, and she did not arrive until the men had made good their landing.

After some consultation, the boats were ordered to proceed under cover of the gun boats only, but our favourable opportunity was gone; and the troops knew it as well as ourselves, for, though there was no murmuring, or attempt to disobey orders, their countenances, so different to what they were the evening before, plainly showed they did not obey the orders with that cheerfulness which confidence inspires. The enemy had nearly 24 hours notice, and had made the best use of their time by minute guns, and expresses, to receive strong reinforcements. It being daylight before the boats shoved off from the ships, our motions were definitely perceived by the Americans, who, not being awed by the shipping, had drawn great numbers of men from the town, concealing them among the bushes, behind trees, logs, and rising grounds, just above the beach, which enabled them to take deliberate aim as we approached the shore; they had likewise brought out four field pieces to annoy us.

About 3 am we formed the line, the gun boats leading the van, and commenced pulling in shore about a mile above the town in order to keep out of the range of the shot from the forts and blockhouses. The boats were heavily laden, and proceeded but slowly, while the enemy kept up an ill directed fire from their* field pieces. When within musket shot of the beach, the gun boats pulled ahead and fired a few rounds of grape and canister shot to scour the beach, but the Yankees had anticipated us, and were so well sheltered, that I believe none were killed or wounded. The batteries and ships' boats then advanced, and I observed to an officer of the 104th Reg[t], who commanded the troops in the boat under my charge, that the Americans intended to let us land unmolested, but it soon appeared I was mistaken, for when about [a] pistol shot from the beach,

---

* Page 9 begins in the original journal.

and we had encouraged each other with the usual salutation of three cheers, they opened [such] a well directed fire from their field pieces and rifles that almost every shot did execution, which for a moment staggered us, but [we] soon recovered from the surprise. Every boat made the best of her way to land, [and] the gun boats kept up a continued fire, but having no other mark than the smoke from the enemy's guns, little execution was done, and in a very short time there was fifteen killed and wounded in my boat, principally picked off from, and about the gun. In passing one of the boats, which appeared in great distress, I hailed the officer, who was wounded, and had but three men who had escaped the effects of the shot of the enemy. As the military officer and myself were obliged to stand up and cheer on the men, we were too prominent a mark to remain long and I took a mental leave of the few friends I had left. The men being so deliberately picked off from the gun, the crew got in some confusion, for as the seamen were disabled, others took their place, and were relieved at the oars by the soldiers. While [we were] occupied in this double transfer, the army officer, with his glass, had discovered a body of men drawn up a short distance from the beach, who being dressed in green, the uniform of all the American foot soldiers, could scarcely be perceived among the trees and underwood. He called me and pointed them out. While [we were] so occupied, the Coxswain of the boat was struck with two balls and fell; the soldier took the tiller, while I went forward to the gun, which being loaded with grape and canister shot, I had it pointed to the spot and made a great havoc among the bushes, if not the men. By this time some of the men had made a precipitate retreat into the town.

When the soldiers were all landed, and the wounded men placed upon the beach, those gun boats, which were not disabled, rowed towards the batteries, and commenced firing, to draw off some of the attention of the enemy from the advancing party. Hence we were kept till half past seven, when we were recalled to the landing place to take on board the troops who were retreating in great haste. They were once in the town, and being dreadfully cut up from some blockhouses, and [with] a great dust seen rising from the opposite entrance, supposed to proceed from a reinforcement to the garrison, a retreat was sounded, but who* gave the orders no one knew, the Governor and his staff positively denying

---

* Page 10 begins in the original journal.

having done so, however, it was not the less obeyed. In a few minutes a smoke was seen rising from their dockyard, which caused an attempt to be made to rally the troops, but [it] did not succeed. Before the soldiers were all embarked it was known to a certainty that, what was supposed to be a reinforcement, was nothing else but the main body of the Americans retreating, leaving some blockhouses manned, until their new ship, and public store houses were on fire, and then [those men remaining were] to follow.

I was informed by several officers of the American army and navy, when I was [later] taken prisoner, that had the attack commenced immediately after we hove in sight the day before, so far from defending themselves, the number of men in the garrison would have scarcely been sufficient to destroy the public works.

We lost nearly 400 men killed and wounded in this disgraceful affair, in every probability the place would have been taken without the loss of a single man had things been conducted as they might. This failure caused a coolness between the Governor and Commodore, [which] at length broke out into an open rupture, in consequence of the loss of our flotilla on Lake Champlain, which, in Sir James Yeo's public dispatches, he attributed to the misconduct of the Governor, who was soon after suspended, and a court martial called, but he died soon after his arrival in England.

The soldiers were greatly disheartened, and it was well for us that the troops at Fort George, the place the Americans had gone to attack, were better commanded, otherwise their ships would have been down upon us, and from our crowded state, most probably would have taken us all. We arrived in Navy Bay the same evening and disembarked the troops and wounded men; thus ended an expedition begun under the most favourable auspices.

I before remarked that, could we get possession of Sackets Harbour, it would have saved an immensity of blood and treasure.[5]

On Lake Erie we had several vessels of war under Captain Barclay, who could not face the enemy for want of seamen; others were similarly circumstanced on Lake Champlain. That the Americans should be kept in check on Lake Ontario, was of the most vital importance to the whole country above Montreal, and probably to within a few miles of Quebec; therefore, had we succeeded in this expedition, Sir James Yeo would have been enabled to send a reinforcement of officers and seamen, to each of the above named places on that lake. Or, even allowing that the enemy should have retaken Sackets they could not, in the course of the Summer, have built and equipped a force sufficient to face us, let their activity be what it might; and they are not deficient in that quality, as far as regards ship building; and the following summer we must still have kept the lead, as by that time reinforcements* of seamen and marines, with artificers, and stores, would have arrived at Kingston from England.[6]

It may be thought that I am somewhat premature in the destruction of the American fleet. I before observed that Sackets was the only harbour they had and without a harbour occasionally to run into, we might have selected our own time, and improved our circumstances in such a manner, that an engagement would have been a morally certain victory. The failure of this expedition may also be said to have caused the loss of our facilities on Lakes Erie and Champlain.

In the autumn of this year, Captain Barclay was forced to engage a superior number of vessels, well manned, equipped, and disciplined. With not thirty British Able Seamen on board, the remainder of his crews made up by soldiers and Canadians, with guns by no means fitted for naval warfare, some of which burst, and others [that] tore their carriages to pieces [with] the first broadside, and though fighting under every possible disadvantage, he did not strike [lower his colours in surrender] until every officer on board his own ship was killed or wounded, himself among the latter, severely; and every officer commanding a vessel in his squadron.

In the Summer of 1814, Captain George Downie lost his life, and ships, on Lake Champlain from being hurried into action by the Governor, against his own conviction, who with the troops under his command was to make a simultaneous attack on shore, but failed to do so. On the borders of Lake Ontario the troops suffered most severely, from our not being able to supply them with provisions, and co-operate with them occasionally. It will be seen from the above of what importance the capture of Sackets would have been to this country [Britain], as well as to Canada.

At Kingston we here purchased a large merchant schooner, which, with some alterations, was made to mount 8 guns. This addition to our

---

* Page 11 begins in the original journal.

little force gave us the superiority on the lake, and the Americans were obliged to continue in harbour till their new ship, which had sustained considerable damage from the fire, was launched and fitted out. Upon our putting to sea the gun boats were laid up and I was appointed to a hired schooner, which acted as tender to the fleet; we proceeded along the American shore, frequently landing, and harassing the enemy. Having received intelligence that a large quantity of government flour was stored at a place called Sodus, a small town standing on the bank of a river of the same name, we made sail for the place, and sending a flag of truce on shore to assure the inhabitants of the security of all private property, provided we were not molested, we proceeded to load the boats and, while performing that duty, we were treacherously fired upon by some of the inhabitants, for which amiable conduct Sir James ordered the town to be destroyed.

After the capture of Fort George by the Americans, our troops under the* command of Gen¹ Vincent retreated towards the head of the lake closely followed by the enemy, until Gen¹ Vincent received a reinforcement, and made a stand, still acting on the defensive. In a few days, the Americans were joined by a strong body of troops under two Generals, and ours made a rapid retreat towards Burlington Heights, when by a bold and gallant manoeuvre [the] General made a night attack upon their camp, completely surprised them, took the two Generals [Chandler and Winder], several officers, and [as] many men prisoners, as his own troops consisted of. After this he [presumably Vincent] retreated further up the country, and fortified his camp, the enemy being still nearly double his number.

Sir James received an express ordering him to return to Kingston immediately to embark troops to reinforce Gen¹ Vincent. We accordingly returned, and took as many on board as the ships could conveniently carry, sailing direct for the head of the lake. On the morning of the 8ᵗʰ July at daybreak,[7] one of our schooners being ahead of the fleet, and close in with the American shore, without the slightest apprehension of an enemy, when to our surprise we were saluted with several shots; and reconnoitering from the mast head, [we] saw a camp with two breastworks thrown up, and several batteries drawn up on the beach. She

---

* Page 12 begins in the original journal.

[the small vessel near the shore] returned the fire, but being crowded with soldiers, was called off by [a] signal from the Commodore, and the troops distributed among the ships. When she returned to the attack, and their works being but temporary, were soon demolished, the guns dismounted, and the enemy driven into the woods. [There] they were attacked by a body of Indians, who being excellently adapted for bush fighting, drove them back to the beach, where those who were fortunate enough to reach, launched the boats, and surrendered, but not before numbers of them had fallen victim to our sable allies who tomahawked them without mercy, as they neither make prisoners, or give quarter, and scalp every one they kill. The boats of [our] fleet were ordered on shore to protect them from the Indians, and parties sent into the woods to secure any prisoners that might want to surrender, which many joyfully did to save their lives. While on this duty, I perceived two American soldiers running with all speed towards the beach, followed by four or five Indians, yelling the war whoop; before our party could get near enough to save them the Indians had killed [them], and we came up just as they had finished scalping them. This operation, which is almost momentary, is performed by giving the deceased a heavy blow on the crown of the head, with the butt end of the tomahawk, and then making a circular incision with the scalping knife (which no Indian is without) about the size of the palm of the hand, they force the skin off. No scalp is considered genuine unless the skin has the hair on where it divides at the crown of the head and the greater number they can show, so much the more are they esteemed above their fellows — this man or demon, had them dripping with blood, which* he held up to me with the most savage exultation. The Indians are such excellent marksmen that they very seldom fail in bringing down their aim, and keeping themselves concealed among the bushes or underwood, the moment their gun is fired, if other objects remain, they shift their places, and keeping them constantly in view, scarce ever fail of completing the work they are upon; after a battle, or with a flying foe before him, the Indian shows himself in all his native ferocity. It is useless to beg for mercy as they are deaf to all entreaties, but stand before them with courage and resolution, and boldly encounter them, they will retreat till some treacherous advantage can be taken.

---

* Page 13 begins in the original journal.

Scene on the Frontiers as Practiced by the "Humane" British and their "Worthy" Allies, cartoon by William Charles, 1812. Wingfield suggests in his journal that the Native allies were discouraged from this compulsive habit by offering them rewards for handing over American prisoners alive. The artist and others suggested that the British were paying bounties to encourage the practice.

Those Indians who have had most intercourse with white inhabitants and traders in furs, are completely degenerated from their brethren in the interior of the country, in courage, cleanliness, and honesty.

The Governor, and different military Commanders have done all in their power to induce the Indians to leave off the abhorrent practice of scalping their prisoners by giving a reward for each [live] one that is brought to the respective headquarters; but as they act in distinct, and separate bodies, and will not submit to any control or discipline, it has but partially succeeded, even in the immediate vicinity of our troops, where it would seem, no motive could possibly prevent them from delivering up their prisoners and claiming such reward. The Americans had likewise their Indian auxiliaries, besides which each citizen is bred up from his infancy to be well acquainted with bush fighting, and also to be perfect master of his rifle.

In the evening the fleet sailed, and I was ordered to York to take in a supply of provisions for the ships, I accordingly shaped my course for that place, and anchored in the bay early next morning.

After arranging with the Commissariat Department, I took a view of the town and its immediate vicinity, but the Americans having paid it a visit as before mentioned, it exhibited but a ruinous spectacle — all the fortifications blown up, and the public buildings lying in a heap of ruins. The skeleton of our ship[8] still remained on the spot where she had been laid down, but not a whole timber left in her, and all her masts and spars, which were ready cut in two and otherwise rendered useless; but the situation that had been selected for building her, showed much ignorance on the part of the managers, for it very doubtful to me, from my own observations, whether she would have been launched, as I had the curiosity to sound in the direction she must have gone off, and found the water too shallow, with a soft muddy bottom for a considerable distance into the lake, that is it is not improbable but she might have stuck fast, and remained as a monument to warn others against the like attempt.

The harbour [in York] is larger than Kingston, but useless except for small vessels in consequence of a bar running across the entrance, with but a narrow* and shallow channel.

On joining the fleet I found that the boats had captured a schooner from the enemy, and she was now fitted up with an 18 pounder upon a swivel and circular platform. I was removed on board her with orders to remain near the army, to convey troops or provisions from one military post to another, as occasion might require, and the next morning sailed for York, with 180 prisoners of war, in boats, under convoy;[9] though the latter place is 60 miles from the Falls of Niagara, justly esteemed the greatest natural curiosity in the known world, yet the spray is distinctly visible on a clear day, hovering over it with the appearance of a small white cloud.

On returning to six mile creek [Six Mile Creek], so named from being about that number of miles above the River Niagara, where the troops were encamped, I went on shore and found them busy in striking the tents, having received an express from Kingston, containing the

---

* Page 14 begins in the original journal.

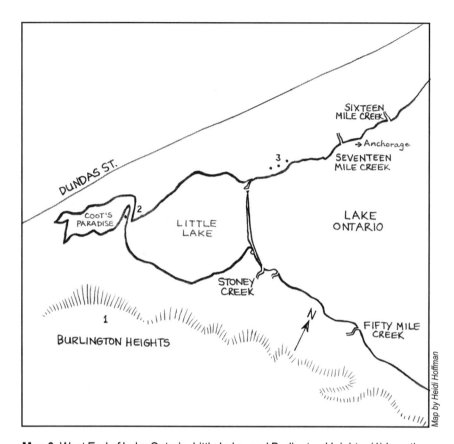

Map 6: West End of Lake Ontario, Little Lake, and Burlington Heights. (1) Location of Burlington Heights according to Pierre Berton in *Flames Across the Border*, and, probable location of General Vincent's base. (2) Location of Burlington Heights Emigrant Hospital, sometimes cited as the location of Burlington Heights. (3) Most logical location of Burlington Heights, according to an old map of the Niagara Frontier, held in the West Point Museum Collection, United States Military Academy Library, West Point, New York. It is the only location of the Heights that meets the requirements of the notes and other materials by various writers of the time.

information that the American fleet was at sea. I received an order from Sir James Yeo to sail immediately for Burlington Bay, or more properly Lake, as the communication with Lake Ontario is only by a narrow passage about 50 yards wide, and then opens into a large basin seven miles long and about four wide; over this passage is a wooden bridge, which shortens the distance from York to Niagara [by] fifteen miles. The channel leading into the bay or lake is very intricate, for NW winds, which sometimes blow up the Lake Ontario, raise the sand, so as to form a shifting bar, and this is only partially removed by the water receding from Burlington Bay. This circumstance took me up a considerable time, in sounding and buoying off the channel, which I found so shallow that it was necessary to get out the gun, all the stores, and provisions, and likewise the masts, to make the schooner as light as possible. This was scarcely accomplished when the American fleet hove in sight, coming up the lake with a fair wind, but towards evening it fortunately fell calm and the schooner being low in the water, and close under the land, we got into the lake undiscovered, and having two boats manned with soldiers from Burlington Heights to assist us, they towed us under the guns of the batteries before daylight. As soon as it was clear day I went on shore and with a glass could discern the enemy's ships at anchor a few miles above Niagara.[10]

After rigging the schooner, getting the stores etc. on board we sailed, down the lake and anchored as near the bridge as we could, for the convenience of making a proper survey of the before mentioned channel, and try if it could be made available for the purposes of navigation, but the sand being risen in numerous banks, and extending a considerable distance into Lake Ontario, rendered it useless except for boats.

I remained in the lake about a month, during which time we were visited by the boats of the American fleet, which anchored at the head of Lake Ontario, with a view to cut out, or destroy the schooner, but in the attempt they found out* we were too well prepared for them, having a party of soldiers on board, besides the crew.[11]

I one morning went on shore early and found the troops busied in packing up, and learned from the Military Commandant, that this post was to be evacuated except by a small guard. I was also informed that there had been an engagement between the two squadrons, in which the Americans were defeated with the loss of four of their schooners, two taken, and two were capsized by carrying too heavy a press of canvas

---

* Page 15 begins in the original journal.

in endeavouring to escape, and every soul on board lost. In the action Sir James Yeo had but six vessels in the whole, while the enemy had thirteen; so well had our brave Commander calculated upon weight of metal, should he be favoured with a strong breeze, and enabled to close with his opponents; and there is but little doubt, if any, but the whole would have been captured, or destroyed, had they not made a precipitate retreat under the guns of Forts St. George,[12] and Niagara, situated opposite each other on the banks of the River Niagara, immediately at the entrance.

A View of Fort George, 1816, drawing by Edward Walsh.

Courtesy of Library and Archives Canada, MIKAN 2837535.

At the same time I received an order from the Commodore to join the fleet; and sailed the same morning. I had to undergo the same routine in getting into the Lake Ontario, as on leaving it, and was ready for sailing the same evening, but detained by a calm.

When a breeze sprang up next morning I proceeded to York, expecting at that place to gain some intelligence of the fleet, but could hear nothing satisfactory, and made sail for four mile creek where some of our troops lay encamped, as the most likely place, but on going on shore was equally as fortunate as at York. Shortly after, a boat came off to inform me that Sir James was hourly expected.

Having been up nearly the whole of the two last nights, I went below to lie down, but had scarcely composed myself to sleep when I was roused by the Quarter Master, with the information that a vessel was coming up the lake, and being close in with the American shore, was certain she belonged to the enemy, I took my glass and soon discovered her to be a large sloop, called a Durham boat. We immediately weighed and made sail, with a stiff breeze, right aft, quite elated with the idea of taking a prize. It being necessary to keep close in shore to cut the boat off her intended port, we were obliged to pass within half gun shot of two of the enemy's forts at the mouth of the River Niagara, but going at the rate of nine miles an hour I knew they could do but little damage. When we had the river in full view I observed two schooners getting under weigh but [was] hoping I should be able to destroy the vessel I was in chase of, or fall in with our ships, before they could clear the river. I did not alter the course, until they were under full sail, and either of them being far superior to us, I felt little inclination to await their coming up, and shaped my course for York; one of the enemy schooners outsailing the other came up with us hand over hand, and had she prudently reserved her fire until she got alongside,* she most probably would have made a prize, but luffing up occasionally to fire her broadside, she gave us an opportunity of getting ahead. After being chased for about an hour, [we saw] our ships hove in sight, and the Yankees returned to Niagara.

The same evening I was ordered to join the *Wolfe*, the flag ship, and the schooner was sent to Kingston, the Commodore being in daily expectation of meeting the enemy, and not wishing to encumber his fleet with so small a vessel. I was kindly received by Sir James Yeo, who told me he had sent for me as he thought I should prefer being in the fleet if a engagement ensued, to going to Kingston and lying inactive. Early next morning we sailed from York in quest of the enemy who were suspected of being at sea.

Our squadron being greatly inferior to the Americans, in guns, vessels, and seamen, the object of Sir James Yeo was, to make up the deficiency as far as he was able, by weight of metal, as before observed, consequently his object was to engage them at close quarters and board, which would, in all human probability, have insured success. The Americans,

---

* Page 16 begins in the original journal.

Courtesy of United States Library of Congress, LC-DIG-ppmsca-01656.

Queenstown at Niagara, painted by Edward Walsh, a surgeon to the 49th Regiment who served in Canada in that period. Travellers on horseback, cart, and foot traverse the wide dirt road, while houses are near the shore of the Niagara River. Queenston is just north of Niagara Falls and the site of the Battle of Queenston Heights on October 13, 1812, when the Canadians and British defeated the American forces that invaded the town.

on the contrary, were armed with long guns, and wanted to engage at a distance, out of the range of our carronades, being fully informed of the state of our ships, as well as of our object. Both sides were eager to engage, but neither would commence, without the advantage of weather gage, that is, by having the wind so in our favour, as to enable to maintain a distance, or come to close action.

As both parties had sailed from their respective ports, determined to engage, we were but a short time seeking each other, and early on the second day after leaving York we came in sight. But light and frequent calms kept us, for above a week, constantly at our guns, alternately chasing and being chased, as the wind gave either the advantage, which is very changeable at this season of the year — a sudden breeze springing up would give us the advantage and, before we could close, either shifting or dying away. Sometimes we were becalmed for hours together, within 5 or 6 miles of each other, so that our minds were worked up to the highest pitch of enthusiasm, and our seamen were in excellent spirits, and eager for the engagement.

Between 8 and 9 o'clock on the evening of the 10th September, the two fleets were becalmed in such a situation, that whichever way a breeze sprung up, an engagement seemed inevitable, and we all adjourned to our berth to take a parting glass together — droll was a Midshipman named Ellery, highly esteemed by all on board, who had frequently expressed a belief that he should not survive the ensuing action, and now appeared particularly low and dejected; having sealed a letter, he threw it among a heap of others and observed, that was the last letter he should ever write. Some attempted to reason with him while others laughed at his foolish presentiment, as they termed it. However, having taken advantage of the hour allowed us — some in writing letters — others in making a Midshipman's will — leaving nothing a year, paid* quarterly — we now filled our glasses and shaking each other heartily by the hand, went on deck to our respective quarters.

Next day a breeze sprang up in favour of the enemy, which allowed them to take their desired distance, so that our short guns would not tell, while their shot flew about us in all directions. After having laid in this galling situation upwards of two hours, we got a breeze in our favour, and immediately endeavoured to close while the Americans made all sail from us.

When the action had apparently ceased, I went to Ellery, who was talking to one of the Lieutenants, and clapping him on the shoulder said, "Well, Bill, you are still in the land of the living." He returned my salute with a melancholy smile, and I had scarce removed my hand when a shot from the *Pike*, the American Commodore's ship, took him about the navel and literally cut him in two. We caught him in our arms but he was a corpse in an instant — so much for presentiment — he was the only officer killed in the whole fleet; our loss besides was but 10 killed and wounded.

The same day the hostile squadrons parted, as if by mutual consent; we went to Kingston, and the Americans into Sackets Harbour.

Upon our arrival, most disastrous intelligence was in circulation from our ship, and army on and about Lake Erie, and likewise from the

* Page 17 begins in the original journal.

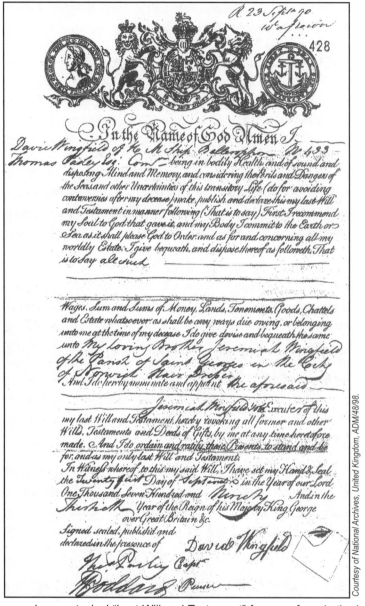

This image shows a typical "Last Will and Testament" for a seafarer in the late 1700s. Ironically, the document, from another David Wingfield, was found during a search of genealogical records for our lieutenant. The wording "… considering the dangers and perils of the sea and other uncertainties of this transitory life …" seems quite suitable to the situation.

troops on the border of Lake Ontario, great numbers of the latter dying daily from a disease caught, in consequence of having been encamped in low swampy ground all the summer, and the only dependence they both had for relief was from the success of the respective squadrons on each lake. Sir James, in concert with the Military Commandant, made an immediate attempt to supply the former by the way of Burlington Heights, as that was the only chance left of saving them, and that now a forlorn hope. For this purpose several merchant vessels were laden with stores and provisions; the men of war, likewise, took on board as much as they could stow, without rendering them incapable of engaging the enemy, should they meet between Kingston, and the head of the lake.

The two schooners, which had been taken from the enemy in a preceding engagement, were ordered to take the merchant vessels under convoy, as soon as the fleet should leave them, for protection against any gun boats the Americans might send out to intercept them.

Before we sailed, I was appointed to the *Confiance*, one of the above mentioned prizes, and superseded the Lieutenant then commanding her, who was appointed to another ship. My appointment took place on the Friday and we were to sail on the following Sunday. I was obliged therefore to engage myself closely to receive, and store away the cargo.

On Sunday morning the squadron sailed, and about 2 pm the same day, we being laden, followed. As Sir James intended to see us to the place of our destination, he hove to as soon as the ships got clear of the land until* we came up, when we all made sail for Burlington Bay, where we arrived in a few days, and immediately commenced handling the cargoes. The fleet sailed down the lake as soon as they had landed what stores and provisions they had taken on board, leaving us to discharge as quick as possible.

On the 27th of Sept a Captn of the Glengarry Regt, a provincial corps, requested a vessel from the Lieutenant commanding the convoy, to carry dispatches of importance to the Commodore; my schooner being unloaded I was to weigh, and proceed immediately. About 10 am I saw our fleet come out of York bay and stretch across the lake under easy sail;[13] shortly after the Americans hove in sight, coming up the lake with a fair breeze, and their line of battle formed. As both parties deemed

---

* Page 18 begins in the original journal.

still determined to engage, it was considered this would be the decisive blow; it blew a stiff topgallant breeze, which gave them both an excellent opportunity of manoeuvring. Finding it now impossible to put the officer on board the Commodore's ship, he was extremely anxious to land; but being ordered to take a position by signals from the flag ship, I made every exertion to gain that point, which I happily accomplished.

After making several tacks we gained the weather gage occasionally firing a fair shot as we passed each other on different tacks. Having now a good opportunity of closing, the ships bore up and took their stations within 300 yards of their opponents, when the engagement begun in earnest, the intention of the Commodore being to board the instant he should perceive any confusion in the enemy's ships. Sometime after the action had begun, an explosion was observed to take place on board the American flag ship, which Sir James Yeo, in the *Wolfe* was engaging. The boarders were in readiness, and orders given to the Master to run her alongside, but while veering around, an unlucky shot carried away the main topmast, and that falling aft, took the mizzen mast along with it. The principal ship in our squadron being now unmanageable, nothing could save the whole but a retreat before the wind; the foremast of the *Wolfe* being the only mast standing, the broad pendant was hoisted to the topgallant mast head, and the signal made to retreat, which was covered in a most admirable style by Captain Mulcaster, in the *Royal George*, who took the whole of the American fire. The officers of the *Pike*, after I was taken prisoner, spoke of his masterly conduct in the highest praise; in this action there were eleven American vessels, and but six of ours, three of the former were so much disabled as to be obliged to run into the River Niagara.

Had the American Commodore followed up the advantage he had gained, our ships must have been destroyed. Indeed these were our bitter reflections, but by [an] unaccountable oversight, after following us a few miles, he suddenly hauled his wind, and hove to though he knew we had no harbour under our lee to run into, nor any roadstead where we could anchor under the shelter of our batteries. Thus, his principal ships being uninjured, in* their spars, might easily have driven us in shore without the interposition of some fortunate circumstance, which in the present

---

* Page 19 begins in the original journal.

state of the weather, for by this time it blew a gale of wind, would be next to miraculous.

When we saw the enemy heave to, we could scarcely believe our eyes, but finding he had given up the chase, by his making sail upon a wind in order to beat up to Niagara, we fully expected he would visit us the next morning. Under this impression, detachments of seamen from each ship were sent on shore, and several guns landed to form batteries, the men working all night, to have them ready for opening by the morning should the enemy attack us.

Being acquainted with the passage into Burlington Lake, I was sent to the Heights, with dispatches. The surf [was] running very high over the bar, [and] through the carelessness of one of the seamen at the oar, the boat capsized, and we had a narrow escape, the sea breaking over us very high. I was obliged to borrow a hat and pair of shoes, having lost my own, as well as my boat cloak, and then we proceeded to the Heights. Having foreseen the possibility of a capsize, I had well secured the dispatches, so that they were scarcely soiled with wet, — immediately on landing I was assailed with the unpleasant intelligence of the loss of our fleet on Lake Erie, and the precipitate retreat of our army under Gen[l] Proctor, under most harassing circumstances. I returned the same

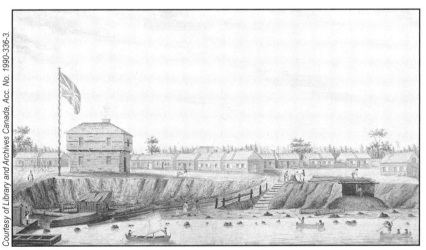

Barracks at Fort York, 1804, painting by Sempronius Stretton. The Americans took York and burned many of the barracks and fort on April 29, 1813, before Wingfield arrived in the Canadas.

Courtesy of Library and Archives Canada, Acc. No. 1990-336-3.

evening with dispatches for the Commodore containing the intelligence of a large number of troops being assembled at Sackets Harbour for a secret expedition, supposed against Kingston.

On the 30th, Sir James sailed, leaving orders for us to proceed to York, as soon as the vessels had discharged their cargoes, and receive on board a detachment of De Wattviller's (a German) regiment for Kingston where we were collecting troops to observe the motions of the enemy.[14]

The 2nd Octr we sailed, and the following morning anchored in York Bay; the Lieutenant commanding went on shore to learn at what time we were to expect the soldiers, and found they would not be in readiness till the evening. About 9 pm they came on board, and we weighed anchor with light airs and a very thick fog; we were, however, detained a considerable time in consequence of one of the merchant vessels grounding upon the bar.

Monday, as the sun got power, the fog dispersed and we were all together except one small sloop, which was nearly over to the American shore, having* steered a wrong course during the night; we had a calm the whole of Tuesday, but in the evening a breeze sprang up, and continued gradually to increase during the night, my schooner and the *Hamilton*, the other American prize, were obliged to keep under easy sail to allow the other vessels to keep up, though we had, each, a vessel in tow: towards noon we had strong breezes with every appearance of a gale, at four it blew a gale and the wind, which had been hitherto in our favour, suddenly chopped round dead against when we were about 30 miles from Kingston: soon after we observed several vessels rounding Long Point which, for some time we supposed were our own fleet, but perceiving by our glasses they were under a heavy press of canvas, and counting nine, we knew them to be the enemy in chase of us.

---

* Page 20 begins in the original journal.

CHAPTER TWO

CAPTURE AND EXPERIENCES
AS A PRISONER OF WAR

We let out our reefs and made all possible sail, but being only in ballast trim, and a heavy short sea breaking, which drove us to leeward without any place to run to for shelter — so it was certain we should be captured. This being the case, I ordered all the arms, ammunition, and whatever stores could be come at, to be thrown overboard, or destroyed, and desired the Master of the schooner I had in tow to be prepared to send his men on board us, and set his vessel on fire. For this purpose she was hauled up to our quarter, and when cleared, she was set on fire and cut adrift.

About half past six the American schooner *Sylph* of 14 guns running up alongside within hail fired a shot ahead, and the *Pike* being close astern of her I hauled down the pendant and hove to; at this time four other vessels to windward had struck.

My feelings, at this moment, I cannot describe. All hopes of promotion vanished at once, expecting the worst of treatment, and what did not add to the amelioration of my circumstances, I was without a dollar in my pockets, except in the proper currency of the Province, called army bills,[1] which bear a premium per diem according to their value; by way, too, of soothing my feelings, while I had been busily employed on deck. One of the men had plentifully regaled himself with rum and, just as the American officer came on board to take possession of the prize, either by accident or design, staggered against me, and would have knocked me overboard had I not been caught by one of the seamen. I sullenly threw my sword and belt on deck and walked down to the cabin; being alone I either sat, or laid down, and could scarcely refrain from shedding tears, however, I was not allowed to enjoy my feelings long, if it could be called

An Army Bill, 1813. This common form of currency used by the British military was available in various denominations. They could be negotiated for cash, even in the neighbouring United States on the basis of a fellow officer's trust.

enjoyment, as the American Lieutenant came into the cabin. I believe he perceived my agitation, which I endeavoured to conceal, for he came to me and offered his hand,[2] at the same time, returning my sword, telling me not to regret, for it might not be long ere he was in the same situation, and true he spoke, for within a year I returned him the same compliment. The Americans captured five vessels, one was burnt, and one escaped, with 200 soldiers of the before mentioned German regiment.*

About half past nine of the same evening, I was sent on board the Commodore's ship where I found a Lieutenant of the Royal Navy, and my old messmate who had commanded the *Hamilton*, who had been on board some time, and I was expected. The officers of the ship were waiting supper, and a cabin was prepared for me in the gun room, among the Lieutenants who, I must own, treated us in a most handsome and gentlemanlike manner.

---

* Page 21 begins in the original journal.

When the prisoners were secured, the ships made sail for Sackets Harbour, where they anchored about two on Wednesday morning.

At daybreak I turned out and went on deck to take a view of the harbour, before the officers were up, and in a few minutes was joined by my friend. We walked the poop together cursing our unlucky stars, and endeavoured to form some line of conduct for the future. Our cash amounted to a considerable sum, but his, as well as mine, was all in army bills and between us both we could not muster one dollar in silver. While holding this conference we were joined by Commodore Chauncey who entered familiarly into conversation with us, and from him we learned that we should most likely get our bills cashed at Albany, through which city we should pass.

After breakfast the First Lieutenant took us round the ship, which appeared to be kept in excellent order. On the starboard, or right hand side, were hung a number of cots and hammocks, for the accommodation of the wounded, which by their own statement amounted to 40, and 19 killed, in the *Pike*, alone. The explosion, which I mentioned in a former page, was caused by the bursting of a 24 pounder under the forecastle, which killed and wounded 15 men. As they had had no opportunity of landing any of their wounded men, or of materially repairing the damages done to the hull and rigging in the late action, we could plainly perceive that our shot had not all been thrown away, and they were still obliged to keep the pumps occasionally going.

Having left our vessels at so short a notice, we were given to understand that a boat would be manned to take us on board them, to collect what, in the hurry, might have been left behind; but when we arrived on board every vestige had disappeared; however, as neither of us had lost anything of consequence we made no complaint.

This afternoon the army officers were disembarked and taken to an inn where they were confined in a room, with an American officer to keep them company and a guard outside the house.

By the conversation after dinner we learned that an expedition was fitting out against Kingston, and we had plainly distinguished by the naked eye a great hustle on shore, and a number of troops. The Yankees made so sure of soon being in possession of that place, that they frequently rallied us upon the subject in a jocose manner. We were still kept on board the ships, and the place of our destination was not yet fixed upon by the Military Commandant of the place.

Thursday, Oct.7th, at breakfast we were informed that the army officers had* been mounted, and had all left Sackets at daybreak under an escort of Dragoons; we much regretted being parted from them as they were eight in number, and only three of us. At noon the Commodore informed us we were to disembark in the evening; the officers of the ship ordered an early dinner and sent on shore to secure beds for us and order a supper being, as they expressed it, determined to give us a treat before we parted. After dinner we were accompanied on shore by the First Lieutenant of the *Pike*, who, on our landing informed us we must consider ourselves on our parole of honour; we gave our word and were then permitted to go where we pleased.[3]

Sackets, at the commencement of the war did not contain above 20 houses or more properly huts, but, like Kingston, had now risen into a place of some importance and a number of houses [had been] run up in a temporary manner, but [as it was] lying in a swamp we were often literally over our ankles in mud, and there being from 10 to 15,000 troops here, for the expedition above mentioned, [it] gave the place the appearance of a large city.

While walking with my friend I was familiarly accosted by an American naval officer, who shook me by the hand, and said he was happy to see me well, but sorry I was a prisoner. Though it was dusk there was sufficient light to distinguish his features, which being totally unknown to me, I answered that he had the advantage of me, never having seen him before to my knowledge. He told me his name was Bowers, and asked if I did not recollect impressing him at Portsmouth eighteen months ago, "but" said he, "I soon gave you the slip." Never having pressed a man in my life I felt awkwardly situated, hardly knowing whether to repel or accept his advances. However, all my protestations to the contrary would not convince him but I was the person, and he pressed us so strongly to take a glass of wine with him that in decency we could not refuse, though we went with reluctance fearing it might interfere with our engagement to meet the officers of the *Pike* at 9 o'clock. He treated us very handsomely, and informed me he was Masters Mate of one of the schooners, [and] after [his] wishing us a speedy exchange, we parted.

---

* Page 22 begins in the original journal.

On our return to the inn we found we had overstayed our time, and caused some anxiety, but upon my relating the anecdote, harmony was restored, and we sat down to an excellent supper. It was late before we separated, when we were shown to our beds, and left to repose without being honoured with a guard.

Friday before breakfast we visited our men, and found they were on the point of marching. They informed us their treatment had been good, but that much persuasion had been used to induce them to enter the American Service, but none complied. On our return to the inn we were informed that we were to set off immediately, and take the route to Utica where we were to receive further orders,[4] and were given to understand that our travelling expenses would be reimbursed when we arrived at the depot for prisoners of war, upon their parole. We were advised by the American officers to accede to this plan or we should be obliged to march with our men, and they were kind enough to procure us a conveyance to Utica by our paying the driver a certain* sum. The only difficulty now remaining was to convert some of our army bills into cash, and on our consulting with the Lieutenant, found he was as bad off as ourselves, indeed, worse as to the amount of cash. We therefore wrote a joint letter to Commodore Chauncey stating our difficulties, and setting forth [the] impossibility of proceeding at our own expense unless some of our bills were cashed. It was after noon when we received an answer to say that the Commodore did not wish to have anything to do with our government bills, but if either of us chose to draw a private bill upon any of our friends at Kingston he would give us dollars for it. The Lieutenant having a brother, holding a high official situation in the civil service at Kingston, drew upon him for 100 dollars, which was immediately cashed.[5]

Before we had finally settled this point it was nearly dusk, but as our waggon had been waiting several hours, and our baggage had preceded us under the charge of our servants, we determined to come up with them and collect it together.

The road leading from this place into the main one had been lately cut through a continued swamp, and the heavy rains, which had lately fallen, rendered it nearly impregnable, so much so that we were frequently obliged to assist the driver in lifting the waggon out of the deep

---

* Page 23 begins in the original journal.

holes. When I speak of a waggon I do not mean one like ours, but a light vehicle built in that form but much smaller, and going upon springs, which are in general use in this part of the country.

We came to the place where the men were stopping about 10 o'clock but could get no accommodation at the inn, and were obliged to go six miles further to a place called Watertown; the road being now much better we soon arrived but found the people of the inn had gone to bed. We soon roused them up and found we were just as far from getting accommodations here as at the last place it being assize time, and every bed in the house [was] occupied. McLean, the Lieut[t], being very ill, with some difficulty we procured a few blankets, and had them laid in a corner of the room for him, while we made a good fire; and getting a good supply of bread and cheese and grog, beer being out of the question, we made our supper and then settled ourselves to sleep the best manner we could. In the morning we found our companion worse, but having procured him a bed we resolved to wait till the luggage came up.

We sat down to breakfast with as motley a group as ever [an] Englishman got into company with; at a very long table were seated two judges, numerous lawyers, multitudes of clients, and more witnesses. I had the honour of sitting next to one of the judges, who in America are styled "His Honor," and as [ever a] plain-dressed farmer-looking man as need be seen. There was nothing whatever in externals to distinguish him and his learned brother from the rest of the* company except [their] being more plainly dressed than the lawyers, and most of the clients and witnesses, but intelligence was in his eye, and I am sure kindness was in his words, for he took a world of trouble in endeavouring to convince me how much better it was to live under a republican government, than to leave my native country and fight for a monarchical one. To all [of] which, of course, I freely assented, and I believe "His Honor" thought he had made a convert, as on parting he heartily shook me by the hand, and gave me a pressing invitation to his house as soon as I should be at liberty to accept it. Here indeed was liberty and equality personified — no one was addressed by his name, but all interrogations began with "I say Mister" — "Squire" or "Honor"; and I believe if His Honor had anything on his plate, that either lawyers or clients wished to partake of, they

---

* Page 24 begins in the original journal.

would not have scrupled to ask to share the dainty with him. And as for our bread, it was necessary to secure it in our hands, for biting it was no protection from its being taken by your next neighbour should there be none more handy.

Having waited till past 11 o'clock, and no signs of our men coming up, the driver, likewise being anxious to proceed, we left Watertown. The roads were but indifferent, and the country all around rocky and barren showing but little signs of vegetation; we met numbers of waggons and carts, laden with all kinds of merchandise for Sackets. This afternoon, from a high hill, we saw Lake Ontario and, as we thought, took a last farewell look at it, not expecting again to join the Squadron.

As evening advanced, I was surprised to hear our driver ask two or three persons we met, "how far am I going tonight?" thinking it strange that our travelling should be regulated by other people. I questioned him upon the subject, which he accounted for by saying, there was no settled town or village near, and we might pass a tavern half an hour before dark, and travel through dangerous and bad roads after night fall. At dusk we put up at a miserable log hut, with no other accommodation than a good fire.

Sunday the 10th was a fine day and we got into somewhat more tolerable roads, the country still very thinly inhabited, consequently but little cleared lands. McLean being still very poorly we travelled slowly for his accommodation, though much against the will of the driver; we found provisions, very cheap and lived well at little cost. This evening we put up at a tavern, so called, and got two beds, but everything belonging to them so filthy that neither of us took off our clothes. Monday turned out thick and hazy, with drizzling rain, however, we started early in hopes of reaching Utica the same evening. Just before noon we stopped to eat, and rest the horses, having nearly 20 miles of woods to go through, without a single house intervening. After performing it over a very bad road, we came into a delightful open country, with numerous farmhouses, and much cleared land, and what pleased us better, an excellent road. Finding we could not reach Utica this evening, we put up rather* early at a very respectable house, and had a good supper with the additional luxury of clean beds.

---

* Page 25 begins in the original journal.

Saturday was a beautiful fine morning, and with the earliest dawn we started, [and] as we advanced the face of the country appeared completely changed. Instead of thick woods, swamps and miserable log huts were now present to our view, [and] large tracts of land in a state of high cultivation, with no more wood land than sufficient to give the scene a more picturesque appearance. About 8 we arrived at Utica, a pleasant and clean little town, and to our great joy found all the officers here who had left Sackets before us; this, to us in particular, was a pleasant meeting, as we should now travel together to the end of our route. We learned they had been here three days, and were waiting a passage to Albany, but the militia officer, who was a magistrate to boot, wanted them to proceed at their own expense — this they, as well as ourselves were determined not to do. After breakfast, which was the only comfortable one we had sat down to since leaving the ships, we went to wait upon the magistrate to procure a conveyance; after much altercation we parted without his

A View of the Boats & manner of navigating on the Mohawk River.

Published by J Riley July 1810.

Courtesy of Craig Williams, Canal Society of New York.

Wing Dam on the Mohawk River, 1810. Wingfield probably encountered such wing dams as he travelled the route of the current New York State Canal System during his adventures as a prisoner of war in 1813. The Western Inland Lock Navigation (WILN) Company constructed such dams to impound water. Boats would pass through an opening in the apex of the dam. Philip John Schuyler, president and leading force in the creation and incorporation of the Northern Inland Lock Navigation Company, constructed the canals that would form the basis of the great Erie Canal System.

coming to any decision. For ourselves we protested that we would not move a step without being supplied with some sort of conveyance by the government, and informed him, on the morrow morn we should wait upon him with our paroles, and no longer consider ourselves bound by them. That appeared to have the desired effect, as in the course of the day we received an order to go on board a barge bound for Schenectady, which would start the next day. We learned from our landlord that we should find this way of travelling very tedious, and hinted, that we, most probably might find it more economical in the long run to hire waggons, and, indeed, so we found it before long.[6]

After dinner, which was excellent, and the wine good, we went to view our barge and found it to be an open boat deeply laden, with no cabin or any place to shelter from the weather, Schenectady being 90 miles distant from this place, and a great number of locks to go through, we had no vast idea of getting there very soon; some were for refusing to go on board, but all being anxious to reach Albany, their objections were surmounted.

The following morning, those who were fortunate enough to retain their baggage, were employed in packing it up, and getting it stowed away on board, while others not so fortunate, amused ourselves by strolling about the town. At 2 pm we started, and the progress we had made by dark realized the idea we had formed of the length of time it would take us to reach the end of our journey, [even] though the current was in our favour. At dark the boat was made fast to the shore and we adjourned to a tavern close by to make our dinner and supper in one; we got plenty to eat and some blankets spread upon the floor to sleep on. With much persuasion McLean, who was now fast recovering got a bed.

Thursday 14th — a cold raw morning with drizzling rain; as there was a good road along the bank of the river, such of us who preferred walking, started off and, having directions from the Master of the where it would be convenient to have breakfast, halted at that house, and had it prepared an hour before the lazy ones came up.* When finished we all embarked, as the current was more rapid and the road diverged too far from the bank of the river; we had some fine views as well as grandeur,

---

* Page 26 begins in the original journal.

which greatly assisted to beguile the tedious hours. At night we put up as before and after supper, began a council [as to] how we should proceed, being tired and much dissatisfied at so slow a method of travelling, [and] being anxious to learn what place was to be our ultimate destination, added to which our money began to wax short and we feared, at the rate per diem we went, our stock should be exhausted before we could get a fresh supply. These reasons induced some to propose hiring waggons, and proceeding at the quickest rate, while others [suggested] to try what another day would bring forth, as the wind might favour us; after some debate the latter was agreed to.

Along the Mohawk River, 1793, etching by Cornelius Tiebout.

Courtesy of United States Library of Congress, LC-USZ62-31797.

The next morning we came to a place called the German Flats, where having to go through seven locks, we left the barge at the first of them, and walked on to the house of an old Dutch woman who got breakfast for us, consisting of broiled chickens, potatoes, tea, and coffee for which we were charged 7½ Sterling each. The barge having cleared the locks we embarked, and from here to the little falls (a few miles) the scenery was truly terrific; the river is very narrow, and on each side the rocky precipices, in many places rise above 100 feet and in some places completely overhang the boat. It seemed, indeed, as if the rock had been formerly rent by an earthquake. About 11 we came to the little falls, a part of the river so rapid, and shallow that no vessel can go up or down; it is estimated from beginning to end as [a] 200 feet perpendicular fall. When we cleared the locks we came into a wider part of the river, with very little current and a strong headwind, so that we scarcely held our own; towards evening it moderated. Putting up for the night, [we] again held a council, which terminated exactly as the last had done, and the next day we again embarked. Having now a strong current in our favour we proceeded merrily along, which made the anti-waggonites exult at having been victorious in council, but at 8 a strong wind rose, and the boat having to discharge part of her cargo, we came to the solution of hiring waggons, and finishing our journey by land.

It was noon before we were ready to start, but the men having good horses promised to take us to Albany the same evening, though 40 miles distant. From this place to the city of Albany we travelled along a fine road, and through a continued orchard, both sides being planted with fruit trees, principally apple; the country is thickly inhabited and the land kept in a good state of cultivation. About half past four we arrived at Schenectady, a populous town standing on the bank of the river of the same name, which communicated with the sea thro' the Hudson; it therefore carried on a considerable traffic inland.

Around 6 we arrived at the city of Albany, and put up at an inn where we had every attendance and accommodation that could be expected at a London Hotel, except the exorbitant charges. After dinner, which had been ordered by a servant sent before while the horses were [undecipherable, possibly "fed and watered"] at Schenectady, we were joined by some gentlemen of the city who were to cash our bills, which proved extremely acceptable to us, and from the information we received at Sackets we enabled [four illegible words] immediately, thereby anticipating our business for* having refused two or three invitations for the morrow. And [having] appointed Monday to meet upon business, we were left to ourselves, and then settled a deputation to wait upon the Governor, inform him of our arrival, and request permission to remain here a few days to rest ourselves from the fatigue we had undergone, and procure several new necessaries we were in want of, after which we were glad to retire to bed.

---

* Page 27 begins in the original journal.

Sunday the 17th. This day, at least, we had determined upon as a day of rest, but the morning was dull and lowering with every appearance of a wet day. After breakfast the clouds began to break, and a party of us sallied forth to view the city, but had proceeded scarcely 100 yards when the rain descended in torrents, and we were glad to return to our inn. The deputation, however, proceeded, but the weather continued so wet throughout the day that there was no stirring abroad. On the return of our deputation we learned that the Governor had it not in his power to grant our request, and had intimated to them that, had he known of our arrival the evening before, he should have been obliged to send us away this morning and, that on Monday at 4 am a coach would call for us to convey us to Pitsfield. This was very unwelcome intelligence, but we were obliged to submit. Our friends were apprised of the Governor's resolution, and waited on us the same evening when they discounted our army bills at 5 percent, which they took care to charge upon the simple value of the bills, without making any allowance for the amount of interest already accumulated upon them, but even this was better than we once expected.

Sketch by Heidi Hoffman.

A stagecoach, one of the many modes of travel used by Wingfield as a prisoner of war.

Sometime before daylight we were called according to our orders, and before we were ready, the coach drove to the door. Imagine to yourself a vehicle somewhat in the form of our stage coaches, but considerably longer in the body — the roof very slight, not sufficiently strong to bear any luggage, [and] supported by slight rods of iron. Suspended from the roof were panels of painted canvas, made either to roll up, or let down, as circumstances might require — when down they were fastened with buttons and loops. It carried 15 passengers, three upon a seat, all of them facing the horses, a most admirable method, invented for the purpose of promoting social conversation — liberty and equality — no outsiders — luggage stowed under your feet to make the travelling more convenient. The coachman hurried us in no very gentle terms, which the reader may be sure, from the good humour we were in at being obliged to rise so early, and our disappointment at not being allowed to remain a few days, was returned with tenfold vehemence, and the fellow threatened to drive off without us. Now this threat, to a person on urgent business, might have wrought wonders, but to us, it would have been the very thing we wished for, however, as the coach was ordered expressly for us, he was obliged to wait. About 6 we were all seated; there were three passengers besides ourselves, which, with the coachman made 15, and I believe no 15 men were ever seated in a coach together in worse humour, and for quite opposite reasons — the three passengers, and coachman, because they were detained, and our party because we were obliged to go.

At Albany we inquired concerning the allowance to be made for our * subsistence, and learned that all commissioned officers from the General to the Ensign were allowed 3/6 per diem; 3 by the American government, and 6 [pence] by ours, being a donation, called "the Queens bounty," — all other prisoners who were admitted to their parole had but half that allowance. This caused some dissatisfaction on the part of my friend, and self, who having no commissions came under the eighteen penny head, which would not support us without the most rigid economy. We came to the determination not to accept it, and if pressed upon us, to give up our paroles and embrace the earliest opportunity of making our escape.

---

* Page 28 begins in the original journal.

We were ferried over the North, or Hudson River, in a floating machine called a scow, and landed in the State of Massachusetts, having been travelling in the State of New York since our first landing. Each particular State has its own currency, that of New York reckons eight shillings to the dollar, and Massachusetts, but six, which, at first occasioned some embarrassment in settling our reckoning, but as throughout the United States the dollar is the standard coin, and divided into 100 cents, a copper coin, we were soon used to it — their gold coin — one eagle, and half eagle — of the value of ten, and five dollars.

Early in the afternoon we arrived at Pitsfield, a small neat town, the residence of one of the Deputy Marshals for the State of Massachusetts, under the charge of whom we were to remain. The whole of us waited upon him and were received in a very gentlemanly manner; he gave us to understand that an exchange was expected to take place in a few days, and it was not improbable but we might be included. We informed him that we wished to come to some immediate arrangement respecting our finances, complaining at the same time at our being obliged to furnish ourselves with conveyances, except in this instance, and that of the barge, and subsistence since we had been taken. To this he answered that he could make no allowance to us, but should pay us our subsistence money from the day we landed. Lieutenant McLean informed how my friend and self were situated; Major Melville replied that, being known British officers, he should pay us under the head of commissioned officers. This of course silenced every objection on our part, and we continued under the three and sixpenny [a] head while we remained on parole though when we were paid at Concord, it made the Midshipmen wince a little, they not being so fortunate as ourselves.

He now signed our paroles for Cheshire, a small town about nine miles off, and [we] were limited to a mile along all lawful roads, the church being made the centre. Upon our request we were allowed to remain here a few days, and the Deputy Marshal cashed some of our army bills, without taking any discount, contenting himself with the premium they bore. A short time sufficiently tired us of this place and, upon application we were provided with carriage to convey us to Cheshire where, on our arrival we found upwards of 20 fellow prisoners all taken on the border of the Lakes. We went direct to the house of a Major Leland, where dinner was provided for us, and where six of the before mentioned officers boarded, but, as he could not accommodate us all, we separated after dinner* though somewhat late; four of remained here, two went to Capt[n] Brown's an old revolutionary officer, and the remainder to a farmhouse about half a mile off, but all in Capt[n] B's family.

The short time we remained here was passed pleasantly and the inhabitants, though all of them were of the war party, paid us every attention; neither were we strictly confined to the limits of our parole, but could at any time procure leave from Capt[n] Brown to extend our rambles to the adjacent villages though we were not allowed to sleep [away] from our quarters.

About a fortnight after we had been here we were joined by the Masters of the merchant vessels, [who had been] taken with us, and who had travelled with the men. They had been anxiously expected, as we confidently supposed they would bring our baggage, and it was a great mortification to learn from them that they were not allowed to do so; though they had made the offer, and that it remained at Greenbush, near Albany, the grand depot for prisoners of war, in charge of our servants. The disappointment was great to all but particularly to my old messmate Jackson, and myself, as the whole of ours was left behind, while the other officers being provided with small travelling trunks or portmanteaux had secured some portion of theirs, and two or three the whole, [although] it would have been impossible for us to have kept our large seachests with us according to the mode we had travelled. We immediately wrote to Major Melville concerning it, and not knowing how long we might be detained here, and finding the want of servants, we wrote for a certain number among the whole [of us]. Our letter was answered immediately, and in three or four days the men arrived with the baggage. I no sooner saw my chest, but knew it had been uncorded, and upon further examination found it had been broken open, and only contained the refuse of my things; [my] bed and bedding had totally disappeared. My friend was somewhat similarly situated, and our united stock might be stowed away in a very small compass. We again wrote to the Deputy Marshall, inclosing an inventory of all the articles missing as near as our memory would serve, but never received any satisfactory answer.

We should not so easily put up with our loss, had not an order come for all His Britannic Majesty's officers to hold themselves in readiness for

---

* Page 29 begins in the original journal.

travelling at the shortest notice. This elevated our spirits to such a degree that had not our baggage arrived at all it would not have detained us.

Early in November we were informed that the 10th of that month was fixed for our departure, and having formed an acquaintance with several respectable young persons of both sexes, we determined upon giving them a ball and supper previous to our leaving, and the evening before was fixed upon for the same; the inhabitants received the invitation with much pleasure. Friday morning Major Melville, who was invited, came from Pitsfield accompanied by his wife and a party of young ladies; he paid our subsistence money and gave us our directions, from which we found that we, who were [the] last taken, were to travel together towards Salem, while the others were to cross the lines into Canada. We had between 30 and 40 couples at our ball, and passed a very pleasant* evening; the Americans in general are passionately fond of dancing, and it was not till the daybreak that the party thought of separating. By the time we had changed our clothes and taken breakfast, our travelling equipages were ready, and taking leave of each other we proceeded to Pitsfield, where we were provided with coaches to take us to Worcester, situated about half way between the former place and Salem, where the cartel was daily expected.[7]

By three o'clock in the afternoon of the following day we arrived at Worcester, the largest town, except Albany, we had seen since our first entering the United States; expecting our stay here would be but short, we put up at an inn kept by a Colonel Sykes of Militia. After dinner we were visited by several naval officers, some of whom had belonged to H.M.S. *Boxer*, taken some time before by the Americans; the others were mates and Midshipmen belonging to different ships, who had been prize Masters, but their vessels recaptured.

We had been here a week, and saw by the papers that the cartel had arrived at Salem, and grounded on entering the harbour, and having received no further notice from the Marshall, we concluded that she had been injured, and it might take some time to repair her damages. We therefore thought of providing ourselves with private lodgings in the town, as the tavern did not suit our finances. On the Monday we were all provided and intended taking possession of them [the new lodgings]

---

* Page 30 begins in the original journal.

after dinner, when about 2 pm an American naval officer arrived at the inn from Boston, and inquired for the British prisoners of war [and] he was shown into our room where I happened to be alone. After the usual salutations had passed between us, he presented me with a note, addressed to the British naval officers on parole at Worcester, containing an order for us to repair to the Marshall's office at Boston with all possible dispatch; I instantly sent to inform them of the arrival of the messenger.

From what we had learned from our fellow prisoners here, we understood that the exchange of prisoners had been concluded previous to, or very shortly after our capture; having, therefore, some doubts, I questioned him particularly, whether the naval officers taken on the Lakes were included, which he positively assured me they were and confirmed the same to McLean and Jackson when they arrived, giving us the Marshall's authority for it. Before he had finished some refreshments I had ordered to be placed before him, he was surrounded by the officers in the town, amongst whom were the army officers anxiously enquiring why they were excluded, but he either could [not], or would not give them any satisfactory answer, and all that could be got from him was, "You had better make as much haste as you can, gentlemen, for the cartel is only waiting for you."

Among the army officers [to be returned to Canada] was a Lieutᵗ of the 8ᵗʰ Regᵗ of foot, who had been serving in the country some years, and had been in most of the actions during the war, which had materially injured his health, added to which he had received a letter from England informing him of the death of a brother, and that a considerable fortune was left him. These circumstances had induced him to apply for leave of absence, which being refused, he tendered his resignation, [but] this not being accepted, he remained in some doubt [as to] how to proceed, when permission was given him to go to Quebec, and lay his case before the Governor; and he took his passage on board one of [several illegible words]* combatant, he [now] determined to accompany us to Boston, and would endeavour to go to Halifax by the cartel.

Our dinner was placed on the table at four o'clock, but no one sat down. McLean, Jackson, and myself were too elated at the prospect of so speedy an exchange, and busily employed in preparation for travelling,

---

* Page 31 begins in the original journal.

while our companions were as much depressed at being left behind and busily engaged in forming conjectures as to the cause.

Only one coach could be procured in the town, and between a stage-coach and a chariot, but four horses being put to it, nine of us contrived to stow ourselves away; at 5 we started and amused the inhabitants by singing "God save the King" in full chorus.

View of Bunkers Hill.
From a Drawing in Possession of the Rev. Dr. Ekleton.

Bunker's Hill, 1790, as illustrated in *The Gentleman's Magazine*, edited by Sylvanus Urban, gentleman in London, 1790.

About midnight we stopped to sup and changed our coach for another, which was to take us into Boston, while the former returned to Worcester for the remaining officers; this carriage being larger than the former, we were enabled to travel more comfortably.

As day broke, Boston and Charleston opened to our view, and as we passed along, the coachman was very communicative, and pointed out the most remarkable spots; among the rest, the famed Bunkers Hill, three or four miles before we reached the town — on an extensive plain, were distinctly seen the remains of several batteries thrown up during the Revolutionary War. About 8 we arrived in the City of Boston and our coach drove up to the exchange coffee house, where we were received with all the officious forwardness shown by masters of hotels, waiters etc., and were shown into a spacious well-furnished room commanding a fine view of the sea, and where for the first time since leaving England, my sight was regaled with a good coal fire. After ordering breakfast, we retired to change our dress preparatory to waiting on the Marshal.

In each of the States, besides the Marshal, is an English Agent, or Commissary whose duty it is to pay the Queen's bounty money and receive any complaints from the prisoners, and report accordingly. The person thus appointed at Boston, to whom we sent [notice] on our arrival, immediately called upon us, and appeared much surprised to see us in the city, observing there must be some mistake as British prisoners were particularly excluded from entering any sea port town. From him we learned that the cartel would sail in a few days, and was not materially injured; some of the officers wishing him to negotiate their bills, he took his leave to enquire the rate of exchange, promising to return before we should have finished our breakfast, and accompany us to the Marshal's office.

We had nearly all assembled in the breakfast room and only waiting for the rest to begin, when in bounced a little fellow, with all the presuming insolence of office, and stood gaping at us, as if struck with astonishment. He soon received a broad intimation that his company could be dispensed with, and he had better leave the room, [however], the fellow retained his position and with a contemptuous smile, said, "Pray gentlemen what brought you here?" He had a variety of answers and two or three stepped forward to show him the door, when he thought proper to announce himself a Deputy Marshal, sent by Marshal Prince to know the reason of our being in Boston against our paroles. [When] he was informed of the note addressed to us at Worcester, he replied "The note I am sure did not order you to come to this city." After entering into some explanation, he broke all short off by ordering us in a very peremptory manner to follow him to the Marshal's* office; this we peremptorily refused to do until we had taken breakfast. "Do you wish me to employ force?" said he — "Do as you please," was his answer — at the same time ringing the bell for the waiter to bring in breakfast. Before it was well placed on the table, we heard the rattle of musquets in the passage and

---

* Page 32 begins in the original journal.

the word "halt." In entered the same man accompanied by a military officer, and our agent; the former asked us if we would come now. We were still in our slippers, our boots and shoes not being yet brought in, when Jackson, a strongly built north country man, surlily replied that we could not go without shoes, he sneeringly replied, "Pray gentlemen, did you come from Worcester without shoes." This was almost too much to bear, and we, with difficulty, refrained from attempting to turn him out of the room, and thereby composing ourselves to worse treatment. After some altercation between him and our agent, we consented to go provided the guard was dismissed, to which the Deputy agreed, and we proceeded to the Marshal's office, leaving our breakfast untouched.

Marshal Prince seemed to be almost choking with ill humour, and appeared to have made up his mind to vent it upon us. He was about the middle stature, very corpulent, and had a remarkable red face, with a sort of savage contemptuousness (if the expression can convey the idea) in his countenance. Before we had all entered the office he sent forth a torrent of abuse, for daring to enter Boston against our paroles, etc., etc., instead of waiting for, or demanding, an explanation. Someone told him they were not used to such language, and we all turned our backs to him, and put on our hats. [When] one of the clerks desired us to uncover, he was told to inform his master that if we were treated as gentlemen, we knew how to behave as such. This appeared to disconcert the Marshal, and he went into an adjoining room followed by his Deputy. On returning, he enquired if any officers taken in Canada were there; we informed him, four, when to our inexpressible mortification he told us we had no business here whatever, as we were not included in the exchange. I immediately stepped forward and particularized the conversation that passed between me and the naval officer who was the bearer of the order, and who was still at Worcester to forward the officers left behind; he requested to see the note, but it being addressed to all, no one thought of securing it. I told him that every officer present had read it and knew it to express "All British naval officers on their parole at Worcester," which was instantly attested by them. Seeing the officer of the 8th Reg[t] in his red jacket, the Marshal told [him] he, however, could have no business here. McMahon stated his case to him, but he replied he could do nothing in it, and that we must return to Worcester immediately. This we positively refused [to do], declaring we would not leave Boston until we had taken breakfast unless we were carried. As we grew warm, Marshal Prince seemed to cool, and taking McLean aside, had a few minutes conversation with him, and coming forward said, [that] the four Lake Officers must leave Boston the instant we had breakfasted, and [he] permitted one of his clerks to bear us company in the room while taking it. To this we could do no other than consent, and took leave of our more fortunate fellow prisoners, who started direct from the office to Salem, while we, attended by the clerk, returned to the exchange coffee house where we found one of our agent's sons waiting, and the old gentleman soon after joined us. From him we learned that we were to be sent to Cambridge, about three miles from* Boston, there to remain till next morning, when a stagecoach would call and take us to Concord, a pleasant little town 18 mile off.

About 2 pm a coach arrived at the hotel and conveyed us to our first place of destination, and at 10 the following morning a stage, somewhat better constructed than our Albany one, took us to the second. There was only one passenger besides ourselves, and though by this time rather used to the inquisitiveness of the natives, this fellow appeared to beat them hollow, and put such a number of impertinent questions to us, that we were soon obliged to make him confine his conversation to the driver.

On our arrival at Concord we found this man to be Major Simmonds, keeper of a tavern, and jailor, or governor of the jail in the said town; he was, moreover, deputed to keep an eye upon our motions while here. At his house the vehicle stopped and with some politeness he informed us we were to remain here, and shewed us into a decently furnished room where a cloth was laid for dinner; after partaking of which, we entered into an arrangement for board, lodging, and a private sitting room, which he furnished at the rate of four dollars each per week. Here we considered ourselves settled for a few months at least, and we had no reason to find fault with the town, or its inhabitants, when we once got acquainted with them, which was the case in a very short time, and in rather a singular manner.

The gaol was removed from the back of the house, by a narrow passage, and we understood from our landlord that there were four English seamen confined therein, as hostages for the safety of as many American

---

* Page 33 begins in the original journal.

View Across the Battleground at Concord. Wingfield passed his winter months in Concord in an "exceedingly pleasant" manner. He attended many "public balls and private parties" during his stay. The location was the site of the first forcible resistance met by the British, in April 1775, at the beginning of the "war of the Revolution." The undated print, of unknown origin, shows the 1836 monument erected to commemorate this confrontation and the small village in background.

seamen who had been taken in a prize belonging to the *President*, an American frigate, and sent to England for trial; there had been originally twelve, but eight of the American seamen returning the same number of hours were released by lot. We visited them the same evening, and found they had been confined 11 months, some part of the time on board a prison ship in Boston, where they had nearly effected their escape, but being detected they were removed to this jail.

A day or two after our arrival, while taking a walk round the town, we were accosted by a lady who, after apologizing for her seeming impertinence, enquired if we were not taken in Canada. On being answered in the affirmative, she told us she was a native of that country, and gave us an invitation to her house, which was a short mile from the town, but through some misunderstanding about the directions we did not go. A short time after we met the same lady, and informed her of our not attending according to [our] promise, and she repeated her invitation, giving us at the same time such directions that we could not mistake her house. After dinner we set out on our visit, and on our arrival received a hearty welcome, her family then at home consisting of two daughters and three sons, the latter quite children; the house very well furnished, and everything indicated a respectable independence. We learned that her husband had been one of the Judges of the lower Province of Canada, but came here in consequence of some estates being let him by a brother, [but] before he could take possession of them he died, Mrs Lee hastened to settle her affairs and return to [undecipherable]* but being detained beyond her expectations, and [with] the war breaking out, she was obliged to remain, much against her will, but having a brother-in-law settled in the town made her situation less irksome.

We had not been here a month before we were introduced to every family of respectability in the town, and were in a manner quite at home. As the Americans devote the winter season to pleasure, [and] indeed no out-of-doors work can be done in consequence of the severity of the weather, we very seldom passed an evening at home, being invited to all their private parties, including the minister, who, in every American town, is considered the first personage; so that between public balls, and private parties we passed our time, exceedingly pleasant.

The first unpleasant occurrence was that [of] one of the seamen before mentioned cutting his throat in the gaol. [When] our servant came running into our room to inform us of the event, we immediately visited him, and sent for a surgeon. He was unable to speak, and bled profusely; the other three poor fellows were in great distress, the tears running down their cheeks while giving us an account of the transaction. It appeared the young man had been in a low desponding state for some time, and for two days previous had taken no food. Towards dusk he [had] retired to the extremity of the room and committed the rash act before anyone of them was aware, and [they] only discovered it by the sudden gush of blood upon the floor. In a short time the surgeon arrived

---

* Page 34 begins in the original journal.

and examined the wound, which, owing to the bluntness of the knife, was not mortal.

This seemed a prelude to a long train of misfortunes, for the next day we saw by the papers that the officers whom we left at Worcester were all confined in the common gaol of the town; the American government journals excused it by alleging the confinement of some of the officers at Quebec. The officers likewise who left Cheshire the same day we did, and whom, we thought, were long since exchanged by the way of Canada, we heard were in Lennox Gaol, about seven miles from Pitsfield, no distinction made between them and the common malefactors, in point of accommodation. The opposition papers inveighed strongly against the inhumanity of the proceeding, and it was strongly deprecated through out the Union, except by those immediately under [the] government. Finding it [this trend to imprisonment] becoming so general, we soon expected to be provided with lodging in the same manner.

The same week we were visited by the same fellow who insolently intruded himself in our room at Boston, and, on being ushered into our apartment by our landlord, he very unceremoniously demanded McMahon's parole, shewing him a letter from the Commissary General for the prisoners of war to Marshal Prince, ordering the latter to deprive Lieut^t McMahon of his parole and confine him in the gaol belonging to the place where he then was. We, of course, could get no sort of information from the Deputy Marshal, who stuck close to the letter of his instructions. By the gaoler's account there was no place fit to receive him, and we jointly begged he might be permitted to remain on parole till the following day, by which time a room in the gaol might be cleaned and got ready, offering to become pledges for his appearance in any manner he, the Deputy Marshall, should think fit, but this he refused, neither would he allow him to remain to dinner until the gaoler assured him it would be at the least a couple of hours before a* room could be prepared for his reception, in consideration of which he was permitted to remain that time.

We sat down to dinner melancholy enough, and about half past five the Deputy Marshal and gaoler conducted McMahon to his solitary

---

* Page 35 begins in the original journal.

chamber. The former left Concord immediately, and through much per-suasion we induced Major Simmonds to admit us into the prison, and pass the evening with our messmate. As our servant had assisted to get the room ready, and from my own immediate observation, the following description of the room may be relied on; but if we might believe the opposition papers, and which I soon after found was too correct, McMa-hon's situation, in point of comfort, was preferable to any officer under confinement. The room, when we went into it stank almost enough to breed an infection, and the floor was covered with hard clots of dirt, though a spade had been used to scrape [away] some of the thickest. A man who had [had] quiet possession of it for eleven years (being con-fined for life), was just removed into another apartment. Our servant attempted to describe the man, and I am almost certain from his descrip-tion neither man or room had been cleaned since he had been an inhab-itant there.

The gaoler, who I before observed boarded us, shifted McMahon's bed and bedding into his new lodgings, and the next morning the men gave the room a thorough cleansing. As we had been permitted to visit the prison, under favour of our landlord, who had no orders to permit us to do so, he advised us to write to Marshal Prince for permission to visit our messmate and pass a few hours with him every day, and our request was granted.

On Christmas Day we had our dinner served up in the prison, being determined to dine together and, as the room had undergone several good washings, it was tolerably comfortable. The Major allowed our friend more indulgence than he would have received from interested motives, [with] more than any habitual flow of kindness being assured, we [made it known that] we should immediately leave his house if any harsh treatment took place.

Early in January 1814 we were joined by a Midshipman belonging to the *Loine* frigate,[8] taken in one of that ship's prizes, [and] also by a Lieut[t] in the Navy who was going to England as passenger in a merchant ship from the West Indies. Several Masters and Mates of merchant ships had likewise arrived, so that by this time our numbers had considerably increased. We had scarcely time to get acquainted with our new mess-mates, before a coach and four drew up to our house with our old friend, the Deputy Marshal, and the officer who had visited us at Worcester. They soon informed us of their business, which was to remove McMahon, and take the Lieut' and Mid. above mentioned with them, but where, or for what purpose we could not learn. The only information they deigned to give us was that it was only a change of place, and they were still to remain on their parole. This none [of us] believed and from what we had read in the papers we strongly suspected they were going to be closely confined, and in a few days after read that they were in Lennox Gaol.*

This removal again reduced us to our original number; and it was no small surprise to us that [since] we had been taken so long before the Lieut' and Mid., should they remain at large, at first we thought naval officers were a privileged caste, but this [latest action] destroyed the illusion, and we now daily expected to follow them.

We had long been displeased at the manner in which our table was served, and had frequently remonstrated with our landlord upon the subject, without any amendment taking place. Indeed, we had no occasion to complain of the small quantity, or bad quality of our provisions, for there was always profusion, yet there was wanting that cleanliness and attention to the cooking and serving up which, if paid, would have made a much smaller quantity infinitely more agreeable. Having now no further inducement to remain at the house, myself and friend removed into a private family, McLean and a Captn of a merchant vessel, who messed with us, were averse to shifting. We had not been long in our new lodgings before the family removed some distance beyond the limits of our parole, and Mrs Lee kindly accommodated us, when we were joined by our old messmates.

On the 2nd March, the person who had the charge of us received a letter desiring him to inform the British prisoners of war that they were to embark on board the cartel at Salem this day [in a] week['s time]. This put us in high spirits, and the week passed rapidly away. On the 10th while sitting in our parlour just after breakfast, we observed a coach and four driving up the avenue and, not doubting that it came to convey us to Salem, we went out to give the officer a welcome as soon as he should alight, when out jumped our eternal torment in the shape of the so often mentioned Deputy Marshal accompanied by

* Page 36 begins in the original journal.

another person, who, by the cockade in his hat we knew to belong to the Marshal's office. Seeing this fellow somewhat damped our ardour, but we had no time to form conjectures as he immediately delivered a letter to McLean informing him he was exchanged for a Master in the American Navy, and then enquired for us, politely informing us [that] they were to accompany us to Pitsfield. We inquired if they were going to conduct us to prison, they said their orders were to take us to the before mentioned place, and conjectured [between] themselves that, as an exchange of prisoners was about to take place between the Canadian government and theirs, and we being taken immediately under the former, it was intended we should be on the spot in readiness to cross the lines; though this tale was plausible enough, we felt well assured there was little, or no, truth in it.

As we had been so kindly treated by the inhabitants, we wished [some time] to take leave of them, as also to settle some little accounts, for which purpose we requested a few hours. Our request was granted and the hour of our departure fixed at 4 pm; an early dinner was provided and we sat down not much pleased. Precisely at the appointed time the coach again drove up to the door, and taking an affectionate leave of Mrs Lee, we mounted, and drove off. When we put up for the night, our conductors informed us we were at liberty to call for whatever we pleased as "Uncle Sam," that is the United States government, paid all our expenses while travelling, and wished to know what we would like for supper; upon our expressing a total unconcern* the inn keeper was sent for, and ordered to provide for four of the best viands his house afforded.

When I had an opportunity of being alone with my friend, I found his sentiments differed from mine, as he was of opinion we were not going to be confined, and situated as we were, we could take no steps toward making our escape with any degree of credit to ourselves. Not being deprived of our paroles, we therefore determined to await the issue with patience, and in the mean time to live well.

The third day we arrived at Lennox, and our paroles being taken from us, we were handed over to a guard of soldiers and escorted to gaol. Here we had sufficient time to reflect upon our irksome and uncomfortable

---

* Page 37 begins in the original journal.

situation, and most severely felt the loss of our bedding (mine never arrived at Cheshire, and my companion gave his away before leaving that place for Boston), on the supposition we were going to be exchanged, and did not wish to be encumbered with so much baggage. We were supplied with two blankets each, and a straw mattress, neither very tempting in point of cleanliness; our provisions were [scarcely] sufficient, but we had to do the best we could with them; however, give a sailor something to cook and I'll answer for it he will not starve.

We were soon removed to Pitsfield to join a large party of officers, prisoners of war, whose destination was [the] Philadelphia Penitentiary, — the Governor and council of the State of Massachusetts, having given orders to the different Sheriffs of Counties to open the gaols on the first of May, and release all prisoners of war, the gaols being only for the use of the State, and not to be at the disposal of the general government.

In a few days we started under the escort of a party of dragoons, forming a cavalcade of thirteen carriages, in each of which we were honoured with the company of an officer or non-commissioned [officer], who likewise attended whenever we stopped. On our arrival at

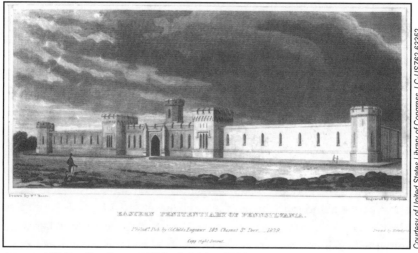

Cherry Hill Penitentiary at Philadelphia, 1829, engraving by C.G. Childs after a drawing by William Mason. This is likely the building where Wingfield was incarcerated, having been removed from Concord, along with a large party of British officers.

Philadelphia we had a large room to ourselves during the day, and at night [were] locked up in separate apartments, or, rather, cells. More than one attempt was made to escape, and at last about 30 got clear of the walls, but only two or three effectually made their escape. Neither the governor's officers of the guard, or the soldiers themselves, had any cause but to wish we were taken out of their custody by some lawful means, for the reader may be assured that we did not allow their charge to be a *sine cure* one.[9]

This retaliating system, as it was called, was carried on with great rancour by the Americans at first, so far, indeed, that in one instance lots were drawn for one of the officers to be hanged in lieu of a British traitor who was sentenced to undergo that fate, which would certainly have been carried into effect but [for] the number of American officers in our custody. The Americans began as before stated, with the seamen of Concord [by] firmly declaring [that] they should undergo the same fate as their citizens, as they called the British traitors, and the few naval victories they [the Americans] at first gained made them suppose they could intimidate the British government from doing itself justice; and about two months after we were taken, things wore rather an alarming appearance; and the British government imprisoned the same as the Americans, which the latter doubled by imprisoning officers. Ours did the* same, and when the Americans found they could no longer keep pace, all officers as soon as taken, were indiscriminately lodged in gaol as hostages, but by this time they had more than thrice our number of officers imprisoned at Quebec and other places, so that it began to lose much of its popularity among the war party, and [with] one of their general officers being sent to endeavour to obtain a mutual release, the Americans discharged two of our officers upon their parole, and soon after we were placed on the same footing as when first taken prisoners.

The officers who were taken in Canada were sent to Pitsfield; and on our arrival we were informed by Major Melville, who had returned to his duty (I should have mentioned before that he was absent on leave when we left here for Philadelphia), that we were still to consider ourselves as

---

* Page 38 begins in the original journal.

hostages, but the government gave us leave to reside at different houses in Cheshire, provided we signed our paroles to confine ourselves strictly within the limits of that farm, and not to walk in any public road. If we refused, we were to be confined in the depot at this place, until the negotiations for a release, or an exchange, was terminated. As the former was preferable to confinement we had no hesitation in complying. After signing our paroles we were informed by Major Melville we might take our own time in proceeding to Cheshire.

We now learned the reason for our not being confined when the other officers were. It seems that the mistake originated in our being sent from Cheshire to Worcester, and there separating from the army officers by going to Boston, and thence to Concord, when none of [us] ought to have been moved from the first place, not being included in the exchange then negotiated, and our being confined at last was owing to a letter from the Commissary Gen[l] for prisoners of war, inquiring what had become of us — if we had made our escape, and when. This, of course, led to the knowledge of our being at large, and our immediate apprehension.

In a few days we set off to take possession of our estates, my friend and self were lodged at a farm house about half a mile from Cheshire. Shortly after our arrival I was seized with a severe fit of fever and ague,[10] and at last reduced to such a state of weakness as to be unable to sit up above an hour at a time. During my illness I was constantly attended by my old friend who proved an excellent nurse, neither did I lack for kindness, from the people in the house, or the inhabitants of the village and, was in fact as much an object of their solicitude as if I had been a sick or wounded officer of their own navy; and I must here remark that, whatever the Americans may be taken in the mass, in their individual character, generally, I proved them to be a very kind and hospitable race, for even while our country was reviled, which was sometimes the case, they were always ready to shew the individual every kindness.

I was strongly persuaded to take exercise, but from the general languor of my frame, the remedy appeared worse than the disease and when I at last tried it, and was sufficiently strong to sit on horseback, my friend stated my case to the Deputy Marshal at Pitsfield, who gave us leave to ride any distance I thought might be conducive to my recovery though not to sleep* from our lodgings. We easily procured horses, and made excursions to every town and village within ten or fifteen miles of Cheshire, which made this the most pleasant time by far, of any we had passed since we had been taken, and I believe I continued it for some-time after I had perfectly recovered, on purpose to have the indulgence continued. While I was in this state we received our paroles with the same limits as at first, and several of the officers were permitted to go to Canada on three months leave, but if not exchanged within that period, to return.

In June we received a letter from Pitsfield informing us that we were at liberty to proceed to Canada on three months leave, and upon the same terms as those who preceded us, also to go with the prisoners who had arrived at Pitsfield from Greenbush, to the number of 400, who were duly exchanged, and would march on the 15th. We were requested to keep near them, and particularly to sleep in the immediate neighbour-hood where they halted for the night.

On the 13th we took leave of our hospitable friends at Cheshire, and went to Pitsfield where, on the day following Major Melville paid us our subsistence money with an additional allowance of 20 dollars each for our travelling expense. On the 13th the men marched at daybreak under an escort of soldiers, and we started after dinner knowing we should come up with them before night; we travelled along good roads, through thickly inhabited country having every appearance of comfort and plenty. On the fourth day we arrived at Whitehall, a small town, situated at the head of a river leading into Lake Champlain, where one of our fleet's [ships] was cruising, on board of which we were to be discharged. On the 20th we embarked on board a steamboat, quite rejoiced at the near pros-pect of being among old friends and acquaintances, not doubting but we should be exchanged on our arrival at Kingston. The following day we passed by the American ships, and the same evening were discharged on board one of ours; the soldiers went on to Montreal and the seamen were detained in the fleet, the ships being much in want of hands.

---

* Page 39 begins in the original journal.

CHAPTER THREE

RETURN TO ACTIVE DUTY
ON LAKE ONTARIO

On the 23rd we arrived at Montreal, and as [we] had only passed through the suburbs of the city on our way to Lake Ontario, we determined to remain a few days, as well to satisfy our curiosity as to [how to] get a new rig out, being destitute of nearly every article of clothing, and, as for linen, we had not one wearable shirt between us, our whole stock consisted only of five, — and they had been washed and mended, and mended and washed, till our washerwoman declared she could mend them no longer, and we desired her to direct all her skills to the frills and collars. A merchant of the city took our bills upon England [the army bills used for cash], and furnished us with every necessary.

While here I accidentally met with a family, whom I had been intimately acquainted with at York, and who introduced us to several others, with whom we formed some parties of pleasure, one of which was to Upper Lachine, where we crossed the St. Lawrence to visit an Indian village called Cognawaga.[1] These Indians were civilized, or more properly, said to be so, for they were infinitely more filthy than I ever saw them in their rude state, though they had changed their wigwams for log huts, and their religion of nature for that of the Roman Catholic. Indeed, from what I have seen of Indians, I consider any plan impracticable to bring them to a* civilized state, — they are too fond of their woods, mountains, lakes and rivers to change their hunting and fishing, though at times they gain but a precarious livelihood by those means, for stationary habitations, and those who have been most in the habit of frequenting our settlements, instead of following

---

* Page 40 begins in the original journal.

the example set before them in cultivating the land and living upon its produce, their only study is how to procure liquor, which they justly term Skittewormba (fire water), and I believe it would be impossible either by threats or rewards to make an Indian do one solid days agricultural work. I had an Indian boy about 11 years of age with me the whole time I was on Lake Huron, and brought him to England where I put him in a good school, but when about 14, I perceived he was miserable though in want of nothing; and closely questioning him, found that his native wilds had more charms for him than every comfort that a civilized life could afford, and when I told him I would send him back under the charge of a gentleman who was going to Canada, an acquaintance of mine, the boy was overjoyed; and I have since heard through a friend that he has become a great man among his tribe.

Having satisfied our curiosity at Montreal, and filled ourselves out with those necessaries we were in want of, we started for Kingston, and arrived at that place on the 15th July. After changing our dress we waited upon Sir James Yeo, who was unwell, [yet] he rose from his sofa and kindly shook hands with us, wishing us joy on our safe return. We informed him how we were situated, and found that the army officers who came before us were under the same circumstances, none of them doing duty with their regiments. He ordered us to go on board the *Prince Regent*, his flag ship, and make ourselves as comfortable as we could, giving us to understand that he could not employ us till we were regularly exchanged.

We found vast alterations had taken place since we left the country; two new ships [had been] launched, one mounting 68 guns, and the other 44, one on the stocks in a great state of forwardness intended to carry 110, and a spacious dockyard, with every convenient storehouses, and a great number of new faces among the officers who had arrived from England, and the town of Kingston as large again as formerly.

We continued to lead an idle life, anxiously hoping each day would bring about our emancipation, until the 12th August, when we were sent for by the Commodore who shewed us a proclamation from the Governor, ordering all the prisoners of war who had left the United States on leave of absence, to return to their duty, as they were duly exchanged. We were ordered to join the *Prince Regent*, and Sir James promised he would not forget us, but there were so many Admiralty Midshipmen sent out for promotion, whom we knew he must provide for first, that our prospect was but dull, unless a death, or court martial vacancy should occur, neither of which at this time was very probable. The patronage of a Commander-in-Chief embraces only the two latter and though he should appoint the officers from among his own followers to a new vessel, the Admiralty seldom confirms them; those also appointed to succeed invalided officers are taken from the Admiralty list, being composed of Midshipmen whose friends have not sufficient interest to get them promoted at home, but influence enough to get them sent out.*

Under some Commander-in-Chief, each of whom has a list, they are promoted according to their seniority on that list; neither my friend or self came under that head, and we had to trust to fortune and our own exertions.

The force that the Americans had now upon the lake, was so much superior to ours that our ships were obliged to be inactive in harbour, until the [new] large ship could be launched, but the boats of the fleet were frequently sent out for days together, to interrupt their merchant vessels coming down the lake to Sackets Harbour. The same evening I returned to my duty, intelligence was received that two American boats were hovering about Grenadier Island, and several boats were manned, and sent in chase of them; about 10 pm I was dispatched in the Commodore's gig to recall them, and with orders for a Lieutenant to remain in a large cutter, and to put myself under his orders, each boat to be supplied with a week's provisions from those that were to return. As soon as we had completed our provisions we rowed further up the lake, and at daybreak hauled the boats

Southeast View of Sackett's Harbor. The undated print of the early 1800s shows a small blockhouse in the right middle, with sailing ships and various buildings in background. Fort Pike is shown on the left, and, in the distant background, right, the artist would have seen Fort Tomkins.

Courtesy of New York Public Library; Digital Collection, Image ID # 809085.

---

* Page 41 begins in the original journal.

up high and dry among the bushes, covering them with green branches, where exposed to view, so that a boat might have pulled close along shore without discovering us. The men lay down around them, well armed, and ready to launch them at a moments warning, if required.

At dusk the boats were launched and commenced rowing close along [the] shore, looking into bays and creeks, using every precaution to prevent our being heard, or seen, from the inhabited parts of the shore bordering upon the lake. At daybreak we hauled the boat up on Grenadier Island, a place famed for the number of men who died belonging to the expedition that was fitting out at Sackets when I was taken, and which totally failed with the loss of nearly 10 [thousand] out of 15,000 men. It was intended to make a descent upon Montreal by the St. Lawrence, and General Wilkinson collected his forces on this Island, but the wind coming on to blow, with heavy rains, and continuing for several days, all communication with the main was cut off. The men being in want of food, and exposed to the inclemency of the weather without proper covering, died in great numbers, indeed one part of the island, at this time looked like the burial ground of a populous city. He conducted his descent down the St. Lawrence with so much prudence that he lost [a] great part of his men in killed and prisoners, for which laudable conduct he was tried by a court martial, and sentenced to be shot, but in consequence of his revolutionary services that sentence was commuted to cashiering.[2]

We were informed by the members of a family who resided on the island, that the American fleet were on the point of sailing, and in the afternoon we saw them standing out of Sackets Harbour, but [because of] the wind chopping around they came to an anchor about 10 miles from us; shortly after we saw two vessels coming down the lake with a fine breeze, which put us in a great state for fear they should pass us before dark, it being impossible to launch the boats without running an imminent risk of being seen by the American ships who would have sent their boats after us, and if not captured them, would effectually prevent our taking the vessels, which on the other hand, we were sure of losing if the breeze continued; but trusting to the light winds, which at this season of the year* generally prevail towards sunset, we still kept our spirits up. With our glasses we could perceive the headmost vessel was a large

---

* Page 42 begins in the original journal.

schooner, and [we] distinguished a number of hands on her deck. From this we thought she had soldiers on board to protect her from any attack, as they knew we were in the habit of frequently sending our boats on these sort of expeditions, from having lost several vessels before. According to our wishes, as the sun sank below the horizon the wind flatted nearly to a calm, and when we thought we were secure from being discovered by the American fleet we launched our boats and pulled towards the schooner, which lay about three miles off. As we advanced we could see the men assembled on the quarter deck, comfortably smoking their cigars quite unconcerned, and got close to them before we were noticed. A boat was run on each side and she became an easy conquest. The other vessel had kept a better lookout and was making every exertion to gain the shore, but there being only a light breeze, she was soon captured; they were both deeply laden with flour, and I was left on board the schooner to take her into Kingston. Her crew and passengers amounted to 22 men who, as they informed us, had come out with the determination of protecting them-selves if attacked by our boats, and if they had kept a good lookout they must have alarmed their fleet, which now lay about 8 miles off in full view.

We hove to till it was quite dark, as it would have given the men of war a suspicion that we were enemies had we immediately altered the course from Sackets to Kingston; the Lieut[t] took the gig to observe the motions of the American fleet, and we proceeded to the latter place where we anchored next morning. A great consolation to us, when we had brought our prize into harbour she was quickly disposed of without the assistance of a prize agent, and numerous other percentages. Also the Commodore had established a rule that the officers and men who were in the boats that captured any vessel should have double prize money, according to their rank, to what the officers and seamen in the fleet had.

When Sir James Yeo came from England he brought two Deal built gigs,[3] one 50 and the other 52 feet long, which had been seized by the revenue officers of that place in the act of smuggling, and being most excellent boats for pulling, they were supplied him from the dockyard. One of them had her back broke at York and was put upon the schooner I was taken in, to be conveyed to Kingston for repair, but when chased by the enemy, I ordered her to be cut in two and otherwise disabled, and then threw her overboard, knowing she would have been esteemed of more value from her swiftness, than the schooner. The other, some time

Photo by Paul Carroll.

Patrolling the Nottawasaga on a small boat — today! Small-scale naval encounters are conducted on the river adjacent to the Nancy Island Historic Site on an annual basis. Shown is the gaff-rigged HMS *Badger* out of Penetanguishene. This vessel may be similar to the swift sailing dispatch boat to which Wingfield refers in the text.

after, was taken by the enemy up a river, and Commodore Chauncey made a dispatch boat of her; she had been frequently seen in the Bay of Quinte about 12 miles above Kingston, and was known to be in the habit of landing a notorious spy, named Johnson. She had been often chased, but we knew no boat in our fleet could touch her; this being the case three boats were stationed in the bay, at different places, so as to cut her off, in one of which I was placed. After two or three days waiting I observed her pulling down the bay chased by* one of our boats, and having everything prepared for launching we soon got the cutter in the water, just before the gig came abreast of us, but she had passed a few yards before we got way upon our boat. Knowing her swiftness I was aware that unless some of the men were disabled she would escape; the Coxswain fired the first shot and disabled the man at the stroke oar, which was instantly seized by the Midshipman. The gig was fast gaining upon us, and I found it necessary to direct the Coxswain to attend to the steering of the boat. As the musquets were stowed in the stern, sheets ready loaded, I had nothing to

---

* Page 43 begins in the original journal.

do but prime, and fire them off and the next that fell was the Midship-man, — I now ordered the after oar to be laid across and the man to take a musquet, as she was still heading us. After firing a few shots we began to come up with her, and distinctly saw the Lieutenant and two seamen throw a man overboard, expecting we should heave to and pick him up, but the boat being our sole object, I directed the spare oar to be thrown to him and continued the chase, leaving him to be picked up by the boat astern. As we were closing the gig fast I desisted firing, and just before we came up, the Americans ceased pulling and we took possession of her. I found the officer commanding her to be the same one[4] who took possession of my schooner when she was taken; five men were wounded and the Midshipman killed. The other boat soon came up and had saved the man thrown overboard, [and] from him we learned that he had been taken off a raft of timber the same morning by the gig, and that the crew had destroyed the raft; the American Lieut[t] excused himself, as he saw no other means of escape, expecting, as he said, we should pick him up and by that delay giving him an opportunity of making his escape. Wishing to get the wounded men on board the *Prince Regent*, we picked a crew out of the two boats for the gig, and about 11 pm arrived on board.

In September the *St. Lawrence* was launched and went off in grand style. This ship gave us the superiority over the enemy and through the

Launching of the HMS *St. Lawrence*.

Courtesy of Royal Ontario Museum, 967-106-1.

indefatigable exertions of the officers and men, we were ready to sail on the 23rd of the same month, and the Americans gave up the contest by going into harbour. Thus we had continued since our arrival on Lake Ontario, neither side daring to risk too much, and going into harbour upon their opponent getting a decided superiority.

Our sailing proved a most seasonable relief to the different garrisons above Kingston, and released a brig and a schooner, which had been blockading in the River Niagara nearly the whole summer,[5] for while I was prisoner our troops had not only retaken Fort George, and possessed themselves of Fort Niagara. The fleet carried as much stores and provisions on board as the ships could conveniently stow, and a strong body of troops to strengthen the forts; but the 25th had nearly proved fatal to our expedition for about 8 o'clock in the evening we were taken by a tremendous squall, and every ship in the squadron had their sails blown to ribbons, which were set at the time; the hands were turned up to clear the wreck, and the quarter deck being nearly full of men clewing [tying up] up the remnants of the sails, a terrific flash of lightning struck the* main mast, cutting through the iron hoops with which it is bound, though nearly an inch thick, and killing seven, and wounding 22, all the hands being knocked down on the quarter deck by the violence of the concussion. We were under the greatest apprehension about a hanging magazine of powder containing several hundred filled cartridges for the 32 pounders, which was situated on the orlop[6] deck just abaft the main mast, — had the lightning communicated to them we should all have taken our departure. The storm continued about a quarter of an hour attended with the most vivid flashes of lightning, the loudest thunder, and the heaviest rain I ever experienced in the whole course of my seafaring life, but no further damage was done than happened at its first commencement. Our business from now to the setting in of the winter was comprised of trying the sailing trim of the *St. Lawrence*, exercising the men at the guns,[7] and supplying the different garrisons with stores and provisions for their winter supply; there were no prizes now to be taken for every harbour was a sealed port, and an enemy not to be seen.

In November the ships were laid up for the winter in Navy Bay and dismantled where they were to lay ice bound till the spring opened.

---

* Page 44 begins in the original journal.

CHAPTER FOUR

ORDERED TO LAKE HURON AND GEORGIAN BAY
Commanding the *Surprise*

In January 1815 Sir James Yeo visited Lake Huron, intending to establish a naval depot at Penetanguisheen, and endeavour to open a communication with Lake Erie, as we had two schooners on the former lake, captured from the Americans. He returned to Kingston on the 19th Feb[y] and on the following day I was appointed to command the *Surprise* schooner on Lake Huron as Lieut[t], with directions to join her as soon as possible, taking with me a Midshipman from the *St. Lawrence*, and [to] get a crew from the *Niagara,* which lay ice bound at York. On the 23rd we took leave of our friends and messmates and about 2 pm started on our route; at this time there were strong reports of peace, and the official intelligence [was] expected soon to arrive, which threw a damper upon my spirits.

As we arrived at Ernestown 20 miles from Kingston, where we put up for the night. Just as we were going to bed we heard a terrible howling and ran out to see what occasioned the noise when, by the moon light we saw a large drove of wolves upon the ice, a short distance from us. We procured musquets, and with several of the inhabitants gave them chase, but after firing a volley or two, they dispersed, and we returned to the inn, where we were occupied about an hour in rubbing the Mid's feet with snow, to cause the circulation of blood, they being frostbitten.

On Friday we travelled 36 miles and stopped at Hallowell, the residence of a Commissariat Officer, who was to provide us with another sleigh, but I learned at the office that every one in the neighbourhood had been impressed[1] to convey stores to York; being compelled to discharge my present [sleigh], I found myself in an awkward dilemma. The next morning I walked back about 5 miles to a magistrate to procure a press warrant, that being the only possible way of getting supplied, and being determined to travel more comfortably* I demanded a double sleigh for the baggage, and a single one for ourselves; the double sleigh is drawn by two horses, and fitted for loads, the single one is drawn by one horse, and fitted for pleasure and convenience. After considerable delay I was enabled to proceed on my journey about noon. It snowed very thick and was intensely cold, and to add to our comfort, the horse took a fit of walking for several miles through a wood where there was no house that we could shelter ourselves in, neither threats, entreaties or personal chastisement, would make him alter his pace, but giving him a good feed of corn the first opportunity that offered, he was induced to mend his pace, and in the evening we halted at a tavern, kept by a justice of the peace, though none of the most cleanly, and His Worship was very assiduous in assisting the driver to unload the baggage.

In the morning I had recourse to our landlord for another press warrant intending to make use of it along the road, but it was such a genuine piece of orthography, that I persuaded the men whom I had with me to proceed to Hamilton, that I might preserve it as a guide to magistrates in England, and a specimen of Canadian literature, for I believe not half a dozen words were spelled correctly and the writing appeared more like a heiroglyphical scrawl, than a magistrate's warrant, but unfortunately it was lost with other papers in the country. Early in the evening we arrived at Hamilton, the largest and nearest town between Kingston and York, and put up at a clean comfortable inn. While our dinner was preparing I waited on the magistrate to procure two sleighs, having promised to discharge my present ones at this place, but his worship was not at home. The following morning I renewed my visit, when he sent a constable out immediately to procure them, who returned about noon with a promise that two would be in readiness on Tuesday morning early.

The idea conveyed by impressing sleighs, may appear somewhat arbitrary but the drivers are paid a certain sum per diem by the Commissariat Department upon procuring a certificate from the officer conveyed; and if any accident should happen on the road whereby a horse or horses should be disabled or die they are remunerated accordingly; and, in fact, it was absolutely necessary, for in some of the districts the inhabitants were of such Yankee principles[2] that, without resorting to this method no sleighs would have been got to convey officers, men, baggage or any sort

---

* Page 45 begins in the original journal.

of stores, however urgent the occasion might be, and as it was, in many places every obstruction was thrown in the way.

Tuesday night after travelling 50 miles we put up at a log hut, which could neither furnish us with a supper or bed, we therefore had but little inducement to sleep long in the morning, and before daylight we were on our road to York where we arrived at 3 pm.

The same evening we went on board the *Niagara* and found that Captain [Edward] Collier was at Penetanguisheen, and the officer commanding could discharge no men without his order. This was a severe disappointment, as the roads were daily getting worse and would soon be impassable in consequence of the heat of the sun melting the snow and drawing the frost out of the ground. I therefore determined to follow him, and on the 4th March arrived at Holland Landing, a naval depot; I here saw Lieut^t Worsley who* commanded on Lake Huron, and was informed by him that an order from Cap^n C. had been forwarded to the officer commanding the *Niagara* to discharge the requisite number of men, which must have passed me on the road. He advised me to return and bring them forward, and the same night I again reached York.

The following morning I went on board the *Niagara* and found the men nearly ready and with some trouble got them clear of the town before night. About 10 I left York intending to join the men the same night but the wind blowing nearly a hurricane and the trees frequently falling across the road made travelling very dangerous, and I took the advantage, which a log house by the roadside presented, to halt the remainder of the night. Early in the morning I was joined by the Midshipman who informed [me] that the drivers of the sleighs had taken advantage of the night and all disappeared. This was a case that frequently happened, as before observed, [and] being desirous of getting sleighs on the spot instead of returning to York, I went on about three or four miles to where the men were stopping in hopes of finding a magistrate.

The man who kept the tavern where the men were stopping happened to be a constable, and volunteered his services to procure as many sleighs as I wanted providing I got a magistrate's warrant. While conversing with him, a worshipful gentleman made his appearance, and when I explained to him how I was situated, he immediately issued his warrant to the constable, and

---

* Page 46 begins in the original journal.

without much persuasion I prevailed on him [the magistrate] to give me his company at dinner. I found him a shrewd sensible man, with more of the gentleman belonging to him than his externals would warrant me to expect, and as no sleighs could be got this day in consequence of the roads being blocked up in many places with the fallen trees, we passed the evening together. I found from his conversation that both he and his constable were located in the midst of a population whose political principles were everything but favourable to the mother country, and theirs being quite opposite made them to be much disliked by their neighbours.

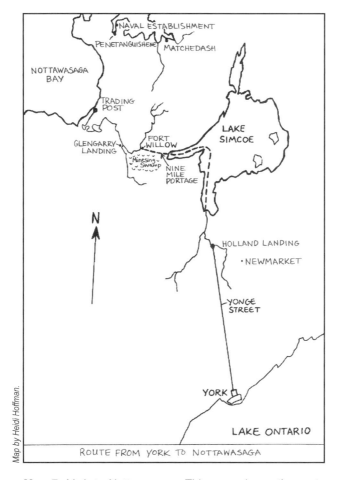

Map 7: York to Nottawasaga. This map shows the route commonly used for the overland passage from York to the Naval Establishment at Penetanguishene on Georgian Bay.

On Wednesday five sleighs arrived, but the roads being nearly bare of snow, I left a party of men to load them and proceeded with the remainder on foot, in many places over our ankles in mud. From the time the snow is worn off the ground, by travelling, till the sun has drawn all the frost out of the earth, the roads are extremely bad, and sometime impassable.

Thursday the men and baggage arrived at Holland Landing, where we had to take the ice to cross Lake Simcoe, having gone through a fatiguing job frequently unloading the sleighs and lifting them over huge trunks of trees, which lay in the road. The same day several sleighs came to Holland Landing to load with stores for Penetanguisheen, and I got a sufficient number to transport us over Lake Simcoe, which I caused to be loaded immediately as each day made the travelling upon ice more dangerous. When nearly ready for starting we were met by a party who had just crossed the lake empty, and had broken through several times coming up Holland River. [Consequently], the sleighs were unloaded, and returned to their respective homes, and I determined to walk across the lake with the men, and leave the baggage until the ice became more firm or broke up entirely. As it would take us more than one day to cross the lake the men* were ordered to cook provisions accordingly, and each to provide himself with two blankets each.

Friday morning we started, our route lying entirely over the ice, which, though two or three feet thick, a sleigh could not traverse with safety. About 3 pm it started to rain, which made our travelling extremely unpleasant, and I judged it better to make for the shore though nearly four miles out of our way, and about 5 pm arrived at a sort of tavern on the border of the lake, where I got the men a comfortable room and good fire to dry themselves by. The whole night it rained fast and when we took the ice in the morning, it was as slippery as glass, and we were all wet through in a short time by falling repeatedly, there being, in numerous places, water half a foot deep lying in large pools. We got to a tolerably dry place to breakfast, and cut up a blanket to tie around our shoes, which, though it did not dry us, prevented any more falls, and we proceeded at a quick rate; early in the evening we arrived at Kempenfeldt, a naval depot, and for the present the end of our journey.[3]

---

* Page 47 begins in the original journal.

This place was badly off for accommodations, as it had only been fixed upon as a naval station since Christmas [1814], and a party of seamen and soldiers were now employed cutting the timber in the direction of Penetanguisheen to form the road, so that there was only one log house, and a few huts covered with branches of fir.

On the 17th Captn Collier arrived here with the men under his command, having received orders to leave everything as it stood, and after completing the schooners on Lake Huron to their complement of men, to return to the *Niagara* with the remainder. The next day he set off not a little pleased to be rid of so unpleasant a job.

I will attempt to describe the route that I had to take to join my schooner, which will make it necessary to go back a little, and treat of some circumstances not exactly connected with my journal, but which will give a better idea of the paradise opening to my view.

At the commencement of the war there were but two islands inhabited on Lake Huron, one called Michilimackinac in possession of the Americans, and considered of great importance, as being the key to all the Indian territory west of the lake, the other named St. Joseph, also of considerable importance as commanding the passage to Lake Superior, on the borders of which lake the fur trade is carried on to a great extent by a company of merchants called the North West Company. They have large settlements, with several forts, or stations, in the interior of the country for the convenience of trading with the Indians. They kept three schooners upon the lake constantly traversing it during the summer months, carrying Indian merchandise and provisions up, and bringing peltry down, leaving the latter in storehouses at the head of the falls of St. Mary, which rapids cuts off the communication between the two lakes for vessels; from whence they are conveyed to Montreal in canoes down the French River.

On each island there was a fort,[4] if they deserved that name, garrisoned by* a small number of troops. When the war broke out, and before the Americans could reinforce the garrison, our troops, assisted by the inhabitants of St. Joseph who formed themselves into a fencible corps, made an attack, and the expedition was so secretly conducted that the enemy had no idea of an assault till they saw our troops drawn up before

* Page 48 begins in the original journal.

Photo courtesy of Mackinac State Historic Parks, Michigan.

A soldier and his lady stroll along the boardwalk. Fort Mackinac (1780–1895) is operated today as an historic site, restored to its 1880s appearance. Some 200,000 annual visitors explore the history of the fort through fourteen original buildings, exhibits, and daily programs as presented by costumed interpreters.

their fort one morning at daybreak. They surrendered without making any resistance. To this place the troops removed, and abandoned the fort on the island of St. Joseph, and were followed by all the inhabitants who settled here; the guns, stores, and provisions were transported to Michili-mackinac and that island put in a better posture of defence.

These islands had always been supplied by the way of Lake Erie, but the Americans soon gaining the superiority there, and we having no vessel on Lake Huron, it was necessary to trace another passage by which they might be supplied, as they entirely depended upon that for subsistence, there being no cultivated land on either of the Islands, except for small gardens. Luckily a large schooner belonging to the North West Company had happened to be on Lake Huron, which they lent to government, by way of indemnifying themselves for their loss, plainly foreseeing she would either be taken or destroyed by the Americans, who were fitting out an expedition to retake Michilimackinac, and a Lieut[t] and party of seamen were sent from Lake Ontario to take possession of her.[5]

Courtesy of the Don Bamford Collection.

The Nancy *Under Full Sail.* The detail for the impressive image by "Chick" Peterson, internationally acclaimed maritime artist, was researched by Don Bamford.

We were now obliged to form a line of communication through York and across Lake Simcoe, that being the only one open to us. The first post was established on Holland River which, I before observed, empties itself into Lake Simcoe, and is a land conveyance from York of about 30 miles. On the opposite side of the lake other store houses were built, as there is a land carriage of nine miles from the border of the lake to the head of an intricate creek, which forms a communication with Lake Huron by emptying itself into Nottawaysagua river; here more store houses were built for the convenience of housing what provisions and stores might arrive while the vessel was on her passage from and to Michilimackinac.

One summer was sufficient to convince us that this was not the most eligible situation for a naval establishment, for the bay into which the river empties itself affords no shelter for vessels, and they were obliged to enter the river. This was attended with considerable delay, and [whenever] the wind blew fresh from the NW, with danger, [the] consequence of a shifting bar of sand, which sometimes had no more than three feet water in the channel — and that channel never to be relied on the second time. We were therefore obliged to sound, and buoy off the passage both on entering and leaving the river, and always to load the vessels outside the bar. This being the case, Sir James Yeo, wishing to establish a naval force on Lake Huron, [sent] an officer from Kingston to find out, and survey a safe harbour, in the immediate vicinity of which a dockyard might be established, and ships built He found Penetanguisheen to answer every purpose and upon his report, seamen, soldiers, and artificers were sent, though in the depth of winter, to open a line of communication between this place and Lake Simcoe by cutting [a] direct road through the wood, which they had nearly accomplished when they were ordered to return in consequence of the peace* and the stores and provisions to be forwarded by Nottawaysagua river.

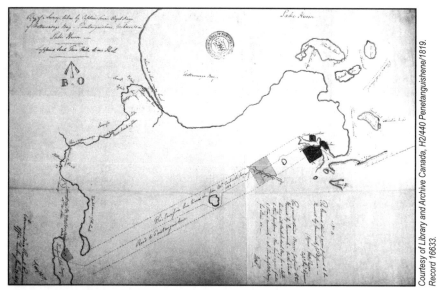

Courtesy of Library and Archive Canada, H2/440 Penetanguishene/1819. Record 16633.

Map 8: "Copy of a Survey taken by Captain Owen, Royal Navy of Nottawasaga Bay — Penetanguishene Harbour, Etc., in Lake Huron." Copy made in 1819 from original (1817). This drawing, shown at a scale of two miles to the inch, illustrates the detail of the shoreline, rivers, and roadway links between Nottawasaga and the military installations at Penetanguishene. The roadway from Kempenfeldt Bay to Penatanguishene is also outlined, as taken from Wilmot's survey of an earlier date.

---

* Page 49 begins in the original journal.

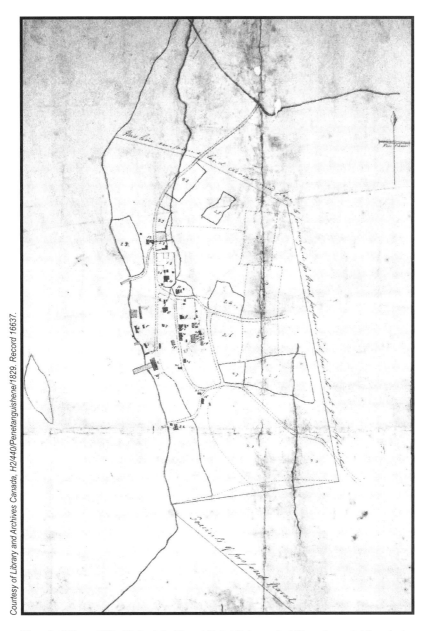

Courtesy of Library and Archives Canada, H2/440/Penetanguishene/1829. Record 16637.

Map 9: "Plan of His Majesty's Naval Establishment at Penetanguishine, Lake Huron, Upper Canada, 1829," showing 27 installations and other detail. The first docks are shown. Origins of this document are not clear; the original is contained in a file of early maps by Owen at Library and Archives Canada.

On the 19th the Mid arrived with the baggage, and we immediately removed to the head of the creek. Here were several log houses scarcely habitable, many a pigsty in England preferable, but much better than the dwellings at Kempenfeldt, which the men took possession of, and the Mid and myself took up our quarters in a small room adjoining the house of the Commissary Clerk in charge of the stores. The frost setting in anew I expected to be detained here some time, and the men having no employment I set them to work to build a house with logs after the fashion of the country, which occupied them till the 29th, and when finished I took possession, but it was something like the house I somewhere read of — "In fine weather it admitted no wet, and when it rained the water was not prevented from running out."

About half a mile from our habitation was an extensive forest of maple trees, from the sap of which the Indians make sugar and this being the proper season of the year, several families were assembled for that purpose, with whom we soon got acquainted, some of them paying us a visit every day bringing game wild ducks, and sugar in exchange for pork, biscuit etc.[6]

These Indians are a remnant of the Mississauga tribe, once a warlike and powerful nation inhabiting the north shore of Lake Ontario and the St. Lawrence, but from their constant intercourse with the European traders in peltry are completely degenerated, now being a cowardly, drunken, and filthy set; these characters indeed are applicable more or less, to the different tribes who live on the border of settlements, and differing entirely from those of the interior who, especially in cleanliness are inferior to no nation. The Mississauga's pass the winter across Lake Simcoe in the settled parts of the county, and in the spring return to their sugaries, as they are termed. Upon their establishing themselves, each family marks as many maple trees, as they have the means of boiling down the sap produced; they then notch the tree with a small hatchet or tomahawk, and insert a wedge to guide the sap into bark basins placed to catch it. When they have caught sufficient to fill their brass kettles, it is boiled down to a proper consistence and let to get cold, when they scrape, or pound it, and put it into baskets made of the bark of the birch tree, called mococks, holding from ten to forty pounds. Some of the sugar I have used was as white as any moist sugar in England; the sap makes a very pleasant beverage, and is esteemed wholesome. The settlers always leave the maple trees on their farms, or a portion of them for the domestic purposes of making sugar, and vinegar, the latter sufficiently strong for pickling. This continues to find the Indians employment till the end of April, when the ice breaking up the creeks and rivers furnish them abundantly with fish and water fowl. When the snow has disappeared the men prepare themselves for hunting, leaving the women and children to proceed to two small settlements they have on the border of Lake Huron near Nottawaysauga River where they plant some Indian corn, and a sort of sweet potato, but never rise anything but a sufficient quantity to serve through the winter, — while we were* here the Indians went in pursuit of a bear, the print of whose feet had been seen in the snow near their camp, and on the second day returned with the carcass. The Chief brought me a hind quarter, the lean of which was tender but the fat most abominably strong, though the Indians ate it with avidity.

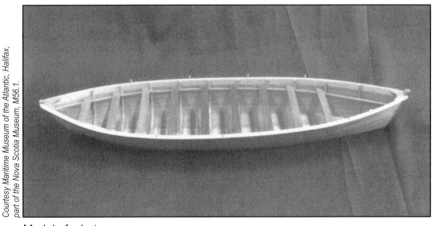

Courtesy Maritime Museum of the Atlantic, Halifax, part of the Nova Scotia Museum, M56.1.

Model of a bateau.

March 30th I sent a party of men down to the creek and directed them to take a boat and proceed as far as the ice could permit, and to break through any short constructions. In the evening they returned having found the ice, in many places two feet thick but very rotten, and the creek open in some places for half a mile in length, but as they had stopped in a place where the ice was strong, and continued so for a considerable distance, I determined to wait till the following Monday, as the

---

* Page 50 begins in the original journal.

sun was getting great power, though every night was attended with frost.

On the 2nd of April I visited the Indian camp to procure a guide, the creek as before mentioned being very intricate, and bargained with the Chief's son, who promised to be with us at daybreak next morning. Monday, after having loaded the boats and waited till 7 o'clock, I started without my guide, who being partly paid had forgotten his appointment. The ice, which had been broken a few days before, being drawn down with the current, had collected in several places and froze together, which gave us nearly as much trouble as if it had not been broken at all. When we had proceeded four or five miles, and conquered many difficulties, the boat came to a very strong patch of ice, though of no great length yet it took a considerable time to break through, and as we proceeded we encountered them more frequently. When night began to close in, the boats had arrived at the beginning of a piece of ice, which, as we could not see the end, appeared to set our efforts at defiance, but sending two light men to reconnoitre they soon returned with the welcome intelligence that when through this piece our difficulties were at an end, as the mouth of the creek was visible at no great distance with the river clear of all ice. This intelligence put us all in spirits, for though the distance from where we started to the river is not seven miles, yet we had nearly one to go. This creek runs through an extensive swamp, so that there was no probability of landing to make a fire, and, the boats being without covering, we could only stow away as thick as possible to create warmth. The rain fell heavily during the night and wet our blankets through and through. Towards morning it cleared up and began to freeze which made us nearly stiff with cold.

Daybreak was hailed by us with no little pleasure, and taking the guide, who joined us the evening before, I walked to the patch of ice where the river was to be distinctly seen. [The] men were set to work at each end and after much fatigue we were quite clear by noon, and entered a fine river with a rapid current in our favour, which swept us down a good rate. A few miles before we came to the vessels, we had to go down several rapids, and being unacquainted with the channel, one of the boats got entangled with a sunken log and nearly capsized, but the water being high we extricated her without any damage being sustained except shipping a little water. About 5 we saw the masts of the schooners, and* soon after got alongside.

---

* Page 51 begins in the original journal.

CHAPTER FIVE

ARRIVAL ON GEORGIAN BAY
Service on Lake Huron

On the 5th [of April] I accompanied Lieut Worsley down the river to the lake, which was free from ice, except immediately round the borders, and having sounded over the bar there was plenty of water, which determined us to sail as soon as we could get the schooners fitted out, as we anticipated that the fine weather had set in and knew our garrison at Michilimackinac was in great want of supplies.

The taking of the two schooners from the enemy was a very daring and gallant affair, and attended with numerous difficulties and privations. The account of their capture may prove entertaining, though it will cause another digression from my journal.

The North West Company's schooner before mentioned, [had] carried up but two cargoes of provisions to Michilimackinac, and [with] the American fleet having conquered ours on Lake Erie in Sept. 1813, it was found [to be] too late in the season to attempt any thing on Lake Huron that year, but the following summer the Americans embarked a number of troops aboard their ships, and sailing up the river St. Clair entered Lake Huron with the intention of retaking that Island, which, St. Joseph being abandoned, would have made them masters of the lake had they been successful. They landed several troops and made many fruitless attempts to gain possession but were always frustrated. While here they gained intelligence of the place where the schooner [*Nancy*] had run too, and expecting to find a quantity of stores and provisions but weakly guarded, they took their troops on board and sailed for the river: Lieut Worsley then commanding the schooner, on receiving intelligence of their approach hauled his vessel as high up the river as the time would allow, and taking out her guns, built a blockhouse with rude logs upon the bank immediately above her, thinking by this means to defend and save her. He had between the blockhouse and the lake about a quarter of a mile — the breadth of the river and a peninsula. The enemy anchored abreast of his battery and landed a party of men who commenced cutting down the trees to make an opening for their ships to take aim but receiving a warmer reception than they expected, were obliged to desist. The [American] fleet then opened a fire at random, under cover of which they landed two howitzers, which soon opened upon the block house with [the] effect, as unfortunately he [Worsley] had built it so near the

Fire One! Efforts to defend the *Nancy* from the attack of the American intruders were unsuccessful. A re-enactment of the original battle of August 1813 was held at the Nottawasaga River site in 2007 by participants in the annual "Wasaga Under Siege" event. Shown here are the British soldiers and their Native allies defending the *Nancy*.

edge of the bank, which is a completely sand, and very high, that the shot and shell of the enemy so undermined it that the guns were rendered useless. Lieut' Worsley now seeing there was no chance of saving his schooner, set her on fire and blew up the blockhouse, retreating immediately into the woods, with the loss of one man killed and one wounded; the latter had his arm hanging only by a small portion of flesh and the skin, the bone being completely cut through and shattered, and felt in so much pain that he begged it might be severed entirely. Wm Sampson, a military surgeon, being accidentally in company performed the operation of amputating it with no other instrument than a razor and common hand saw, and made a perfect cure without his being obliged to undergo another operation. The man was Cook on board one of the ships at Kingston, and the above fact is well authenticated by the examination of the man before a medical board held at the above place.*

After three days rambling, Lieut^t Worsley and his party reached the store house at the head of the creek more dead than alive, having undergone excessive fatigue. He found here a party of troops waiting for a passage to Michilimackinac, and proposed loading all the boats then in the creek with the stores and provisions, and by keeping the shore close on board, to proceed to that island, where they arrived after a tedious pull of upwards of 400 miles. [They] narrowly escaped being taken by those two schooners, which had been left on this lake by the American Commodore to look out for the canoes laden with peltry coming from Lake Superior, while with the remainder of his ships he returned to Lake Erie, not thinking anything was to [be] apprehended from the force on Lake Huron.

When Worsley had ascertained there were only these two vessels on the lake, he fitted up the largest bateau as a gun boat, placing a 6 pounder in her bow. With this, and two other boats manned by seamen belonging to the late schooner, and some soldiers from the garrison, he pulled to the bay of St. Joseph where one of these schooners lay, and before daybreak carried her by boarding, with the loss of one seaman and two soldiers. He immediately sent the boats back with the prisoners under a sufficient guard and remained with his prize in the same position waiting the arrival of the consort. The following evening she hove in sight but the wind failing she anchored some distance off. Lieut^t Worsley thinking this would be an improper time to attack her, resolved to remain till next morning, when at day dawn, taking advantage of a fine breeze, he ran directly alongside and captured her without any resistance being made. Thus, for the loss of one schooner, he added two to the service, and was promoted for his brave conduct.[1]

---

* Page 52 begins in the original journal.

To return — we immediately commenced fitting out the vessels, and on overhauling the rigging of mine, I found the principal part so rotten that I was obliged to cut a cable to convert into running rigging; the decks, from being exposed to the weather during the winter season, leaked much, and the sails wanted to be made new altogether, and not a yard of spare canvas on board; however we had them ready for sailing by the 15th.

On the following day we took up seven large bateaux[2] to the head of the creek, to load with stores and provisions, and returned on the 18th, when we cast off from the shore and dropped down to the mouth of the river. I here received a Mid from the *Confiance*, who had been twice up the lake, and who was to serve me as a pilot, [and] likewise an old chart, and some verbal directions from Lieut Worsley in case we should part company, and then sailed with a fine breeze.

The 22nd from 2 to 7 am we had a calm, and were within a few miles of some islands we passed yesterday, and had a long range on our right, called the Manatoulin Islands, accounted very dangerous, from the number of shoals and sunken rocks among them. Between 9 and 10 am the wind chopped round and freshened, accompanied with sleet, which froze as fast as it fell; with much difficulty we got the sails lowered down to close reef them and when finished could only hoist the mainsail and jib; the rope which hoisted the foresail was frozen in the block. We had lost sight of our consort, and I found myself awkwardly* situated. The compass would not traverse, night [was] approaching, and the weather so thick that we could not see a hundred yards ahead; a heavy short sea [was] breaking over the deck, which froze so as to make the vessel appear like a lump of ice, and it was extremely dangerous to traverse her from one end to the other, for the slightest false footing would have been inevitable destruction.[3]

The sails were totally useless, for had our lives depended on moving a rope through a block it could not be done, the sleet [having] settling upon them, they were frozen to an enormous size. I enquired of the pilot if there was any probability of our getting entangled with the land; he informed me we had 200 miles drift — this made me quite easy, knowing that as long as we had sea room we were safe. I therefore ordered

---

* Page 53 begins in the original journal.

Drawing by Heidi Hoffman.

Sailing in the Freezing Rain.

all the men below, except three to keep a look out, relieving them every half hour in consequence of the excessive cold. About 9 when I thought everything snug, land was reported right ahead, and at the same moment the jib blew to ribbons, which rendered the vessel a perfect log upon the water. We all instantly ran upon deck, and our utmost exertions to get the remnants of the sail down or prevent it from flapping about were of no avail, and after a quarter of an hours work we desisted, and the men were sent aft. I now expected every minute to run aground or strike upon a rock, either of which must have been death to all hands, from the intense coldness of the weather. I remained forward anxiously looking out, for by this time we had drifted past the land reported, and none was in sight when I heard a confused noise on the quarter deck, where the men were assembled, and going to inquire the cause found the boatswain's mate senseless from the wet and cold. He had been the most active in endeavouring to secure the jib, and had received more ducking than any one else, though we were all tolerably well soaked. He was conveyed to bed and covered up warm; nine others were frost bitten more or less.

I was convinced in my own mind that we must strike, expecting we were entangled among the Manatoulin Islands. The vessel was totally unmanageable and I remained some hours in this state of anxiety, when about 2 am the weather cleared up so as to be enabled to see about a mile around us, and not discovering any land, I was in hopes we had drifted clear of it. As the day broke the gale abated, and we had an opportunity seeing the peril we had escaped, having been running directly upon an island, and had not our jib most providentially blown away when it did; took all headway from the schooner, and she dropped to leeward not above twice her own length off it.

The next day the sun rose in a cloudless sky, but it was 5 pm before the vessel was under proper canvas, though several coppers of boiling water had been used to thaw the ropes. I was now at a loss what course to steer, for I soon found my pilot quite ignorant, or uncertain, of the headlands frequently mistaking them, and he at last confessed he did not know where we were. At dusk we hove to with her head to seaward, and prepared for a good nights rest;* next morning we made sail to the westward, and the following day anchored in the bay of Michilimackinac, where the *Confiance* had arrived two days before, having brought up under the lee of an island — at the commencement of the gales Lieut[t] Worsley began to be alarmed for our safety and intended to sail in quest of us had we not arrived as we did.

The Island of Michilimackinac is about 6 or 7 miles in circumference, and is situated at the westernmost end of Lake Huron, one side washed by the lake and the other by Lake Michigan. I before observed, that it was a place of some importance, and under the present Commandant, Colonel MacDowall [McDouall], it has received numberless advantages, so that, could he be certain of supplies, he might have set the whole American forces at defiance. This place with all its improvements, as well as other forts taken from the enemy during the war was given up,

---

* Page 54 begins in the original journal.

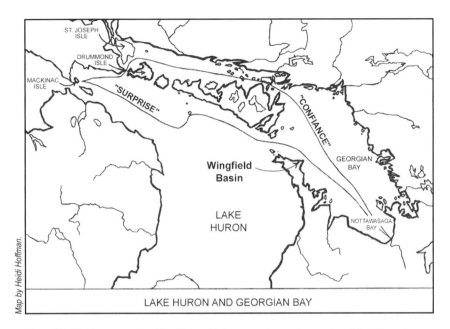

Map 10: Nottawasaga to Mackinac. This map shows the route of the *Surprise* as described by Wingfield in his journal notes. It is apparent that the *Confiance* took the sometimes more challenging but more protected route north of Manitoulin Island, through the many smaller islands and passages of the North Channel.

which caused strong remonstrances from the western tribes of Indians. The poorer may be said to live entirely upon fish, but the number is few and confined to those of Indian extraction, as both rich and poor depend entirely upon Government, or casual supplies from speculators; when they have an opportunity they exchange their fish for pork biscuit etc., etc., — and salt was so scare an article among them that what was left in a cask after the pork had been taken out would [be] a supply sufficient to last the whole crew for three or four days. The principal sort of fish on this lake are white fish, very large trout, jack, and sturgeon, — the former is peculiar to the Lakes, and is a most delicious fish weighing from 6 to 10 and 15 pounds; the inhabitants and Indians make it into stew or soup. The trout run very large, and I was informed by the officers of the military mess that they had one of 60 pounds weight at their table: I have frequently bought them from the Indians [at] 30 and 40 pound. The jack likewise runs very large and has not that strong a flavour of an overgrown jack in England. I cannot say whether sturgeon are plenty or not, as I saw but three, which were brought alongside by some Indians, and having read the first caught in the River Thames, in season, was presented to the King by the Lord Mayor, I was anxious to purchase them, thinking they must necessarily be super excellent, and the Indians perceiving my avidity rose the price accordingly; but wishing to give the sailors a treat with what was so much consequence in point of "a delicacy" that a Lord Mayor of London should forego the pleasure of treating the corporation, to present it to His Majesty, I considered the seamen should not but relish it. I therefore served out part of one of them, and had some cooked for my dinner, but having no proper ingredients, and the cook never having read *Monsieur Ude upon Cookery*,[4] I suppose, was the cause of my dislike of it when served up. A slice or two of fat salt pork was put into the lid of a camp kettle, which serves for a frying pan, and the sturgeon done brown, but I no sooner tasted the dainty than I thought I was swallowing train oil, and spewed[5] it accordingly; the crew relished it as much as I did, — a sturgeon might be got for a sprat, and the whole three for herring, however the largest I took with me to the Island,[6] and presented to a French lady, the wife of a Captain in*the Indian department with whom, in company of some officers of the garrison I dined, and made an excellent dinner off the despised sturgeon — so much for the difference in cooking. The Indians were beginning to assemble at the island from the westward, some to remain and assist in defending it, while others proceeded to join the army, being ignorant of the peace. I believe there was not one man, out of between two and three thousand then collected, that was under 6 feet high, and well proportioned in all their limbs, and remarkably clean in their persons and dress, which consisted of the skin of the moose made into a sort of frock coat fringed all around and with the same material, and leggings coming half way up their thighs. Their moccasins, or shoes were made of the hide of the buffalo, and worked in various rude devices with porcupine quills, dyed of different colours, for which they use some particular roots, and were ingeniously and handsomely done. The women are handsome and finely proportioned, and of a lighter complexion than those I had seen, many of them might be called handsome brunettes, and from the

---

* Page 55 begins in the original journal.

cleanliness of both sexes, formed a striking contrast with the Indians I had before seen.

While here I had the opportunity of seeing the burial of a murdered Indian and the trial of the delinquent. The quarrel originated in one of the wigwams while the parties were under the influence of liquor, and one young Indian stabbed another with his scalping knife, who lingered three days, and expired without the least apparent concern, having shown no symptoms of pain during his illness. I have visited him in company with the surgeon, who said he must experience great pain, from the nature of the wound, particularly while it was being dressed, and I attentively watched his countenance while his wound (in the head) was undergoing that operation, and not a muscle was changed, though he was quite sensible, and answered a few questions through an interpreter. When dead, he was wrapped in his blanket and laid in a grave about three feet deep, lined with birch bark, his arms deposited by his side, with powder and shot. The hole was not covered over with earth, but a little below the surface of the ground, a sort of arch was made over him, and covered over up to the height of a common grave in England. In the centre was a hole about six inches square, that the spirit, as they superstitiously suppose, may have ingress and egress; the funeral was attended by his relations and friends, the oldest of whom made a speech or funeral oration.

The next day, according to their custom, the murderer delivered himself up, and was attended by his relations, and the oldest men of his tribe, or nation, bringing various presents. The prisoner was quite naked, except a piece of cloth around his middle, and blacked from head to foot with a composition of grease and charcoal in token of mourning. His friends were without armaments, and their faces unpainted; they drew up a short distance from the wigwam where the relations and friends of the deceased were assembled, who, Capt[n] Askin[7] informed me, were deliberating whether they should accept the presents, or dispatch the prisoner. If the former he had nothing to fear, but these murders sometimes run to great extent, one revenging the death of the other, [with] much blood spilled; if the presents are not accepted their method* of punishment is summary, for the murderer is immediately taken to the grave of the deceased, and tomahawked by the nearest relation.

* Page 56 begins in the original journal.

After the prisoner and his friends had waited nearly an hour, the opposite party emerged from their wigwam, having all parts of their person, visible, blackened; the nearest relations and oldest men of the tribe formed a line and sat down immediately opposite the delinquent and his party, the former occupying a space in the centre smoking his pipe with the unconcern imaginable as if he was not at all interested in the ceremony.

After a short pause the business was opened by an old chief of the prisoner's tribe who continued speaking a considerable time, not in a hurried tone, but slow and calm, frequently making a full stop for a minute together, accompanying his words with many gestures, rather graceful than otherwise. He was answered in a speech by the opposite party of about the same length, the whole ceremony being conducted with the greatest solemnity; when after a long consultation the presents were accepted, consisting of blankets, scarlet cloth, gunpowder and shot, some provisions and a small quantity of spirits issued from the government stores by order of the Commandant, whose duty, as well as interest it was to keep them quiet if possible. The pipe of peace was now lighted with great ceremony, and handed round to all the parties, the prisoner taking it last. From that time he was perfectly absolved and looked upon by both nations as if nothing had happened more than ordinary, but there are frequent instances known of the relations proving inexorable however great the quantity or valuable the quality of the presents offered, the condemnation or acquittal of the culprit resting solely upon the nearest relation who is never censured, the oldest men merely acting as mediators.

When the Indians understood the island was to be given up to the Americans with its important fortifications, they formed, in their council, a strong remonstrance to the Government at Quebec, insisting upon their original right to it, as it was never purchased from them, and upbraided the "Great Father," as they call the Governor, with leaving them open to their enemies, after having drawn them into the war. This remonstrance was drawn up in plain though forcible language, for the Indians, like the Spartans of old, have no idea of wasting words, by adding them as ornaments of speech. I read several of their "talks" literally translated, by the favour of Captn Askin, the principal officer of the Indian department, and they were all comprehended in strong energetic language.

Sackets Harbor at Sunset, September 1813, Peter Rindlisbacher artist. In this artist's rendition the ship in the stocks is the *General Pike,* under construction as the new flagship for the American Navy. *Reprinted with permission of the artist.*

Erie Barge Canal, watercolour, 1829, John William Hill artist. Wingfield travelled on a canal, passing through several locks, in the winter of 1813–14. In 1817, legislation was passed to start construction of the Erie Canal. There were many changes in both canal and countryside in the intervening years. One can visit the ancient remains of the early locks, now on dry land, in parts of the countryside. *Courtesy of I.N. Phelps Collection, Miriam and Ira D. Wallach Division of Art, Astor, Lenox and Tilden Foundations, New York Public Library, No. 54577.*

Engagement in the Gale, Peter Rindlisbacher artist. On September 28, 1813, the British and American fleets came to battle on Lake Ontario. From left to right: the *General Pike*, USN, under Commodore Isaac Chauncey, the HMS *Royal George*, under Captain William Howe Mulcaster, the HMS *Wolfe*, the British flagship under Commodore St. James Lucas Yeo. *Reprinted with permission of the artist.*

HMS St. Lawrence *Under Full Press of Canvas*, painting by Oswald K. "Ozzie" Schenk. She was the largest wooden ship ever built and launched on the Great Lakes. *Courtesy of the Don Bamford Collection.*

Indian Encampment on Georgian Bay, oil on canvas, Paul Kane artist. Canadian artist Paul Kane (1810–71) undertook two journeys in the latter part of the 1840s to sketch Native people and the Canadian landscape. He returned to Toronto in 1848 and for the next eight years worked on formal oil-on-canvas paintings based upon the information he recorded in his sketches. This painting is based upon three sketches taken in 1845 among the islands of Georgian Bay. Wingfield encountered Native people in their settlements on a number of occasions during his travels in Upper Canada. He makes reference to his involvement with the "Indians" on numerous occasions in his journal notes. In fact, he arranged for a young Native lad to return to England with him after Wingfield's period of naval service on the Lakes. No doubt he would have encountered villages such as the one pictured here. *Courtesy Royal Ontario Museum, 2005_5136_1, Image 912.1.8.*

John Bull making a new batch of ships to send to the Lakes, 1814, by William Charles, artist. A satire on British efforts to recover after major naval losses on the Great Lakes in 1813 and 1814. In the centre, King George III feeds a tray of small ships into a bread oven, as two other men stand by with additional trays of ships and cannon. A Frenchman stands to the left, holding a trough of "French Dough." King George: "Ay! What — Brother Jonathan taken another whole fleet on the Lakes — Must work away — Work away & send some more or He'll have Canada next." Frenchman: "Begar Mounseer Bull. Me no like dis new Alliance — Dere be one Yankey Man da call 'Mac Do-enough' Take your Ships by de whole Fleet — You better try get him for I never get Do-enough made at dis rate!!!" Englishman: "Here are more Guns for the Lake Service. If ever they do but get there — I hear the last you sent were waylaid by a sly Yankey 'Fox' and the ship being a 'Stranger,' he has taken her in." Second Englishman: "I tell you what Master Bull — You had better keep both your Ships and Guns at home — If you send all you've got to the Lakes, it will only make fun for the Yankeys to take them." *Courtesy of United States Library of Congress, LC-DIG-ppmsca-10753.*

Peace, ink and watercolour, *circa* 1814, by John Reubens Smith, artist. In an allegory of the Treaty of Ghent, signed on December 24, 1814, Britannia and America hold olive branches before an altar. Sailors, holding British and American flags, hold an uninscribed banner; through drapes and pillars a dove flies out of a triangle. The metaphorical symbolism has been interpreted in various ways. *Courtesy of United States Library of Congress, LC-USZC4-3675.*

A Greenwich Pensioner Saluting the Admiral. This charming oil from the Collection of the National Maritime Museum shows the love, respect, and esteem in which Admiral Nelson was held and continues to be held throughout the naval and seagoing community. *Courtesy National Marine Museum, U.K., Item # PZ7615.*

On the 9th May the *Confiance* sailed for Lake Erie and the *Surprise* was the only useful vessel left on the lake to supply the station to be occupied when Michilimackinac should be given up, as also to move the stores from that island, so that we had no respite from loading and unloading cargoes, except when we were sailing between the river and the island.

On the 16th a large boat was discovered from the fort,[8] which soon after landed a Captn of the navy and party of seamen sent by the Commodore to examine and survey a place, which had been pointed out, and strongly recommended to the Governor of Canada by the North West Company, who were interested in fixing the particular spot which we pitched upon as our future military post on* Lake Huron. This place lay about 40 miles from Michilimackinac, and was discovered by the crew of a schooner coming from Lake Erie to St. Josephs, which was wrecked; they took to their boat and pulling between the islands, came into a fine harbour protected from all winds.

Captn Collier was to consult with the Military Commandant who, with the engineer were to accompany him, and report upon its eligibility as a permanent military station, and also sail round the Island of St. Joseph, to survey, and mark out the proper ship channel leading to the Falls of St. Mary, about which there was some dispute between the Canadian and American governments.

On the 20th I received the party on board, and sailed upon a voyage of discovery; in the evening we anchored about half a mile off what was the town, or village of St. Joseph, and taking our guns went on shore. The Americans had entirely destroyed the fort, if it was ever worthy of such a name; the barracks, and several of the houses, and but two or three of those were left tenantable, as the lake had risen three feet above its usual height, and the lower part was covered with water. At this time there were no inhabitants, and a sportsman would have been induced to take up his temporary abode here, if fond of snipe shooting, for they were thick as larks in a stubble field, and we bagged several brace for our sea stock. The next morning we weighed [anchor] and stood round the island with a light breeze, and soon got entangled among numerous islets and sunken rocks, which obliged us to use the utmost circumspection

---

* Page 57 begins in the original journal.

to prevent the schooner from striking upon any of them. On the 22nd I found we were carried by a strong current into a very narrow channel, which obliged us to anchor, and the boat was sent ahead to reconnoitre, when we found ourselves upon the verge of some dangerous rapids, which would have considerably damaged the vessel had we proceeded. Taking the advantage of a strong breeze we returned the same evening anchored off the town, about as wise as [when] we went.

The 23rd we sailed upon another exploring cruise to view and survey the before mentioned harbour, and from our ignorance of the proper channel, grounded upon a dangerous reef of rocks, but the wind being light we soon got off without sustaining any damage. And [by] sending the boat ahead to sound, we got in safe, and found a spacious basin, with good depth of water and perfectly land locked, or to render a sea phrase intelligible, so surrounded with land as not to be able to see any outlet to the lake. The next day the Commandant, Captn Collier, and the engineer went to make their observations on shore, while I took a boat and rowed in different directions of the harbour to sound the depth of water, observe the anchorage, passages etc. For two or three days we were busily employed in making discoveries, and taking observations; and on the evening of the third it was determined that this should be our future military post[9] on Lake Huron. The following morning weighed with a light breeze, and [we] stood out of the harbour by different passage, where we found greater depth of water, and much more safe than the former, though [because of] light airs and baffling winds, we did not arrive at Michilimackinac till late in the evening, and I was not a little pleased to get rid of my passengers, as the cabin was too confined to accommodate us all comfortably.

We left here the next day for the river, and in our passage down the lake I found the schooner to make more water than usual, and on our arrival careened her over* a few rocks to examine her bottom, and found the seams nearly open, the oakum having pulled out.

She did not leave the river till the 10th June, the men having to take the empty boats up to the Commissaries store, and the melting of the snow had so swollen the river, and made the current so rapid that they had great difficulty in getting them up. After loading the schooner I

---

* Page 58 begins in the original journal.

found the leak increased materially, and on the 14th when we arrived at the island it would have been unsafe to cross the lake again unless the vessel underwent some repair. I requested carpenters and caulkers from the garrison, and sailing into the harbour we had surveyed, she was laid alongside a small island and we prepared to heave her down.

Courtesy of Library and Archives Canada, C-011665.

Commander's House on Drummond Island, circa 1820, artist J.J. Bigsby. It is most likely that there were no permanent buildings at the time Wingfield visited here.

This harbour was formed by several islands belonging to the range called the Manatoulin Islands, which runs along the north shore of the lake from the river Nottawaysauga to Michilimackinac, a distance of 300 miles. As this range is composed of many thousands, some large, some small, and others mere islets, or rocks, numerous bays and harbours are formed, doubtless some very safe and commodious, but the *Surprize* being the only vessel on the lake, and she not sufficiently large to supply the garrison with their winter stock, my time was entirely taken up with running backward and forward and, though I much wanted to explore some of the bays, and creeks with which the lake abounds, I had no opportunity of devoting any time to that purpose. Indeed though water fowl were here in great abundance I could spare no time for shooting or allow any of the men for that purpose, but employed an Indian to

supply the seamen and, though 25 in number, a few hours was amply
sufficient to supply them each day with fish, wild fowl and pigeons. The
latter appears to migrate from East to West, in June and the early part of
July, and return in September, when they fly in such flocks that, though
it may appear a la Munchausen,[10] of a fine clear day they appear in the
distance like a low black cloud, many millions I have no doubt being in
a flock. At this time they fly so high that a common gun is useless, but
if the morning is lowering and foggy, they fly so low that any number
may be killed. There is on the Island of Michilimackinac a very high
rock, which, towards the east is perpendicular, and I have it from a good
authority that on a foggy morning thousands of pigeon may be picked
up, stunned by flying against it.

Hunger it is said is an excellent sauce, and that is the only sauce we
had, except pepper and salt, so that our cooking was very simple. Broiled,
fried with salt pork, or boiled in the copper, was the only plan we could
adapt, but the latter being more convenient [it] was the general method
for ducks as well as pigeons, and the sauce aforesaid, and the additional
luxury of the latter pungents we never failed to allay a well created appe-
tite, for we had but those hours for rest which darkness afforded.

As the schooner was only employed in sailing from Nottawaysauga
River to Drummond Island, the name given to our new military post, it
would be uninteresting to enter into minute details of each voyage; I shall
therefore only confine myself to those circumstances which occurred
during the summer worth noticing.

The latter part of August we sailed from Drummond Island with only
four day allowance of biscuit, and two of meat, through the negligence
of the Master's* Mate whose duty it was to inform me that the provisions
were short — and I was not aware of the circumstances until the next day,
but having a good breeze and never having been more than four days
running the distance, I took little notice of it. Fortune, however, seemed
to embrace this opportunity of spiting us all she could, for it was the
eleventh evening before we anchored in the bay of Nottawaysauga. The
first day's sail took us above sixty miles in a direct road; it then fell calm
and so it continued with the exception of a few light breezes for nine
days. During the whole of that time we did not see a single canoe, which

* Page 59 begins in the original journal.

Courtesy Woodward Lighthouse History Collection.

Courtesy of Ann Method Green, Public Relations Chair, DeTour Reef Light Preservation Society.

LEFT: De Tour Reef Light, *circa* 1931. The dangerous reef, over which David Wingfield travelled as master of the *Surprise*, was originally marked by a light tower on the adjacent shore. It is now easy to avoid due to the presence of a large structure built offshore over the actual reef. In Wingfield's time, of course, avoiding the treacherous obstacle called on the skills of the ship's navigator, along with the sharp eye of a diligent lookout. RIGHT: Original De Tour Reef Shore Light. This was the first beacon set in place to warn sailors of treacherous passage by the nearby De Tour Reef. The original light dates to 1847. This 1930-era photo of the original light station at De Tour Passage is part of the Woodward Lighthouse History Collection.

I believe is the only passage up or down that we did not see several. The sixth day being close in with the land, one of the men pointed out several small animals drinking at the water's edge, which at first sight I thought were bear cubs, and at that time nothing could have come amiss. The boat was immediately hoisted out, but as we approached the shore the animals ran into the woods; we landed a small distance from where we saw them, and walking softly to the place I decried three raccoons in a fir tree, [and] having a sailor with me we fired and killed two of them. We then traversed the woods some time and killed a partridge; this bird differs from the English partridge, being larger, and the flesh not so white; the other men joined the boat without any game. When we got on board, they [the game] were all boiled together in the coppers and equally distributed amongst us, but formed a very scanty meal.

The following day we anchored opposite a long sandy beach, and taking our guns went on shore, — on landing we were agreeably surprised to find the beach, which was composed of a fine white sand, literally covered with cherries,[11] growing on small spreading bushes, the highest of which would not stand above two feet, but at this time the weight of the fruit had bent the branches so low that they lay upon the sand in such quantities that we gathered three or four bushels. This fruit appears to be peculiar to the country for, though in flavour, size and colour they differ nothing from the largest black cherry in England yet, as before mentioned, the bushes are very low and do not appear to attain any greater height. I removed the sand from several roots, but there was not the slightest vestige of earth, and farther from the water, as the earth mingled with the sand, so the bushes lost their vigour, and where the mould ran down to the water's edge there was no appearance of them. Sometime in the following month I brought the schooner to an anchor about a mile off a long sandy beach, and here again I observed the same appearances, but the fruit nearly all decayed. I saw several cherry trees in the woods but the fruit not good to eat, being nearly all stone, and very husky. The eleventh day a breeze sprung up, and the same evening we anchored in our destined port where I immediately went on shore to send off provisions for the crew, and found the clerk in charge of the North West Company's store busily employed stewing ducks, which happened very opportune.

Since I was last at this place a store house had been built, and stores and provisions brought down the river in readiness to load the schooner when she arrived, also that the time and labour of going up the river was saved. The work* was of itself sufficiently fatiguing, but the mosquitoes, which infest woods and swamps are so large and venomous, that the work appears ten times as great; indeed so venomous are they that two men whom I sent up in the summer with a party, returned with their faces so swollen that they had hardly any vestige of humanity. The sand fly is also very annoying, for though so small as to be almost indiscernible, they are nearly as venomous as the mosquito.

---

* Page 60 begins in the original journal.

I had plainly foreseen that the *Surprise* alone would not supply the garrison with more than what would be almost immediately required, in consequence of having to send the men up the river each time till this, though I had frequently written to the Commissary at York urging him to forward stores etc down the river to save time; and now [that] autumn [was] fast approaching, I knew that without further assistance the garrison would not obtain the winters supply. I now wrote the Commodore requesting another vessel might be sent, which was soon complied with.

In September I left three men at the former wintering place[12] to cut down trees and prepare logs for building huts for myself and the men, intending to lay up the schooner in this river, as it would have been impossible for us to live on board so small a vessel during the winter months. I also sent two men across Lake Simcoe to purchase some livestock for myself and get such things as the men required to make them comfortable through that dreary season; we also landed all the men whenever we came into the river to build the houses, as the Indians, or some other kind friends had set fire to those we occupied last winter, as likewise to procure fuel, which would be difficult to come at for snow.

On the 3rd November I got two or three casks of lime from the garrison to build chimney stacks, but excepting one in mine, none were built, in consequence of the difficulty of procuring stone, — and having taken leave of my friends we sailed the same day, that being the last time of my seeing Drummond Island. On the 5th we arrived at the mouth of the river, and found the water so shallow on the bar that we had to batten down the hatchways and force the schooner over, through a heavy surf that completely washed over her.

I had sometime before received an intimation that the naval force on the lakes was to be reduced to a peace establishment, and had been in expectation of receiving orders to proceed down the river St. Clair to winter on Lake Erie; but just as we entered the river, a boat came alongside with a Captain of the navy, and I learned to my surprise that there were several officers arrived and an establishment fixed here, all the houses I had built taken possession of and the one intended for myself converted into a Purser's storeroom.

About the middle of December we had formed ourselves on shore, and the river being open, the men begged permission to send across to Lake Simcoe for some live stock for their Christmas dinner, — and the officers wishing to make some addition to their stock, I and a Lieut of Marines,[13] with a party of men went up the river in a small boat, and crossed Lake Simcoe for Newmarket, where we remained three days, collecting what was required, and as the winter was daily expected to set in, I was anxious to join the Establishment.[14]*

An American winter differs somewhat from an English one, in as much as when the former sets in there is no fear of mid-winter weather until the spring commences and snow lying upon the ground in December is the signal for a most dreadful slaughter — start not gentle reader, I do not mean of human beings — but those other beings which one considers company for the preservation of our being. Each farmer now makes as near calculation as he can of what may be necessary for the supply of his family through the winter, and being sufficiently erudite to know that dead carcasses consume no food, he begins the slaughter; pigs are generally cut up and salted for pork, sheep, fowls, etc., etc., are hung up in some place of safety where, exposed to the frost, they become as completely secure from putrefaction as if cooked and hermetically sealed. When any part is to be dressed it is immersed in cold water to thaw, which makes it as supple as if newly killed, neither is the flavour deteriorated; but as soon as a natural thaw commences, it is necessary to devour whatever is left, or it spoils in a very short time, so that the American farmer keeps nothing through the winter except his store stock.

To return — When we came to the nine mile portage I was detained two days transporting stores for the use of the Establishment, the travelling being exceedingly difficult in consequence of the late rains. About 2 pm we went down the creek in the small boat, leaving the marine officer to proceed the following morning in a bateau that was destined for the Establishment. We had on board four sheep, three large hogs, and nine or ten small pigs. It was raining fast at the time, and no spirits in store to give the men, but making sure of joining the schooner the same night, I did not trouble to take any provisions with me. About dusk we arrived at the mouth of the creek, and here I found a Mid with a party of men, and a bateau, sent to our assistance; he had a tent pitched, a good fire, and three days of provision, and we were all wet through and totally unprepared to stop out all night. I ordered the men to refresh themselves, intending

---

* Page 61 begins in the original journal.

Sketch by Heidi Hoffman.

A Long Winter Portage. If he knew the tales of it, Wingfield must surely have recalled the rigours of the Great March, January 1813, from New Brunswick to Kingston, during his own winter travels to and from the Establishment.

to proceed, but the rain descending in torrents, and thinking one night would make but little difference I altered my mind, and putting the livestock into the bateaux, we all huddled together in the tent to keep ourselves warm, the rain having by this time totally extinguished our fire. In the course of the night the rain changed to snow, which fell in large flakes freezing hard at the same time, so that at daybreak we found the mouth of the creek completely blocked up.

The snow continued to fall thickly during the day, attended with a most severe frost, and after a great deal of fatigue we got the boats into the river, which from its width, and the strong current in our favour, gave us no room to doubt but we should arrive at the Establishment before night fall. We went on rapidly for about a mile, when, the river taking some short turnings, we found the snow had accumulated in vast quantities from drifting down with the current, and in consequence of its freezing so intensely, had become a compact mass of ice. Finding the bateau a great encumbrance we left her here and embarked in the small boat with* all the live stock except the four sheep. The evening began to close before we had cleaned this obstruction, and all of [us] being much fatigued and benumbed with cold, we put up for the night. Fearing the sheep might stray, I sent two men to kill them and leave their carcasses in the boat, but one of them made his escape into the woods and was given up for lost. Above a fortnight after, when we sent two men, with Indian guides to fetch them and the meat we had hung on the branches of trees on our passage down, the lost sheep was standing quietly in the boat, alive by the side of his more fortunate companions, and I am morally certain, during the time elapsed it could procure no food, the snow everywhere covering the ground some feet deep.

We landed on the edge of a large forest of firs, and commenced clearing away the snow from the place where we intended to take up our night's lodgings. One party of the men was employed in cutting fuel for our fire, and another in lopping the thickest branches of fir to make a bed, as also to screen us from the severity of the weather; a third party was no less busily employed in killing the pigs, which we had found to be troublesome through the whole of our days' journey. Having spread the branches on the ground and lighted a fire, we began to enquire what there was for supper, but having too confidently expected to reach the Establishment this night, particularly after discharging the bateau, little attention had been paid to the husbanding of our provisions, and there was barely sufficient to satisfy our hunger at the present time. The same evening we put the feet and some of the heads of the pigs into a camp kettle, which had fortunately been brought out of the bateau, and stewed them to be ready for our breakfast the following morning so as to lose no time; the liver etc was fried to serve for bread, but at the best our first meal was rather unsavoury, not having any salt. Before daylight we

---

* Page 62 begins in the original journal.

had breakfasted, and with the earliest dawn started. The stoppages now became more frequent, and in some places the snow had frozen so hard as to be able to bear the boat, which, by means of rollers placed under her stem, we got out of the water, and soon rolled her over, though this method was attended with great risk, the men being in constant danger of falling through the ice. The most difficult places we had to encounter were those where the ice would not bear, the breaking of which was attended with much labour, and our progress [was] slow. During the whole of this day we had not advanced above four miles, though we delayed no time for any meal, and when we put up for the night we were so excessively fatigued that we could scarcely get in sufficient fuel for the night. By way of drying the ground a little we collected a large quantity of wood and fired it, which melted the snow, and when we wanted to lay down, the embers were raked in a heap and fir branches spread for our bed. This evening we had some more pork boiled, but it was by no means unpalatable as the morning meal, hunger seasoning it most deliciously.

Sketch by Heidi Hoffman.

Hauling a Fully-laden Bateau. Wingfield and his men made a perilous crossing of the Nine Mile Portage at a time when the seasons mingled between freeze and thaw, leaving both the waterway and the land crossings dangerous. The trip to pick up livestock to ensure that meat was available for Christmas dinner turned out to be a precarious adventure.

The Midshipman and myself consulted upon the expediency of leaving the boat and walking down, but none of us being provided with snowshoes, and* the ice not to be depended upon, we determined to try another day, though from the exhausted state we were in, rank did not exempt us from an equal share of toil we knew it would be improper to continue much longer.

The next day we found the ice in many places firm, but the water between them so considerable that it proved no relief to the men, and toiling till after noon, some of the men had broken through the ice, and [were] finding it altogether a heartless job. I determined to leave the boat, and cook provisions for the march, which I knew would be attended with much fatigue.

After the necessary work of getting in firs and providing our bed, we commenced cooking; the pigs were cut up somehow, the smallest roasted and the largest hung upon the branches of the trees around, to be out of the way of any animals that might pass that way, till we should have an opportunity of sending for them. Here one of the men was so severely frostbitten in the leg as to be incapable of walking, yet so stubborn that he would neither rub it himself or let others do it for him; knowing the consequence of its remaining in that state, I ordered him to be forcibly held, while others rubbed the part affected with snow, which soon caused the circulation of blood, though attended with excessive pain as his struggles and cries proved, but his leg was saved and he was able to walk on the morrow.

I divided the men into two parties, sending the lightest men on ahead, and two men a distance before to give warning of any danger, and when to take to the woods; each of us had a portion of the meat slung over our shoulders, some cooked and some not. We had to leave the river several times and take to the woods where it was either open or the ice dangerous; the snow in many places, where it had drifted was breast high with no sure footing, the ground being naturally swampy.

Just before we halted for the night, one of the men who had been furthest ahead returned with the information that we were not far from the little lake, a wide place in the river about a mile and a half broad, and three and a half long. This put us all in good spirits as we knew we were

---

* Page 63 begins in the original journal.

not above ten miles from the Establishment, and [we] began preparing for the last night's rest under the canopy of heaven, our tent being left where it was first pitched, so stiff with the wet and frost that it was impossible to take it with us. One of the men who had broken through the ice was here taken ill and unable to proceed, which put me in a dilemma, and in the morning he was worse. We were, therefore, obliged to make a hand sleigh to lay him on and drag it over the ice and snow. About four in the afternoon we arrived at the Establishment like so many chimney sweeps, and I believe two or three days more wandering would have made some havock amongst our party; as it was some were laid up several days, and the man who was taken ill died three days after our arrival. Thus ended our expedition for live stock with the loss of one man and the principal part of our errand hanging upon trees in the woods, however the Captn and officers gave up all claim to their share of favour of the men who were no losers.*

We were now cut off from all society and obliged to form some[thing] to pass away the time; racing upon snowshoes, and cutting down trees being the principal amusements; leap frog was likewise one of our pastimes in which men and officers indiscriminately joined and I must say that during our sports when we were hail fellow well met I never found the slightest liberties taken by the men, or dereliction of their duty, but I believe the reverse was the case, though when at play at the above sports, or snow balling, when we could persuade the snow to stick together, no favour was shown to any one, and to give an officer a snowball under the ear was the greatest delight of Jack, and we were not far behind in returning the compliment for, nearly one hundred miles one way or two the other, from any civilized society made strange alterations amongst us all, and cemented a sort of friendship malgre[15] the rank, which by me, and I believe others, is remembered now. And I can say with pride and pleasure that, though the duty we had to go through, from the time I took command of the schooner, was severe to the extreme and in many instances I was obliged to work as hard as any foremast man, I had no occasion, during the eighteen months I commanded to punish any man.

A whist club was likewise established under the directions of our excellent Captain P.S. Hambly, and I shall take the liberty of making the

---

* Page 64 begins in the original journal.

rules public, at the same time much doubting whether they will be followed. Our sittings were on alternate nights, [the] exception being Sunday, of course, playing to commence at seven o'clock, and no game to begin after ten — stakes one dollar the rubber, and quarter dollar points — making any irrelevant remark during the game, quarter dollar fine — swearing one dollar, betting upon the rubber above one dollar, the same, — one quarter of the winnings, and all the fines collected each night to provide a fund for such of the men who might be ill, to supply them with such things as the service did not allow, and in many instances could not be procured without such fund.

A weekly paper was also established and unlike the ephemeral papers of the present day, no personalities were allowed that could cause unpleasant feelings to anyone. Thus the winter passed away imperceptibly, with the addition of as many officers as the service would allow to be absent, taking it in turns to cross Lake Simcoe for York on a fortnight's leave to enjoy the pleasures of the capital of Upper Canada.

Our stock of books were very limited; in the novel line we had Miss Porters *Don Sebastion* and that was read till we could quote any part. The only other books, except bibles etc were *Timmerman on Solitude* and an old magazine, the former was often intruded upon one or the other, and as often thrown at the offender's head, with some kind remark about solitude, but in a moment of ennui[16] I put the volume in my pocket, and took it to my log house, where I read a few pages and was so pleased with the work, that a brother officer who lived with me, awoke about 2 or 3 o'clock and was surprised to find a candle burning, [that] he broke into my solitude by exclaiming, "What the devil are you about at this hour." On the next day I was obliged to leave on a surveying expedition up the river, and when I returned it was with difficulty *Timmerman* was to be procured, he [had] become such a favourite, and to this hour he is occasionally my companion.

Upon Christmas Day according to the etiquette of the service, the Captain dined with us and we had delivered ourselves of some luxuries to enjoy this day; we were* all assembled in the messroom fully prepared to do honour to the feast, dinner on the table, and just going to sit down when the alarm of fire was given; the back of our mess house was in

---

* Page 65 begins in the original journal.

flames. Water it was next to impossible to procure, and snow became the only substitute, which was eagerly collected by the whole of us, as well as the men who had been called. The fire was, without much difficulty, extinguished, but alas! when we looked upon the viands, cold and covered with ashes, a regular gourmand would have fallen into hysterics, but we being only plain sailors, had that portion washed in hot water, which would bear the ordeal, and made up the deficiency of the dinner by a few extra portions of good wine.

Early in January 1816, I left the Establishment upon an exploring expedition up the river Nottawaysauga to ascertain how high it might be navigable for boats, as we had received some vague tradition from the Indian that it rose, or ran, but 15 or 20 miles from York, and the direction of its course seemed to favour the idea. It would form a much more eligible passage for supplying our military station on Lake Huron, saving much time and expense, from there being but one land carriage from York and that considerably shorter than to Holland Landing.

Our Indians had all left us some time, and gone over to the settled parts of the country, and as this expedition had been planned for some time, two Indians had been victualled at the Establishment to serve as guides. They had no idea of remaining longer than suited their own pleasure, or convenience, and had left soon after their brethren, so we were obliged to start without, but being almost as good bush rangers as the natives, it did not delay us, although from our want of a perfect knowledge of the warm springs it was necessary to proceed with caution.

These warm springs are a singular phenomena both in the lakes, as well as the rivers and creeks, and in some places, so numerous that it is difficult to avoid them, for unless they are extensive there is generally a thin crust of snow or ice over them, which causes the traveller to walk with confidence until he find himself immersed in water, which at this season of the year and in this country is far from agreeable. I once attempted to leap an open space that extended a considerable distance up the creek and jumped in, where I had the supreme felicity of remaining nearly a quarter of an hour before the men came up to assist me out, my toes barely touching the bottom, and the ice around me so smooth that after floundering about some time in endeavouring to extricate myself I was obliged to be contented with exercising my lungs to hurry on my party. Before we were shewn a short cut through the woods by the Indians, our route was always up the river and one time the Captain, with a dozen men was trudging over the ice, and being ahead of the rest, in he popped; a rush took place to assist him, when he had six companions all floundering about in the same hole. A change of clothes or house shelter in these circumstances are entirely out of the question; there only remains to fell wood and make a good fire as quick as possible, for a few minutes will suffice to freeze the clothes stiff, but every party small or great in number were always provided with axes.

On the second evening we arrived at the mouth of the creek, and the following morning pursued our route up the river, which we found about the same width* namely from 90 to 120 yards, the banks in each side high and covered with very fine timber, which indicated a deep rich soil, but few fir forest. As we depended upon the fir branches both for our bed, and shelter from the inclemency of the weather, they would have been a more welcome sight to us, though the general observation in the country is that where there are large forests of fir, the soil is sandy and very poor. Indeed we were enabled to verify the same, as our houses were built on the edge of an extensive fir forest and for more than five feet deep there was no appearance of mould,[17] while the trees were gigantic, and straight as a line, many of them sufficiently large for the main mast of a second and third man of war.

The fourth day brought us to a small island in the middle of the river but not large enough to obstruct boat navigation; [on] the fifth the obstructions became more numerous and the river narrowed, — these obstructions appear to have been caused by the grounding of large trees swept down by the current; the sixth day we lost the track of the river in an extensive swamp with numerous islets. But about 20 miles above the mouth of the creek it became unnavigable, and all idea of opening a communication with York vanished, [and] having ascertained this point we had to return to the Establishment.

From this time till May I remained at the Establishment, with the exception of a trip to York for a few days. On the fifth of the month we commenced fitting out the schooner and preparing for sea, as the sun had great power, and the river and creek open, but for miles on the lake the ice remained firm, so that it would have been worse than useless

---

* Page 66 begins in the original journal.

to attempt to run through it. On the 20th I thought we might force our way through, the ice beginning to be detached but totally failed and was obliged to return into the river. On the 20th March[18] 1815 the lake was completely open, except a small quantity of ice round the shore, but nothing to prevent our sailing, had the schooners been ready, and the creek sufficiently open to allow the transport of provisions.

CHAPTER SIX

RETURN TO KINGSTON AS MASTER OF THE *BECKWITH*
And Home

This month I was superseded in my command, and ordered to proceed to Kingston to take command of the *Beckwith,* a ship of 450 tons burden, which was nearly ready for launching, and to be employed in all duties relative to the army, such as conveying stores, provisions, troops etc. from and to the different military posts bordering on Lake Ontario. It [had been] found by experience that the ships of war were not calculated for purposes of that kind; [it placed] the officers of each service under unpleasant circumstances as to accommodation and messing, and the troops took up too much room in the event of an action. This had been well understood during the war, but from the immensity of business constantly on hand, it could not be remedied.

I was not much pleased with the exchange as it was strongly rumoured that she [*Beckwith*] would be taken into the service and made a post ship of. On my passage to join her, I was ordered to preside at a survey of a large quantity of naval stores at Holland Landing, which were to be transferred from one storekeeper to another. This I knew would detain me some days, and on the 2nd June I left Lake Huron, still covered with ice for several miles from the shore, though the heat of the sun made bathing in the river [Nottawasaga] quite a refreshing amusement.

On the 15th June I arrived at Kingston and found that the *Beckwith* would, when launched, make one trip to Niagara merely to try her trim and then be taken into the service in lieu of a brig, which was out of repair, and the Captain officers and men turned over to her, while I remained on board the *Prince Regent* till she was launched.*

---

* Page 67 begins in the original journal.

Having nothing to do in the interval, I obtained leave to take a small vessel, used as a pleasure boat, and pay a visit to Sackets Harbour. I was accompanied by the Master of the ship, and two military officers who had never been there, and felt the same curiosity as ourselves. On our arrival we were handsomely entertained by Capt. Wolsey the American senior officer, and invited to dinner. In going over the fort, which the fears of others had made impregnable when we attacked Sackets in 1813, caused much merriment between the army officers, who had long served under the Duke of Wellington, and as it had been considerably strengthened since the attack, [the fort] must at the time have been little better than a mud battery. As a naval man my attention was more particularly taken with their dockyard, and [on] examining the two ships[1] on the stocks, which, had they been launched, [they] would have been larger, and carried more guns than any ship in the British navy. The largest was pierced for 130 guns, and the other would have been scarce ten guns short of that number; the larger of the two on the docks at Kingston would have mounted 136 and her consort 130 guns. Thus, had the war continued, the mill pond Lake Ontario, compared to the ocean, would have had the largest ships in the world, or, perhaps, the largest ever built, upon the bosom of its waters. As to the number of ships launched, that would have depended upon the length of the war, for, from the time of the arrival of the shipwrights, carpenters, and other nautical artificers, the ways were never unoccupied, but as soon as a vessel was launched, down went the keel of another. I had the curiosity of taking and noting down the length, breadth of beam, and thickness of portals in the largest American ship but lost it. Her symmetrical proportions were beautiful — the Americans at this time certainly beat all our ships in symmetry — After dinner we were shown a curiosity[2] by Capt[n] Wolsey, in the shape of a pistol barrel that discharged seven bullets successively at the interval of a few seconds. Upon the same principal, he informed me, they should have armed the tops of their ships with swivels of a large calibre.

It was now fast on for three years since I was here a prisoner of war, and it appeared almost incredible the improvement that had taken place in the town. For unlike Kingston, which is on high firm ground, this was little better than a complete swamp as before mentioned. To reclaim the ground must have been attended with much labour and perseverance, but now there were many substantial houses, and in the suburbs several elegant villas, and the inhabitants had changed from ephemeral visitors to decided settlers.

On the 8th July the *Beckwith* was launched, and in consequence of many alterations being necessary, she was not ready to sail till 25th August when we embarked part of the 99th Regiment on board to relieve the garrison at Fort George. As soon as I conveniently could leave the ship, I proceeded to the Falls of Niagara, but the description given by travellers, though I have read many, give but a very faint idea indeed of the reality. The effects of the view are too astounding to give an idea of the feelings of a person viewing them. For though the Almighty power may be seen and felt in the earthquake, whirlwind, and storm, here His works preside in most tremendous majesty without the attendants of danger. And I will defy the skeptic to view this work of the God of Nature without being humbled in his contrite heart* and inwardly contemplating that there must be an overreaching Providence who conducts all things for the best. The work of [the] man who constructed the artificial Falls of Virginia waters was swept away, and did immense damage, but the works of the Almighty are always under control, though I must beg pardon for making a comparison between the stupendous falls of Niagara, and the pigmy one of Virginia water, which is about the difference between a mite and a mammoth.

There are some wonderful traditions of Indians going over the falls and being dashed to pieces, and one was told me with wonderful gravity, of an Indian, who once got into the current leading to the falls and, seeing of necessity he must go down, deliberately drank the contents of a bottle of rum, and laid himself down quietly in the boat to wait the event. I remarked to the veracious personage who related the story that he ought to have added "In the presence of a vast number of spectators," and advised him to make the addition to the next curious person for whom he should act as cicerone.

The traveller who views the water rolling down from Lake Erie will at once see the fallacy of any tale of the kind, as above two miles above the brink, there is continued rush of water over rocks many six feet high, and he will naturally perceive the moral improbability of any, even the strongest vessel to approach the precipice of the falls, except in detached parts, as they must be dashed to pieces before they reach them.

---

* Page 68 begins in the original journal.

The Splendour and Fascination of Niagara Falls, 1854. Platt Babbit, an early photographer, commemorates the ongoing fascination of all comers to the "stupendous Falls of Niagara" in this early ambrotype image. Wingfield waxes eloquently about the intrigue of the falls and reflects on comparisons with other sites of much lesser significance.

The whirlpool, a few miles below the falls, in the river, is almost as good a natural curiosity as the falls themselves. It is formed by an elbow in the river and the current running extremely rapidly, finds its course obstructed, and then meeting the main stream forms an astonishing vortex. When I visited it there were several large logs, apparently part of a raft, whirling around, sometimes totally disappearing, and others rising on end four or five feet perpendicular out of the water. The river below must be supplied from an under current as but a small portion of the water, comparatively speaking, finds its way through the natural channel. Having remained two days, which rather whetted than satisfied my curiosity, I was obliged to return to the ship.

On my arrival at Kingston, I found that a further reduction in our naval force was about to take place, and I was among those who were ordered to England, and on the 30th Sept. 1816, I bid adieu to Lake Ontario.

The final page of the Wingfield journal.

PART TWO

POSTSCRIPT TO THE JOURNAL

That is as far as Wingfield goes in his memoirs. He seems to cut his story rather abruptly, but details of the balance of his life are more obscure. We know that he returned to England on the supply ship *Prevoyant* and took up a commission as lieutenant at half pay.

Wars always produce heroes, and many heroes are not recognized in their lifetime. They do their duty; they fight hard and smart; they live or die according to the decrees of fate. They are the grunts of America, the doughboys[1] of past wars.

Canada remembers and honours great leaders such as Sir Isaac Brock, hero of the Niagara Campaign in 1813. Sir William Howe Mulcaster, a daring naval officer of the same period, was a hero several times during his career, as was Sir Edward Collier. However Barclay, Worsley, McDouall, Roberts, and Wingfield comprise just a few of the many brave, stalwart, committed, and hard-working figures of the same era who were not so recognized.

David Wingfield did not win any glorious battles, nor did he perform in any outstanding way on the battlefield. He did his duty to King and to Country. However, during his four years in North America he had many adventures, some of them outstanding. His exploits are worthy of greater attention. He proved he could cope with almost anything that fate might put into his path — even losing his ship, his career, and his freedom.

No monument has been erected in his honour. Sailors of Lake Huron will remember him every time they visit a lovely little harbour by Cabot Head at the northeast tip of the Bruce Peninsula in Ontario. The harbour is named Wingfield Basin. Also, his memoirs are worthy of emphasizing to students of history, and should be read by anyone wishing to get a better sense of the life and times in the military in the early part of the nineteenth century.

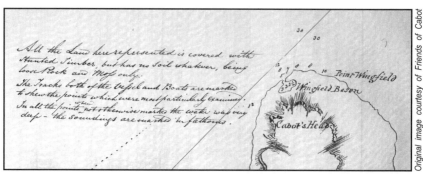

Map 11: Section of original hydrographic chart. The chart section is from the field notes and drawings collected by William Fitz William Owen, the son of naval officer Lieutenant William Owen. In 1815, the junior Owen began a survey of the east shore of Lake Huron and of Georgian Bay to the area near present-day Victoria Harbour: in the latter survey, land forms, timber resources, and navigational hazards were observed and the site for a naval base was sought. David Wingfield accompanied Owen on this venture and assisted in the work. Wingfield Point and Wingfield Basin are named in his honour. Nearby Fitzwilliam Island perpetuates the name of the junior Owen while Owen Sound is named after his father.

PART THREE

THE BIOGRAPHY OF DAVID WINGFIELD

Devising a detailed biography, rich in descriptives and elaborate in particulars, for a little known Canadian historical figure with British roots presents a formidable challenge. The primary source document for information about David Wingfield is his journal or diary, kept while he was in the naval service on the Great Lakes in the period from 1813 to 1816. Virtually nothing has been known about his personal life, other than a few genealogical gleanings and brief peripheral references to his naval service on behalf of England before his transfer to Upper Canada as a Royal Navy midshipman.

What follows, therefore, is fleshed out from our research, using material provided by members and resources of the Wingfield Family Society (www. wingfield.org), in particular, Jocelyn Wingfield, Norfolk, UK; Le Bron (Lee) Preston, Long Beach, California, USA, and Robert Wingfield, Buffalo Grove, Illinois, USA. The original connection with members of the Wingfield Family Society was made for us by Patrick Folkes of Tara, Ontario, an esteemed Bruce County historian, and John Weichel, of the Southampton and Tobermory, Ontario, areas, another noted local historian and author of several important Bruce County works, especially his two-volume marine history of Southampton and the Bruce Peninsula shores, *Forgotten Times*.

While one can bring many family connections together, in the absence of anecdotal information, the data is cold and factual, devoid of flavour and the personality that enriches the tale. It becomes necessary to seek out secondary, and indeed, tertiary sources upon which presumptions and speculations might be boldly made.

For example, can you imagine a family with so many diverse branches: According to Jocelyn Wingfield, "The Wingfield Family Society had to be a one-name Society since, when we discovered that Wingfield was spelled in some 150 ways in the records, thereby making it difficult for would-be members to prove their descent from the Wingfields of Suffolk from which spring several cadet lines[1] including those of Powerscourt, and those of Tickencote — whence spring the Virginia and Georgia lines — we agreed that all Wingfields and those interested could join, 'bringing their records' so that we could sort it all out on the computer."

The "Wingfields of Wingfield" spawned, in order of seniority, the following cadet lines: Letheringham & Easton, Crowfield & Coddenham (Jamaica: Spanish Town and Orange (near Montego Bay) from 1677 to the tsunami & earthquake in 1692); Worcester & Staffordshire; Temple Bruer (Lincolnshire); Great Dunham (Norfolk); Powerscourt (County Wicklow, Ireland) and Rhodesia, now Zimbabwe; and Ampthill (Bedfordshire); and Barrington (Gloucestershire); Kimbolton and Stonely (Jamestown, Virginia; Brantham & Wakefield (Yorkshire); Upton & Tickencote and (from 1680) Virginia; and other cadet lines in the United States. Indeed, it is a complex family network.

Such poses part of the dilemma in creating an appropriate biography for David Wingfield. Should his surely most colourful family life and intriguing military career rest only on cold data and dates; or should it be enriched in a sometimes-speculative manner, based on bold interpretations and assumptions built upon reasonably careful research and estimations constructed from that research base?

Our choice is to pursue the latter course. In doing so, we risk the challenge and critique of the pure historian, but most surely would omit the opportunity to honour yet another of our countless unsung Canadian heroes from days gone by. So be it.

This is our David Wingfield.

Origins

An overview of the population of England, Scotland, and Wales in the year 1801, according to the census records of the day, reveals that of the 10.5 million residents, just under 200,000 men had joined the ranks of the army while just over 126,000 men had enrolled in the naval service, including the marines. Another almost 145,000 identified themselves as seamen registered in merchant shipping. There were 1,410 convicts on board the hulks! Persons employed in trades, manufacturing, and handicrafts roughly equalled the two million residents still involved in agriculture. These figures are taken from the official census records available from the General Records Office of National Archives.

The United Kingdom census documents[2] identify that our David Wingfield lived in the County of Gloucestershire in mid-west England during his retirement there. He claims, according to the census records of 1841, while he was living in Painswick Parish, Gloucester, that he was born in Windsor, County Berkshire. It is not known how much of his

Courtesy of National Marine Museum, PAG 7012.

A Convict Ship at Portsmouth, etching by Hunts after an original by Edward William Cooke, undated. The image shows a typical convict ship, similar to the "hulks" mentioned by Wingfield in his journal. This is a seventeenth-century prison ship hulk at Portsmouth. No longer suitable for active naval service, such battered hulks were used to house prisoners. They sometimes grew like topsy, sprouting disorderly buildings and rooftops to supplant once-elegant lines and standing rigging with slum-like lodgings.

childhood might have been spent there. His later years, again according to census records and other notices published in the *London Gazette*, were spent in Painswick and Ruscombe near Stroud, and in Bussage near Bisley, also in the Stroud district. One report shows him resident at No. 12 Type-street, Finsbury, in Middlesex, but we suspect that may well be a namesake, not our lieutenant, for there is no other corroboration that would remove him from Gloucestershire, even during his financially troubled years in the 1840s and 50s.

If his death certificate is accepted as being accurate for the date of his demise, February 23, 1864, at Horsley, then we must discount dates other than 1792 or 1793 (depending upon birth month) as his birth date. However, various records show his birth date as being 1796 or 1799, according to Wingfield genealogist Lee Preston. The 1841 Census, for example, shows David as age forty-five, with his wife, Abiah, at age thirty. This would give us a birth date of 1796. The census of 1851 shows him as age forty-eight; therefore, he would have a birth date of 1793. Yet again, the census of 1861 shows him at age sixty, giving a birth year of 1799! Given his sea travels to Denmark as early as 1806 as a seaman, the 1792/1793 date range seems to be most realistic, giving him at most the modest age of thirteen or fourteen by the time he entered the Royal Navy as a second-class volunteer in 1806. Even Wingfield's journal adds a degree of confusion to the question. Notes at the conclusion of his manuscript offer a speculated birth date of 1798, with his first year "went to sea" at 1810. These notations, however, may not be in Wingfield's own hand.

Wingfield's Birthplace

Windsor is a suburban town and tourist destination in the Royal Borough of Windsor and Maidenhead in Berkshire, England. It is best known as the site of Windsor Castle. The town is situated twenty-one miles west of Charing Cross. It is immediately south of the River Thames, which forms its boundary with Eton. The village of Old Windsor, just over two miles to the south, predates what is now called Windsor by around

Courtesy of Jocelyn Wingfield.

Market Street, Windsor, Berkshire, by Frederick L. Griggs, 1906. This street may have been frequented by Wingfield's family, or indeed by David when he was a child. From James Edmund Vincent, *Highways and Byways in Berkshire*, London: Macmillan & Co., 1906.

three hundred years; in the past Windsor was formally referred to as New Windsor to distinguish the two.

In 1870–72, John Marius Wilson, gazetteer, reported Windsor (New), as "...a parish in Windsor district, Berks; containing the greater part of Windsor borough-Post town, Windsor Acres, with Windsor Castle, 3,237. Pop. in 1851, 6,553; in 1861, 6,728. Houses, 1,142."[3] It was much smaller and much less industrial than Gloucester.

There is an element of romance about Windsor. Its difference from Gloucester, described in Wingfield's era, becomes evident in notes further below.

In his remarks about Windsor, made in writings dated 1776, a German traveller, one Karl Moritz, offered these observations about the Windsor of the day as he first entered the city:[4]

> The green hills of Windsor smiled so friendly upon me, that they seemed to invite me first to visit them.
>
> And now trudging through the streets of Windsor, I at length mounted a sort of hill; a steep path led me on to its summit, close to the walls of the castle, where I had an uncommonly extensive and fine prospect, which

so much raised my heart, that in a moment I forgot not only the insults of waiters and tavern-keepers, but the hardship of my lot in being obliged to travel in a manner that exposed me to the scorn of a people whom I wished to respect. Below me lay the most beautiful landscapes in the world — all the rich scenery that nature, in her best attire, can exhibit… I seemed to view a whole world at once, rich and beautiful beyond conception. At that moment what more could I have wished for?

And the venerable castle, that royal edifice which, in every part of it, has strong traces of antiquity, smiles through its green trees, like the serene countenance of some hoary sage, who, by the vigour of a happy constitution, still retains many of the charms of youth. Nothing inspired me with more veneration and awe than the fine old building St. George's Church, which, as you come down from the castle, is on your right. At the sight of it past centuries seemed to revive in my imagination.

In a moment of disappointment, he continues:

But I will see no more of those sights which are shown you by one of those venal praters, who ten times a day, parrot-wise, repeat over the same dull lesson they have got by heart. The surly fellow, who for a shilling conducted me round the church, had nearly, with his chattering, destroyed the finest impressions. Henry VIII, Charles I, and Edward IV are buried here. After all, this church, both within and without, has a most melancholy and dismal appearance.

I now went down a gentle declivity into the delightful park at Windsor, at the foot of which it looks so sombrous and gloomy that I could hardly help fancying it was some vast old Gothic temple. This forest certainly, in point of beauty, surpasses everything of the kind you can figure to yourself. To its own charms, when I saw it, there were added a most pleasing and philosophical solitude, the coolness of an evening breeze, all aided by the soft sounds of music, which, at this distance from the castle, from whence it issued, was inexpressibly sweet. It threw me into a sort of enthusiastic and pleasing reverie, which made me ample amends for the fatigues, discourtesies, and continued cross accidents I had encountered in the course of the day.

I now left the forest; the clock struck six, and the workmen were going home from their work. I have forgot to mention the large round tower of the castle, which is also a very ancient building. The roads that lead to it are all along their sides planted with shrubs; these, being modern and lively, make a pleasing contrast to the fine old mossy walls. On the top of this tower the flag of Great Britain is usually displayed, which, however, as it was now late in the evening, was taken in.

As I came down from the castle I saw the king driving up to it in a very plain, two-wheeled, open carriage. The people here were politer than I used to think they were in London, for I did not see a single person, high or low, who did not pull off their hats as their sovereign passed them.

This description provides a truly romantic introduction to the borough of Wingfield's birthplace.

Windsor was an area, in nineteenth century England, where it seemed that social mobility, according to census summaries, was greater than in many other shires across the land. According to those provided by the University of Portsmouth, larger numbers of lower-class workers seemed able to elevate themselves into middle-class labours over the period of the early 1800s. Was it that the economy was less industrial, and more favoured to occupations of a higher order?

Wingfield's Windsor Roots

We know nothing about the family of David Wingfield at this time. It was thought that he might be part of a family branch known as the Sunningdale Wingfields, but that quest for information has proven to be fruitless by family genealogists. The search for family connections continues.

Early Military Service

It is likely that he made early entry into the military service, perhaps from Windsor. Certain records[5] seem to indicate that he joined the Royal Navy on November 23, 1806, as a second-class volunteer, without any known patronage or sponsorship, on board the HMS *Ruby*, a 64-gun ship. His service record, however, indicates that he joined as a first-class volunteer. He served under Captains John Draper, Robert Hall, and Robert Williams. It was on this ship that young Wingfield, *circa* age fourteen, accompanied the expedition of 1807 to Copenhagen. He saw action with the Danish gunboats in the Little Belt, a strait between the Danish island of Funen and the Jutland Peninsula.

The HMS *Ruby*, launched at Woolwich in 1776, was a 64-gun, third-rate ship-of-the-line. She carried 159 feet 6 inches at the upper gun deck, and sported a beam of over 44 feet. She was about 1,369 tons burthen and carried thirty-eight 24-pounders on her main deck and twenty-six 18-pounders on her upper deck. The *Ruby* was converted to a receiving ship in 1813 and finally broken up in 1821.

In his short time on board the *Ruby*, Wingfield would have learned the ropes, so to speak, moving on to the HMS *Agincourt*, as an ordinary, then able seaman, under Captain William Kent, where he removed after only a few short weeks as a midshipman in March of 1810. Once again, his service record shows him as a master's mate during part of this time.

The HMS *Agincourt* was a 74-gun ship-of-the-line, presumably a third-rate. Prior to the Battle of Dover in 1805, she was part of the Channel Fleet. Stationed just off Ushant, it was part of the British blockade of the port at Brest, France. The *Agincourt*, at that time, was under the command of Captain Briggs and part of Admiral Lord Gardner's fleet.

Wingfield joined the HMS *Fylla* 20 under Captain Honourable Edward Rodney, on the Guernsey Station. This vessel is listed under the Welsh "Forgotten Fleets" shipping lists being compiled by one P.M. Heaton, 1989, but no data is otherwise available. According to the William R. O'Byrne *Naval Biographical Dictionary*, published by John Murray in 1849, Wingfield was present during an unsuccessful attack on two French man-of-war brigs, under covering fire from the gun-brig *Firm*. From August 1811 until March 1813, he was attached, according to the same sources, to the *Diadem*, a 64-gun ship-of-the-line, under Captain John Phillimore, during which time he visited Lisbon, cruised the North Sea, and was actively employed with the patriots of the north coast of Spain. The *Diadem* was a 160-foot, Intrepid class ship-of-the-line that gained notoriety as part of the victorious British Mediterranean fleet that defeated Portugal in the Battle of St. Vincent on Valentine's Day 1797. He is shown as a midshipman at this time.

On leaving her, according to Murray, David Wingfield joined the Lake Service of Canada in 1813 where he served "commanding gunboats and schooners,"[6] serving as master's mate on the HMS *Prince Regent*, and on the *St. Lawrence* in 1814, following his capture by the Americans.

His naval record, including the times in Canada detailed later, summarizes the length and nature of his "Services performed in the several Ranks" as follows: "Eight years and three months as Vol., Ord. S., Midshipman and Master's Mate, of which three years were passed Cruizing (*sic*) in the North Sea, Great Belt, and off Lisbon, three months in the Downs, Eighteen months cruizing in the English Channel. Eighteen months cruizing off the North Coast of Spain. Two years on Lake Ontario and (nine months) Prisoner of War in the United States of America. Fifteen months on Lake Huron and three months in the *Prince Regent*, Lake Ontario."[7]

Service in Canada

His life and times in Canada are addressed in the main body of the text. His intriguing journal is the one piece of evidence attesting to his adventures in that period, including a period of incarceration as an American prisoner of war, commencing October 5, 1813, having been taken when he was in command of the *Confiance*. In Canada, he also served on the flagships of Commodore Yeo, and later commanded the *Surprise* as a newly promoted lieutenant, serving in the waters between Wasaga on the east and Mackinac and Drummond islands on the west. His final assignment was to serve, presumably as master, on the recently launched *Beckwith*, but it is apparent that he was withdrawn to England before that was possible. However, he did get to join the *Beckwith* for its shake-down cruise to the "Falls of Niagara." He spent his final three months on the "Lakes of Canada" on the *Prince Regent* from June 1816 until September 30 of the same year.

Return to England

His residency, post-childhood, and following his return to England on half pay after military service in the Canadian colony, was in the Painswick Borough of Stroud, in Gloucestershire, a few miles south of Gloucester city. He returned to England on the supply ship HMS *Prevoyant*, most certainly the French storeship *Prevoyante* captured in 1795 by the HMS *Thetis* (1782), a 38-gun fifth-rate vessel; 700 tons; 38 guns; 238 men.

According to his journal, upon his return to England, Wingfield brought with him a young Indian lad who must have gained the lieutenant's favour during his assignment on Lake Huron. Wingfield knew him from age eleven. He does note that his intention was to educate the young man with a good English schooling and help him become comfortable in British society. But he observed, by the time the young man was fourteen that he was "miserable," and, upon questioning him,

The Prevoyante *Dismasted.* The *Prevoyante* – later the *Prevoyant* – carried Wingfield home after his service in the Canadas. The ancient pencil image shows Cochrane, a British naval leader, attacking five French storeships, May 17, 1795. This was to become the store ship on which Wingfield travelled.

found that he was quite homesick for his native wilds. He was sent back, quite overjoyed, under the care of an acquaintance travelling to Canada. Wingfield later heard through a friend that "… he has become a great man among his tribe."[8]

Information as to why Wingfield chose this area in the Painswick Borough of Stroud for his residence could not be located. It may well have been the proximity to the sea, via the River Severn, and the extensive marine activity in a period of much growth and development in that area north and west of Berkshire, the county of his birth. It may have been a family connection through his wife, Abiah Wood. In any event, he and his family resided in the heart of the Cotswold hills and villages in west-central England at a time when the area was thriving with a growing wool industry, in the midst of an economic boom that saw the development of trade, industry, and shipping facilities taking advantage of the ocean access provided by the mighty Severn. Canals and bridges were under construction throughout the area to establish waterway connections with the river. The region is dotted with picturesque villages, rolling farm fields, and hundreds of houses, other buildings, and fences built from the underlying "Cotswold stone," a yellowish limestone, rich in fossils from along the escarpment edge that creates the natural beauty of this area. Today, the Cotswolds are designated by the government as an "Area of Outstanding Beauty," covering some 780 square miles, and given the same status for protection as the British National Parks.[9]

Courtesy of Jocelyn Wingfield.

TOP: Bibury, Gloucestershire, with the famous Arlington Row of houses.
BOTTOM: Calcot, Gloucestershire, Cotswold gables and stone walls.

There is evidence that Wingfield moved around in the County of Gloucestershire, particularly in his later years when he had become poverty stricken. This series of images portray the nature of the countryside in the Cotswold Hills area. There is conflicting information that suggests Wingfield was both a country villager and also a city dweller at times. All images as originally published in *Cotswold Villages: English Villages and Hamlets* by Humphrey Pakington. London: B.T. Batsford Ltd., 1934.

Life on half pay, said to be the sum of six shillings per diem, in spite of the apparent good times around him, was not easy for Wingfield. He was married, had a growing family, and was required to provide for their support and accommodation. With an annual income of just under £100, it was at a time when a four-pound loaf of bread could cost up to a full shilling or more, and a modest suit of clothing might be as much as £8. It was generally understood that one could not live comfortably, with a family, with an annual income of less than £100. At the time, the boundary between income levels for the middle class and the simply rich was considered to be about £500. At the level of income of Wingfield's "half pay," even with the modest additional revenue that might have been possible as a shopkeeper, his life must have been a struggle. Accommodation costs might have been as much as £40 for a comfortable set of rooms, although he was likely able to rent a modest house in the more rural villages for as little as £10 per year.[10]

As the decades of the nineteenth century ensued, the prices of manufactured items such as shoes, clothing, and children's apparel did tend to fall as the manufacturing processes extended to more household goods. But there is little doubt that Wingfield's family expenditures were increasing as the size of his family grew quickly to levels that were not manageable to support the daily living needs of as many as eleven children with his first wife Abiah. Even the cost of food alone might require fully one half of the family income.

An examination of the court reports for debtors shows our David Wingfield as being financially insolvent on at least five occasions between 1842 and 1854. In the earliest reports, he is listed as a shopkeeper at Bussage, near Bisley, and his creditors are "informed that a Dividend of three shilling and nine pence in the pound may be received, by applying to Mr. Paris, Solicitor for the Assignee, at Stroud, Gloucestershire, on or before the 1st of June next — Bills and securities to be produced."[11] Given that a dividend was assigned payable to his creditors, Wingfield would have declared or would have been forced into bankruptcy. As time unfolded over the next twelve years, he was noted to be "out of business" and had pled insolvency on at least four occasions with assignments in various amounts ordered by the courts. One record, September 7, 1850, for a David Wingfield, a saddler of Finsbury, Middlesex, shows him to be "In the Debtors' Prison for London Middlesex," listed with others, "on their own Petitions."[12] Whereas the 1851 census still shows Lieutenant David Wingfield as resident at Stonehouse, Stroud, in Gloucestershire, the authors have concluded that this David Wingfield is simply a namesake, perhaps even the same David Wingfield whose Seaman's Will is shown elsewhere.

Gloucester City

John Marius Wilson, the Imperial gazetteer of England and Wales (1870–72), reports in his voluminous records of the city from that era,[13] that the distinguished municipality of Gloucester stands on the River Severn, just over thirty-seven miles NNE of Bristol, and a little more than one hundred miles by railway or road, WNW of London. The Severn is navigable past it; a ship canal gives aid to its commerce; a canal connects it with the Thames; and several railways give it communication with all parts of the kingdom.

Its geographically central location, its easy association with the sea, and its function as a major port on the River Severn, joined to the Thames, would surely make it attractive as a retirement location, close to family, to anyone with a naval background.

Gloucester is one of the old cities, originating from the ancient city of Caerglou, or "bright fort." It is known that the Romans, under Emperor Claudius, took it over in AD 44 as a key protectorate to fend off invaders from South Wales. It was a city suffering from fractious civil discord amongst its inhabitants and suffered from the incursions of the marauding Scots up to the time of Edward the Confessor who enter-tained there. The city was often visited by William the Conqueror who held court at this site. Henry III was crowned there, in 1216, at the age of ten years. The parliament of 1278 is notable for the passing of acts concerning the liberties and franchises of the nation, known as the Statutes of Gloucester. Gloucester Cathedral houses the tomb of Edward III.

"The city," writes J.M. Wilson:

> "stands in a beautiful valley, sheltered on the east by a range of hills; and it occupies a gentle eminence rising from the Severn, at its division by the Isle of Alney. The

Courtesy of Jocelyn Wingfield.

Westgate Street, City of Gloucester, by Hugh Thomson. The heart of the city has not changed since Wingfield's time. It remains a picturesque setting to this day. From *Highways and Byways in Gloucestershire,* by Edward Hutton. London: Macmillan & Co, Ltd., 1932.

surrounding scenery and the various approaches, are, for the most part, highly ornamental. Gardens, orchards, parks, and elegant villas adorn the environs; and pleasant villages, agreeable hamlets, well-conditioned farms, and many pieces of good close scenery are in the neighbourhood.

Views of the city, from the best vantage-grounds in its vicinity, show the summits of its rich ecclesiastical architecture, striking upward from surrounding wood, in a magnificent group of towers and spires; whilst the near sheltering hills, cultivated to their tops — the most conspicuous being 'the famous hill of Robin Hood'— display unusual variety and ornature."[14]

The docks are accessible from Southgate Street, one of the four main streets in the city's cruciform configuration. No doubt, the returned Wingfield would spend time in this area, surveying activities, vicariously supervising undertakings, particularly if they were military in nature. The harbour facilities were enlarged in the early 1800s, a new basin was formed, and numerous warehouses were added to support economic needs that coincided with the arrival of the railways. The old houses, built of wood, with projecting second stories, present at the time of Wingfield, have, for the most part, entirely disappeared.

Wilson writes, "The old streets, which formerly were very narrow and disagreeable, though still irregular and far from straight, are now, in general, broad, well-paved, picturesque, and pleasing; and the atmosphere of the place, which formerly was foul and noisesome, is now kept pure by means of good drainage and a plentiful supply of water."[15]

The architectural remains of the Middle Ages are numerous and extremely fine. There remain even today many instances of ancient British architecture, including many examples of straw-thatched roofing so typical across rural areas of the time.

An instance of the rapid rise of land values, also noted by the Imperial Gazetteer Wilson, occurred in the autumn of 1861, when a plot of ground, which had been purchased in 1815, for £70, was sold for £2,000. Economic growth seemed to be rampant. On a reconstruction of the ancient south gate to the old city, an inscription reads, "A city assaulted by man, but saved by God."[16] A spa, discovered in 1814, possessed considerable medicinal virtues, and gave occasion for the erection of a handsome pump room, and hot, cold, and vapour baths. There were also a theatre and assembly rooms.

At the time of Wingfield's residence in this area, the city hosted several well-known schools

Chalford, Gloucestershire: A Stone Village Near Stroud, shows how the local stone was used in the construction of many buildings, fences, bridges, and aqueducts. From *Cotswold Villages: English Villages and Hamlets* by Humphrey Pakington. London: B.T. Batsford Ltd., 1934.

Courtesy of Jocelyn Wingfield.

of church and grammar origin, one founded by Henry VIII. There were several hospitals of renown, a house of refuge, a reformatory, and a lunatic asylum. There were also a house of industry and a penitentiary. The chief imports for the area were corn, wine, spirits, and timber; the chief exports were iron, coals, malt, salt, bricks, and pottery.

The County, Gloucestershire, was described in 1914, by J. Charles Cox in his travel guide for the area, with a quotation by William of Malmesbury, "The villages are very thick, the churches handsome, and the towns populous and many."[17]

Stroud, the specific town of Wingfield's retirement residence, southeast of Gloucester, was heralded as a large market town, the chief seat of the West of England cloth trade. "The district has been long celebrated for the excellency of its scarlet dye," claimed Cox.[18] This area provided the source for the famous red wool cloth used in the scarlet uniforms of the British military for generations.

Painswick, north of Stroud, was the site of the St. Mary's Church of England, attended by Wingfield, in which he was married to Abiah, his first wife. The impressive structure, with a tower and lofty spire, dates back to 1480.[19] The church was the site of a battle in 1653, at the time of Charles I, when the Parliamentary forces took refuge in the church, but the Royalists subdued them, bursting in the doors and throwing in hand grenades. The church is

Courtesy of Jocelyn Wingfield.

St. Mary's Church of England. Wingfield was married to his first wife, Abiah, here. The church has a long and colourful history. Over the centuries, since it was built in 1480, much lore has developed about the building and its grounds. The image, *Painswick Church & Yews*, is from *Gloucestershire* by J. Charles Cox. London: Methuen, 1914.

surrounded by a longstanding cluster of ninety-nine yew trees, whereby, according to local legend, every attempt to plant just one more to make an even hundred, has failed, the newcomer always dying. Every year, at the Nativity of Our Lady, September 8, these mystic trees are clipped. In a ceremony the following Sunday, known as Clipping Sunday, the parishioners encircle the church, join hands and listen to the sermon preached from the tower door.

Painswick was included in the town sites that flourished as cloth-trade centres beginning in the mid-1600s.

Harbour Works, Canals, and Shipping

At this time, there was considerable activity in the establishment of England's first canal networks in this area. Construction of the Gloucester and Sharpness Canal, originally called the Gloucester and Berkley Canal, started in 1794. The project faced financial difficulties and work was temporarily halted in 1799. With the assistance of government funding, the project re-started in 1819 and was finished by 1827. In the same period, a junction was created to join the Stroudwater Canal, which finally interconnected the Parish of Stroud, the River Severn (1779), and the new waterway. There is little doubt that a man of Wingfield's background, well connected to the sea, would monitor all of these developments.

One would suspect that Wingfield would have also been familiar with much of the following Gloucester shipping and marine traffic detail as itemized by the Imperial Gazetteer:

> The vessels belonging to the port, at the beginning of 1863, were 279 small sailing-vessels, of aggregately 7,756 tons; 72 large sailing-vessels of aggregately 9,097 tons; 5 small steam-vessels, of aggregately 129 tons; and 2 large steam-vessels, of jointly 154 tons. The vessels which entered, in 1862, were 169 British sailing-vessels, of aggregately 43,720 tons, from abroad; 425 foreign

sailing-vessels, of aggregately 78,484 tons, from abroad; 4 British steam-vessels, of aggregately 1, 043 tons, from abroad; 1,396 sailing-vessels, of aggregately 59,048 tons, coastwise; and 30 steam-vessels, of aggregately 1,837 tons, coastwise. The vessels which cleared, in 1862, were 49 British sailing-vessels, of aggregately 12,786 tons, to British colonies and foreign countries; 67 foreign sailing-vessels, of aggregately 17,648 tons to British colonies and foreign counties; 3,525 sailing-vessels, of aggregately 139,700 tons, coastwise; and 30 steam-vessels, of aggregately 1, 833 tons, coastwise.[20]

The David Wingfield Family

While his family roots are unclear at this time, an examination of various census data helps us to piece together the information about David's immediate family.

In census records for 1841, 1851, and 1861, for Stroud, Gloucester, he indicates "not born in same County," claiming Windsor in Berks (Berkshire) as his birthplace.

He was married at age thirty-six to Abiah Wood, fifteen years his junior, on July 8, 1828, in Painswick. Naval records confirm that the marriage was recorded for any potential Royal Navy widow's pension that might be required. Their first child, Amelia, was born in 1830.

The 1841 Census reveals that he lived in the Painswick Borough of Stroud, Gloucestershire, with six children. By 1851, residency was stated to be Stonehouse Parish in Stroud. There were ten children by that time. In 1861, three years following the death of his wife Abiah in 1858, he was noted to be living with one son, Aurthur, age nine, at Newmarket Parish of Stonehouse, in the Township of Horsley, Stroud. Census data confirms the names of his children as follows. There is some information, according to historian Jocelyn Wingfield that indicates two infant daughters, not listed, died in 1845 and 1846:

Amelia	ca. 1830		
John[21]	ca. 1831/32	Tailor & Draper	
Lydia	ca. 1834		
Sarah	ca. 1836	School Teacher	d. June 1903 Winchcombe
Emma Lawson[22]	ca. 1837		
Thomas George	ca. 1840	Fireman	
Louise Ann	ca. 1842/43		
Ellen Jane	ca. 1846/47		
Henry Eggleton [23]	ca. 1849/50	Fleet Engineer, RN, 1901	
Aurther[24]	ca. 1851	(probably Arthur)	
Christiana (Christina or Christa)	ca. 1855	School Teacher (said to have transferred the Wingfield diary to Library and Archives Canada, 1932/33)	

Portion of page from 1851 Census, Stonehouse, Stroud. The details of David Wingfield's family, resident with him at Stonehouse at this time, are shown.

Courtesy of General Records Office, United Kingdom.

David Wingfield's Second Marriage

As noted earlier, his second marriage, at age sixty, to Penelope (née Corbett), age *circa* forty-three in 1861 is documented in volume 6a, page 511, of the UK Census Records: July–September 1861, at Stroud. They had only a few years together. Wingfield died February 23, 1864, according to the death certificate. A separate burial record at the Parish of St. Martin, Horsley, confirms the date of his interment two days later, on February 25.

The details of David's death are shown in this death record. This is one of the two sources that show him with the rank of "Commander" at the time of his death. The other is in the information transmitted from the trade commissioner at Bristol who, in 1932, accepted the 68-page handwritten manuscript comprising Wingfield's memoirs from his time in the Canadas. Notations show the cause of death as "Disease of 2 Lungs – Certified" and the presence of Wingfield's second wife, Penelope, at the time of his death.

It is noteworthy, but most certainly unclear, why various census records show Wingfield's post-retirement promotion from Lieutenant on half pay, to "Commander on half pay, Greenwich Pensioners" as we find noted on his death certificate. This has been discussed in detail elsewhere in this text.

The records indicate that he died at age seventy-one. His second wife Penelope, age circa forty-three, was noted to be present at the time of his death. Wingfield's cause of death was noted on his death certificate to be "disease of the 2 lungs — Certified." This was most certainly consumption, or tuberculosis, as we know it. Tuberculosis was the great killer of the ages in nineteenth-century England. Records indicate that it accounted for nearly 20 percent of all deaths of the time, an even higher number in Europe. Large numbers of those afflicted, died. We have seen estimates of death rates from 20 to 40 percent.

APPENDIX A

The David Wingfield Family Tree

Descendants of David Wingfield

30 Aug 2008

1. David Wingfield (b.1792;d.1864)

sp: Abiah Wood (b.1810;m.1828;d.1858)

  2. John Wingfield (b.1832)

    sp: Jane (b.1846)

      3. Ellen Wingfield (b.1862)

      3. Frederick William Wingfield I (b.1863)

        sp: Anne (b.1868;m.1887)

          4. Frederick William Wingfield II (b.1890)

          4. Victor Wingfield (b.1892)

          4. Percy George Wingfield (b.1893;d.1894)

          4. Bessie Myrtle Wingfield (b.1896;d.1897)

          4. Norman Edward Wingfield (b.1899;d.1918)

      3. Christiana Wingfield (b.1866)

  2. Sarah Wingfield (b.1836;d.1903)

  2. Emma Lawson Wingfield (b.1837;d.1861)

  2. Thomas Wingfield (b.1840;d.1901)

  2. Louisa Ann Wingfield (b.1842)

    sp: Robert Shill (m.1873)

  2. Ellen Jane Wingfield (b.1846;d.1885)

  2. Henry Eggleton Wingfield (b.1849)

    sp: Mrs. Henry Eggleton Wingfield (m.1886)

      3. Arthur Eggleton Wingfield (b.1887;d.1892)

      3. Gladys Irene Wingfield (b.1888)

      3. Edith Maude Wingfield (b.1892)

      3. Dorothy Seymour Wingfield (b.1896)

  2. Christina Mary Wingfield (b.1855)

sp: Penelope Corbett (m.1861)

Wingfield Family Tree. Prepared by Wingfield Family Society with the assistance of Jocelyn Wingfield and Zella Morrow. *Note: Since the family tree for David Wingfield was created, additional genealogical research has identified three additional children. These names and their birth order are shown in the text listing on page 192.

APPENDIX B

The Wingfield Family Society as submitted by Jocelyn Wingfield

History of the Wingfields

In most of the British Isles, from around AD 1300, surnames began to be used. These family names were taken from professions of the male head of the household, e.g., baker, archer, miller, etc., or, from a manor or village name. Therefore, on leaving a place — if the lord of the manor indeed permitted it — called Wingfield, young John would be called John de (from) Wingfield. There were two main places called Wingfield in England.

Perhaps nearly half the Wingfields are descended from the Germanic-cum-Scandinavian family (of DNA Haplogroup I1b2a)[1] that lived in Suffolk, England, from before the Norman Conquest in 1066. Close to another half are derived from the Shropshire and northern family — who likely took their name from South Wingfield in Derbyshire (those of DNA Atlantic Modal Haplotype R1b). Both families are visible in medieval records. The manors or estates of both Wingfield (Suffolk) and South Wingfield (Derbyshire) figure in the *Domesday Book* of 1086–87. Wingfield families from both these places were "armigerous" or had their own coat of arms. Many descendants of these families are today traceable to medieval times — through the Wingfield Family Society. Hundreds of Wingfields have trekked home to Britain and Ireland to see their family heritage sites, such as the fourteenth century Wingfield Castle, or Powerscourt House in County Wicklow in Ireland, or the Kimbolton Castle in Cambridgeshire, which the Suffolk Wingfields owned in the sixteenth and seventeenth centuries.

The Wingfield Family Society (WFS) (www.wingfield.org) was founded in Virginia, United States, in 1987, adopting the basic arms of the Tickencote (Rutland — now Leicestershire) Wingfield cadet line of the Letheringham (Suffolk) Wingfields as the Society's logo.[2]

Courtesy of Jocelyn Wingfield.

Logo of the Wingfield Family Society.

While there are many regional Wingfield reunions held periodically throughout North America and in England, this is the first society formed to encompass all Wingfield families into a single worldwide unit. In addition to those living in North America and the United Kingdom, there are also members in Australia, France, Ireland, Italy, and New Zealand. The Society is a non-profit, one-name organization of over four hundred families, whose goals are to record the different family lines via paper/microfiche records cross-referenced by DNA, to document roles the various Wingfields played in history, to preserve and acquire items of family significance, and to publish and disseminate such information to Society members and the public at large. Assisting members in their personal heritage search is a major activity. For those seriously interested in family heritage, the Society has proficient genealogists to advise and assist members in their searches.

Many Wingfields of Suffolk were knights, two of whom were knights of the garter. These included comptrollers of the household for Kings Edward IV, Henry VIII, and Edward VI; and captains of the guard for Kings Henry VIII and Edward VI. One was the chief of staff for the Black Prince at and around the time of Poitiers, 1356. Two Wingfield knights married sisters of Edward IV's Queen, Elizabeth Woodville, and many were lords of the manor in scores of places in England, as well as in Wales and Ireland. Captain Edward Maria Wingfield was founding father of and first president of the Jamestown Colony, 1607.[3]

Photo from Wally Goodman, Wingfield Family Society.

EDWARD MARIA WINGFIELD
OF STONELY PRIORY
(1550 - 1631)
FOUNDER OF AND FIRST PRESIDENT
AT JAMESTOWN, VIRGINIA
"where English civilization was first established on American soil"

Son of Thomas Maria Wingfield, MP for Huntingdonshire,
and grandson of Sir Richard Wingfield, K.G., of
Kimbolton Castle, Captain Edward Maria Wingfield, an
experienced soldier, was one of eight grantees for the
Virginia Charter of 1606. Sailing with 105 settlers he was
elected first President of the Council in 1607, building the
vast James Fort in a month. Still active in the affairs of
the Virginia Company when aged 70, he was buried at
Kimbolton Church on 13th April 1631.

"I rejoice that my travells and daungers have done
somewhat for the behoof of Jerusalem in Virginia...
I could not forsake ye enterprise of opening so
glorious a kingdom unto ye King."
E.M.W., 1608

Memorial to President Wingfield at Kimbolton (Cambridgeshire). This famous Wingfield was Captain Edward Maria Wingfield, founder and first president of the Council of Jamestown, Virginia, 1807, "where English civilization was first established on American soil."

The Wingfields of Shropshire include the inventor, marketer, and patentee of lawn tennis, Major Walter Wingfield, son of Major Clopton Wingfield and Jane Wingfield, nee Mitchell. Clopton had served in the 66th Regiment, the Berkshire Regiment, in Quebec City in 1827, and then in Kingston 1831–33, and again in Quebec City 1834–36, where Jane died in 1836.[4]

Courtesy of Gail Lee Wingfield Mansfield, artist.

Major Walter C. Wingfield
Inventor of lawn tennis

A sketch of Walter Clopton Wingfield who patented lawn tennis equipment in 1874 (U.K. Patent No. 685). A bust in his memory stands at the entrance to the Lawn Tennis Association at Barons Court, London. According to the *Encyclopedia Britannica*, "There has been much dispute over the invention of modern tennis, but the officially recognized centennial of the game in 1973 commemorated its introduction by Major Walter Clopton Wingfield in 1873. He published the first book of rules that year and took out a patent on his game in 1874, although historians have concluded that similar games were played earlier..."

Henry Colsell Wingfield of the Westminster Wingfields was the founder of the Wingfield Sculls, the famous rowing race for men living in England. Formerly a pupil at Westminster, a keen rowing school, he presented, in 1830, a trophy of a pair of miniature silver sculls (oars) to be raced for on his birthday, August 10, "forever." Henry Wingfield, the first of three Henry Wingfields, was an attorney, the grandson of a rich hatter. In 1842, his wife Jane divorced Henry for adultery, which was all reported in the *Times*. Henry emigrated, almost at once, to farm near Picton at South Marysburgh, Ontario, Canada, for twenty years, occasionally visiting England. In 1861, he embarked for Liverpool and on June 4, at noon, four miles off the north point of Newfoundland, just like the *Titanic* fifty-one years later, his ship, the SS *Canadian*, struck an iceberg in the fog, and the Wingfield Sculls Founder (and about thirty others of the crew of three hundred) went to the bottom of the Atlantic. In 2007, in his memory, the four-hundred-plus members of the Wingfield Family Society (WFS) presented the Wingfield Sculls Committee (uniquely comprised of past winners only) with a US$2,500 silver trophy matching the men's one, for the "Women's Wingfields." The Westminster Wingfields are connected to the Worcestershire Wingfields, but the researchers in the WFS have found no male descendant to take a DNA test to help prove whence Henry came. He is unlikely to be a Suffolk Wingfield, but may well be derived from the Shropshire/Derbyshire branch of the family.

Another family of Wingfields, not yet placed or traced further back than the early 1790s, includes David Wingfield, RN, after whom Wingfield Point and Wingfield Basin are named in Georgian Bay, Lake Huron, Canada. David's line is traceable back to his father in Windsor, Berkshire, but, although he is not thought to be a Suffolk Wingfield, the WFS cannot verify his connection without finding a male descendant. David Wingfield is buried at Horsley, near Stroud, in Gloucestershire, England.

Family Information

A database of over 150,000 names is maintained in the Society's computer in Lynn Haven, Florida. These records have been acquired through the dedicated cooperation of members so that considerable information is now available to all. Data goes back to 1087 — where some of it is admittedly a bit flimsy, but everything that is cross-referenced dates back to the 1330s.

The Wingfield Immigration Register is accessible on the WFS website under the subsection Immigration. Periodically updated, it lists Wingfield emigrants from the United Kingdom up till about 1914, to every continent of the world, most of them to North America from 1607 on. Contributions to the database are welcome and members share their research.

Coat of Arms

With the introduction of armour in the twelfth century, identification of military men became more difficult as much of the body and face was covered. Of necessity, an emblem or insignia was required for identification of knights in battle or on the jousting field. The markings on the soldier's shield became known as his coat of arms and the distinguishing "figure" atop his helmet was called his crest, which did not necessarily relate to any feature on his shield. From the fourteenth century onward, it became fashionable for social purposes to join one's personal arms with the arms of one's wife, provided that she was a heraldic heiress (i.e. heiress of an armigerous gentleman or knight). It was, however, the personal arms alone, those which appeared on a knight's defensive shield, which continued as the nominal arms of the family.

Heraldry is the science of Coats of Arms. The College of Arms in London was established in 1484 and is responsible for regulating and approving Coats of Arms in England and Wales. John Wingfield, of the Suffolk-Tickencote Line, was York Herald of the College of Arms from 1663–74.

From "The Three Dozen Anecdotes"

An intriguing review of historical anecdotes about members of the Wingfield families can be found on the WFS website under the sub-section Publications. This collection of stories, gathered and presented by Jocelyn Wingfield, covers a nine-hundred-year period and brings together an unusual collection of tales about Wingfields across the continents. One rather humorous episode is provided below:

> Richard Wingfield, the 6th Viscount Powerscourt, 31, having lost his (1st) wife, Lady Frances Roden, the year before, on Sep 3rd in 1821 invited the new King, the intelligent, witty, immoral George IV, in this, his coronation year, to visit Powerscourt Waterfall. The Dargle [River] was dammed, so that after lunch the dam could be blown up and the King would see the water in full spate. There was a very boozy lunch; the family saga has it, so the King (with Lord P. [Viscount Powerscourt, Richard Wingfield]) staggered to his coach to drive off

to his ship without visiting the Waterfall. The mine was then exploded, producing such a spate that the specially constructed royal viewing bridge was swept away. If the demonstration had taken place as planned, the Wing-fields would have assassinated the King!

When King Edward VII came to see the famous 300 foot waterfall, a drought had put it out of existence; but Wingfield readiness was equal to the occasion. Relays of workmen were set to carry buckets of water to pour down the dry Dargle drop, so that His Majesty was not disappointed!"[5]

APPENDIX C

Place Names

List of Lesser Place Names from Wingfield Journal

Bay of Quinte runs along the shorelines of Trenton, Belleville, and Deseronto, at the eastern end of Lake Ontario. This area is steeped in rich Loyalist history.

Bunkers Hill, also called Bunker Hill, or Breed's Hill, or Charleston Heights, is located in Suffolk County, Massachusetts.

Burlington Heights is discussed in the Notes section in some detail. Historians have not been consistent in specifying its location. We believe it is to be found at the top of the bluffs above the now Hamilton Harbour. A map is included in the text.

Cabot Head is the most northerly section of the Niagara Escarpment overlooking Georgian Bay at the northeastern tip of the Bruce Peninsula, Ontario, and provides shelter to Wingfield Point and Wingfield Basin below.

Cambridge, Massachusetts, according to the local Historical Commission, known as Newtowne until 1638, was laid out in an orderly grid of streets, bounded today by Eliot Square and Linden Street, Massachusetts Avenue, and the Charles River. Each family owned a house lot in the village, planting fields outside, and a share in the common land. Boston, accessible only by ferry in the early days, was about eight miles away.

Charleston, near Boston, established in 1628, was the site of the battle of Bunker Hill, fought on June 17, 1775. The Bunker Hill Monument in the town's midst continues to celebrate that most famous first conflict of the American Revolution. Wingfield commented about the location as he passed through during his time as a prisoner of war.

Cheshire, in western Massachusetts, about ten miles from Pittsfield, was settled in 1766, by Baptists from Rhode Island, apparently the first settlers in the area who were not Puritans.

Chippawa, a town within present-day Niagara Falls, Ontario, was the extent of navigation possible before goods had to be unloaded and carried between Lakes Erie and Ontario, prior to the construction of the Welland Canal.

Cognawaga, or Kahnawake, as shown on a present-day road map can be found in New York State, on the shoreline of the St. Lawrence River, immediately south of Montreal.

Concord, Massachusetts, first established in 1635, was the site of the first shots being fired in the American Revolutionary War in 1775 during the Battle of Lexington and Concord. Then, in the mid-nineteenth century, Concord was the centre of the country's literary renaissance and home to some of that nation's most influential writers, such as Ralph Waldo Emerson, Henry David Thoreau, Louisa May Alcott, and Nathaniel Hawthorne.

De Tour Passage is found near the mouth of the St. Marys River where it empties into Lake Huron. The spelling is shown several ways. It seems that the current interpretation of the meaning of De Tour is "detour," a temporary route around a passage. The original name came from *passage de tour*, meaning "passage of the turn." There is a sharp turn in this route.

Drummond Island, located at the eastern end of the North Channel, above Manitoulin Island, is the location of Drummond Island Historical Museum where one can review the colourful history of the area. The island was named after British Lieutenant-General Sir Gordon

Drummond. In August 1813, he was appointed commander of the troops in Upper Canada.

Ernestown, near Kingston, Ontario, was originally known as Second Town, having been surveyed after the Town of Kingston.

German Flats, also spelled German Flatts, was one of the original towns of Herkimer County, New York, lying along the Mohawk River and the Erie Canal. Its infamous history was marked by bloody carnage initiated both by Natives and by settlers in turn during the 1700s.

Greenbush, near Albany, New York, derives its name from the Dutch *groen bosch* that described the stand of pines that originally covered this location.

Hallowell, an area within Prince Edward County, near Kingston, Ontario, where an heroic Captain John Prinyer tricked a band of American soldiers into surrendering to save them from a certain death by nearby Native warriors hiding in the bush.

Hamilton, at the time of the War of 1812, as mentioned in the Wingfield journal, was a small community located near the current-day Town of Port Hope on Lake Ontario.

Holland Landing, first known as St. Albans, was the extreme northern terminus of the extension of the end of Yonge Street, York. It was envisioned as the most direct route to the Upper Great Lakes via roadway from Toronto.

Kempenfeldt, or *Kempenfelt*, originally the site of a naval supply depot, has evolved into the site of the present-day Barrie at the head of the some ten miles long bay of the same name. An interesting bit of trivia, as it relates to our story of Wingfield, is the location of two villages nearby: Stroud and Painswick.

Lennox (now spelled *Lenox*), in Massachusetts, was a prosperous farming and mill town in the early 1800s. There is no apparent information about the gaol located here that housed British prisoners of war during the 1812–14 encounters.

Little Belt is a strait between the Danish island of Funen and the Jutland Peninsula. It is the area purported by earlier historians where Wingfield first served as a second class volunteer beginning in 1806.

Navy Bay, in eastern Lake Ontario, near Kingston, was the site of the first Fort Henry built during the War of 1812 to protect the Royal Navy dockyards. It was the site of the shipyard for the construction of the HMS *St. Lawrence* and other British vessels used in the War of 1812.

Courtesy of the Don Bamford Collection.

The HMS *St. Lawrence*, a line drawing.

Navy Point is the site of a modern-day marina by the same name, near Sackets Harbor.

Penetanguisheen, or *Penetanguishene*, commonly known as Penetang, is a well-known tourist destination on southern Georgian Bay, richly steeped in history from its early days as a British naval installation.

Pitsfield, Massachusetts, correctly spelled Pittsfield, lies along the meandering banks of the Housatonic River in a largely rural part of the state.

Presque Isle is a spit of land in Erie, Pennsylvania, that creates a natural harbour, well-known as a place of refuge for mariners on Lake Erie since early times.

Put-In-Bay, Ohio, is in a group of islands known as the Bass Islands. Today one can find, on South Bass Island, where United States Naval Commander, Captain Oliver Hazard Perry, rendezvoused his fleet, a striking 352-foot marble monument to commemorate the Battle of Put-In-Bay and Captain Perry.

Sackets Harbor, New York, the early 1800s headquarters of the United States Navy and the site of major shipbuilding facilities, has a number of historic sites to commemorate its important role in the War of 1812. Spelled in various ways by Wingfield and also by various writers, Sackets Harbor was founded in 1801 by a Mr. Augustus Sackett, a land speculator from New York.

Salem, Massachusetts, was one was one of the most significant seaports in early America, famous for whaling.

Schenectady, New York, lies near the confluence of the Mohawk and Hudson rivers, not far from Albany.

Sodus, located in Wayne County, New York, takes its name from the Native word for silvery water, which described the nearby bay.

St. Joseph Island, located at the westerly end of the North Channel beyond Manitoulin Island, is well-known to Canadian historians, and to tourists, for its dozens of historic sites dating back into the early history of British and American efforts to dominate this area.

Upper Lachine, at the site of Montreal, became the environs for the Lachine Canal, proposed following the War of 1812 to support shipping and navigation in a period of a rapidly expanding economy.

Utica, the county seat of Oneida County, New York, established in 1773 on the site of old Fort Schuyler, was originally settled by a small number of Welsh families who introduced dairy farming and brought Welsh butter into prominence as a valued commodity in the New York markets.

Watertown, some ten miles distant from Sackets Harbor, has been the site of military activity at present-day Fort Drum since the early 1800s.

Whitehall, on the shores of Lake Champlain, known as the birthplace of the American navy, has a long history dating back to its founding by a Scotsman Philip Skene, in 1759. Today, one can find the preserved hulk of the U.S.S. *Ticonderoga*, a steamer converted to a war sloop for use as Commodore Thomas Macdonough's flagship at the decisive Battle of Plattsburgh in 1814.

Wingfield Basin, a small protected basin at the northeastern tip of the Bruce Peninsula on Lake Huron and Georgian Bay, was first sounded under the direction of Captain William Fitz William Owen, and named for our David Wingfield, who assisted in the endeavour.

Worcester, mentioned by Wingfield, was one of the early towns founded by the English in Massachusetts. It is noted for its development of affordable triple-deckers, a compact form of three-storey housing for working class people in the nineteenth century.

APPENDIX D

Glossary of Maritime Terms and Related Items

This selected glossary contains definitions and explanations of words and phrases used in Wingfield's journal that will be of use to students and to newcomers in the study of naval history in the era about which we have written:

Artificer: A skilled worker, in this case, employed in the art of shipbuilding.

Batteries: A grouping of guns or artillery positioned and used in one location.

Boats: The term, as used by Wingfield, denotes a smaller craft, often pulled by oars and carried upon a larger vessel and deployed for manoeuvres in shallow waters and tight quarters.

Breastworks: A low protective wall, perhaps to protect fortifications and often devised as part of a harbour works to divert waves or the course of a river or stream.

Canister shot: A metallic cylinder packed with shot and used as ammunition.

Careen: A term used to describe the action of hauling a vessel into shallow water or ashore, and pulling it over as far as possible onto its side, to allow bottom cleaning, re-caulking, or repairs.

Coppers: A word used to describe various kinds of cooking vessels, usually large pots, some of which were crafted of "copper."

Dragoons: Technically, a heavily armed cavalryman but loosely used to refer to armed guards taking persons by force or coercion.

Durham boat: Refers to a boat originally built by the Durham Boat Company of Pennsylvania, flat-bottomed, with a shallow keel, used to transport goods or troops; some were up to sixty feet long. They were propelled by oars or poles. Variations of this design were built across Upper Canada and used on Lakes Ontario and Huron. The remains of one were found on Russell Island, near Tobermory, by Orrie Vail in 1955. Vail, C.H. Snider, and others claimed it was the wreck of LaSalle's *Griffon*. It was later confirmed that it was the remains of a Durham boat, apparently built at Penetanguishene.

Express: Wingfield uses the term to refer to a letter or message, hopefully delivered in a fast and efficient manner.

Expresses: Wingfield uses the term to refer to a means of transportation on a specific mission headed to a specific location, presumably by a direct route.

Man-of-war: A war ship intended for combat. The Royal Navy used a "rating system" to classify its ships. Internet research on the topic of ships' rating systems is an instructive pursuit.

Military Commandant: In the British context, usually an officer in charge of a training unit; in the American context, an appointed official rather than a military rank. Wingfield makes numerous references to the position of commandant in both British and American contexts.

Minute guns: A military gun capable of being discharged at least once every minute; used to describe guns fired at a funeral. At Sackets Harbor, the minute guns were, and still are, used for sounding an alarm or calling for assistance.

Overhauling the rigging: Wingfield uses the phrase twice: once to address the inventory of rigging and fixtures in a captured vessel and again to describe his findings about the state or condition of the rigging on a number of British ships that required considerable overhaul before going into battle.

Post ship: A ship of the Sixth Rate, smaller than a frigate, carrying at least twenty guns, under the command of a post captain, rather than a lieutenant or a commander.

Purser: An officer aboard a ship who keeps accounts and tends to matters of the crew's welfare. The purser also keeps watch over the spirit locker! A world famous brand of rum, called Pusser's is derived from the word *purser*. Rum and the sea are inseparable. For more than three hundred years, from the earliest days of wooden ships and iron men, sailors of Great Britain's Royal Navy were issued a daily ration — or "tot"— of rum. Prior to 1740, the men's daily tot of rum was a pint a day, which they drank neat, that is without water! Before battle, they were issued a double "tot," and always after victory for a job well done.

Quarantine ship: An older vessel used as accommodation for passengers and seamen who have just arrived in port after visiting a country known to have a plague. They must stay aboard until possible contagion is eliminated.

Receiving ship: An elderly man-of-war, at anchor in port, ready to accept new recruits and other seamen awaiting assignment. The ship provided hammock, food, grog, etc.

Ship's furniture: Those items such as sails and running rigging, and even portions of the standing rigging that might be removed, in this case for winter storage.

Stocks: The framework that supports a ship under construction.

Strike: As used by Wingfield, to haul down the ship's flag (colours) as a sign of surrender. There are stories of some captains nailing the flag to the mast as a sign that his ship would never surrender.

Topgallant breeze: A light breeze; sufficient to fly a light-weight sail from the topmast or upper mast of a sailing vessel.

Top-hamper: Refers to sails, spars, and rigging far aloft, which encounter wind resistance that can be harmful to the operation of the ship, heel it over excessively or even prevent her going to windward as she should. Top hamper can also include ice.

Under weigh: Having hauled or "weighed" the anchor, and in motion.

Vessels: In the nautical sense, larger ships; as opposed to smaller "boats."

Weather gage: Having the favourable position for manoeuvrability with respect to the wind direction, particularly during a sea battle on sailing ships. Weather gage, more specifically, is being upwind of the enemy fleet.

The System of Royal Navy Ranks

It seems appropriate to clarify, in part, the system of ranks in the Royal Navy as referred to by Wingfield so many times. The system of naval rankings has evolved over time.

Wingfield makes reference to many of the ranks in place during his era. At the top of the hierarchy are found the flag officers. At this time, there were admirals, vice-admirals, and rear admirals. He mentions none but refers several times to the Admiralty and to Admiralty Lists.

Next in order of hierarchy are the commodores. He also refers to Commodore James Yeo as a commander-in-chief, not specifically a rank, but rather an appointment. He refers several times to the American Commodore Chauncey, and speaks many times of commandants but is not likely referring to flag officers. While it is apparent that the Royal Navy did not use the term *Commandant*, both the Provincial Marine and Americans did. The appointment as commodore could have been temporary, assigned to the senior captain in charge of a fleet, and removed after such an assignment was completed. The rank and its definition have changed over time.

With respect to commissioned officers, the next in line, he makes reference to captains, post-captains, commanders, first (senior) lieutenants, and lieutenants. Some larger ships had several ranks of lieutenants, each with specific duties. When a captain was selected to command a vessel of sixty-five or more guns, he was "posted" on the Admiralty List and became known as a post-captain. Some sources believe that it was only this rank or higher who could be advanced in rank automatically whenever anyone on the list above him died. This practice carried on even while he was in retirement. We have spoken elsewhere about one opinion that suggested that our Lieutenant Wingfield could have been promoted to commander in this manner.

Wingfield served as master's mate or sub-lieutenant on several vessels. He never referred to the next broad category of warrant officers, but referenced masters, surgeons, pursers, and quarter masters. The master was considered to be captain if there was no officer who out-ranked him on board. On a man-of-war, he was responsible for navigation and pilotage.

Wingfield arrived in Canada as a petty officer with the rank of midshipman and referred to his fellow "Mids" on numerous occasions. Other petty officers included cooks, clerks, and boatswain. The boatswain, in the days of sail, was the one who administered punishment on board. When he refers to "coxswain" on a number of occasions, he is referring to the person assigned to the tiller. He refers many times to a commissariat officer (or department), typically the person or section in charge of food and other supplies for the army. Wingfield refers to "other inferior officers" in his journal, a term that would apply to ranks below that of lieutenant. The term "superior officer" is still used to describe ranks above lieutenant.

According to some records, Wingfield joined the Royal Navy as a second-class volunteer, presumably without the patronage of a ranked overseer who might have shepherded his more rapid promotion. We believe that his first captain, on recognizing his abilities, recorded him as first-class volunteer, as shown in his service record, as cited elsewhere.

There are many Internet sources from which to study the evolution of Royal Navy ranks over the centuries since Wingfield's time.

A List of Ships' Sails and Rigging:

Suffice it to say that there are numerous ships' sails and as many components of the standing rigging to carry them. The study of sails and
rigging is the substance of a book in itself. Students of the topic will want
to search out books and electronic resources that illustrate the many
variations of ships' rigging through the ages. Brief reference to the topic
can be found in *Freshwater Heritage* by Don Bamford. For our current
purposes, the following list of masts and yards, each carrying a sail of the
same or similar name, is provided, if only to set down categories and the
numerous sub-sets into which they are divided:[1]

Bowsprit	Spritsail topsail yard
Sprit Topmast	Fore yard
Fore (lower) mast	Fore topsail yard
Fore topmast	Fore topgallant yard
Fore topgallant mast	Main yard
Main (lower) mast	Main topsail yard
Main topmast	Main topgallant yard
Main topgallant mast	Mizzen yard
Mizzen (lower) mast	Mizzen topsail yard
Mizzen topmast	Crossjack yard
Spritsail yard	

The sails carried on a ship with such standing rigging are varied. The
vessel is rigged according to wind conditions; the actual sail plan being
different for light, heavy, and storm conditions.

Fore and aft sails are those that run fore and aft, and are generally
easier to control. A square sail is set crossways to the mast. A gaff-rigged
sail is like a cut-off triangle, supported by an upper "gaff" or boom. A
staysail is a sail, usually with two sides attached to the rigging for easier
control. Triangular sails are usually called Bermuda or Marconi rigged.
There are numerous variations of most sails.

Today's sailing vessels used by recreational sailors carry jibs, lappers,
genoas, gennakers, spinnakers, storm jibs, and staysails, to name a few.

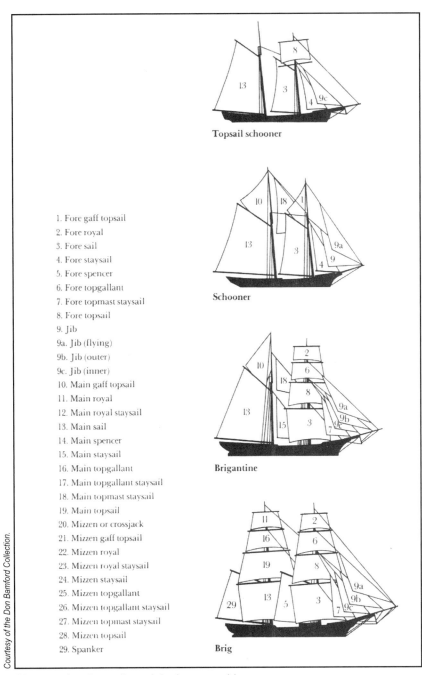

1. Fore gaff topsail
2. Fore royal
3. Fore sail
4. Fore staysail
5. Fore spencer
6. Fore topgallant
7. Fore topmast staysail
8. Fore topsail
9. Jib
9a. Jib (flying)
9b. Jib (outer)
9c. Jib (inner)
10. Main gaff topsail
11. Main royal
12. Main royal staysail
13. Main sail
14. Main spencer
15. Main staysail
16. Main topgallant
17. Main topgallant staysail
18. Main topmast staysail
19. Main topsail
20. Mizzen or crossjack
21. Mizzen gaff topsail
22. Mizzen royal
23. Mizzen royal staysail
24. Mizzen staysail
25. Mizzen topgallant
26. Mizzen topgallant staysail
27. Mizzen topmast staysail
28. Mizzen topsail
29. Spanker

Topsail schooner

Schooner

Brigantine

Brig

Diagram showing sails and rigging on a ship.

Mains and headsails can often be reefed by furling systems. The sailor in Wingfield's time, however, was a hard-working crewmember who had to be muscular, agile, and often brave. To climb to the "tops" above the fighting top platform, and to balance like a tight-rope walker on the ropes slung below the yards was a feat that not all could easily master. Nevertheless, in all kinds of weather, but especially in raging storms, energetic seamen could be called upon to fulfill their duties reliably at the call of the ship's master.

The study of sailing ships and their rigging is an intriguing and instructive adventure for those who wish to gain a better understanding of the sea and the men who plied her.

List of More Significant Ships in Wingfield's Journal

Beckwith HMS: Wingfield was to be in command of this ship but politicians ended the war and she was only used a few weeks at the most.

Confiance, ex *Julia*, USS: Wingfield was given command for a period in 1813. The British used it as a transport. The *Confiance* attended at the Burlington Races but saw no action. On October 2, 1813, she was transporting soldiers to Kingston when captured by the *Sylph*, USN, near the False Ducks. The USN *Pike*, the American flagship, attended at the capture. This was not the same *Confiance* we encounter during Wingfield's travels on Lake Huron and Georgian Bay.

Governor Tomkins USN: Fought in the battle known as the Burlington Races. The USN *Pike* was Commander Chauncey's flagship in this battle.

Lady Washington: Captured by the British and renamed the *Vincent*. Used as a transport by Canada. David Wingfield put in charge. He used it for a month-long charting of Little Lake in June 1813.

Nancy: Served as armed transport in the Upper Lakes during the war. Supply ship for forts Mackinaw and St. Joseph. Burned and sunk in the Nottawasaga River.

Niagara HMS: Mentioned only because Wingfield went aboard at York to get some seamen to take up to Wasaga.

Prince Regent, HMS: Was Yeo's flagship in 1815. Wingfield was supernumerary for a short time while still technically a United States prisoner of war. In the book of Officers Services[2] he is shown as master's mate from August 12 to September 1814. He is also recorded on this vessel, with the rank of lieutenant, again from June 1816 to September 30, 1816.

Royal George HMS: Captain Mulcaster was commander during the Burlington Races. His brave actions won him high praises from both sides.

St. Lawrence, HMS: Just launched during September of 1814. Her maiden voyage began October 14, 1814 and she immediately became Yeo's flagship. Wingfield is listed[3] as master's mate, from September 1814 to March 21, 1815.

Surprise and *Confiance*, ex *Scorpion* and *Tigress:* Captured from the Americans near DeTour Passage. Wingfield was appointed lieutenant and placed in command of *Surprise*; Lieutenant Worsley was put in command of the *Confiance*.

Wolfe, HMS: Wingfield was transferred to this ship for a short period. This was Yeo's flagship. The *Wolfe* fought in the battle off the mouth of the Genesee River, September 10, 1813.

APPENDIX E

A Timeline: A Wingfield Chronology

Where dates have not been specifically provided in the Wingfield diary, or may have been given in error, we have tried to verify from other sources to make the chronology as accurate as possible.

1792/93: Birth of David Wingfield in Windsor, Berkshire. (No birth certificate has been found at this time.)

March 23, 1806: Wingfield joined the Royal Navy as a Second Class Volunteer.

July 12, 1812: America declared war.

July 17, 1812: British, under Captain Charles Roberts, captured Fort Mackinac.

August 16, 1812: British, under Sir Isaac Brock, captured Detroit.

March 31, 1813: David Wingfield sailed on the *Woolwich* out of Plymouth.

April 27, 1813: Americans, under Major General Henry Dearborn, attacked York.

May 5, 1813: Wingfield arrived at Quebec.

May 16, 1813: Yeo arrived at Kingston, followed by his troops a few days later.

May 28–29, 1813: British attacked Sackets Harbor.

June 16, 1813: Wingfield promoted to master's mate and put in command of the *Vincent*, recently captured from the Americans.

June 19, 1813: Attack on Sodus Bay.

July/August 1813: Wingfield entered Little Lake for the first time, to conduct a survey. Spent "about a month" there. He does not provide specific dates.

August 13, 1813: The schooner, *Nancy*, burned and sank at Wasaga.

August 27, 1813: Wingfield joined the *Wolfe*, Yeo's flagship.

September 10, 1813: Battle of Genesee River.

September 10, 1813: Battle of Lake Erie. Captain Oliver Hazard Perry, USN, defeated the British fleet under the command of Captain Robert Heriot Barclay, RN.

September 16, 1813: Wingfield appointed to *Confiance*; took stores to Burlington Heights. This *Confiance* was a transport on Lake Ontario.

September 23, 1813: The *Scorpion* and the *Tigress*, American armed transports are captured by the British near De Tour Passage where the St. Marys River enters Lake Huron. They were renamed the *Surprise* and the *Confiance*.

September 27, 1813: Wingfield took despatch to Commodore Yeo.

September 28, 1813: Beginning of event known as the "Burlington Races." Wingfield did not participate but stood by as master of the transport *Confiance*.

October 5, 1813: Americans captured the *Confiance*; Wingfield taken prisoner by the Americans.

October 14, 1813: Wingfield travelled on the Mohawk River in an open barge.

October 15, 1813: Wingfield and companions arrived at German Flats.

October 17, 1813: Arrived at Albany.

November 10, 1813: Wingfield and companions attended a dance at Concord, Massachusetts.

December 25, 1813: Celebrated Christmas with dinner in prison at Concord.

Mid-March 1814: In jail in Lennox.

May 1, 1814: Wingfield released from jail, but incarcerated at Philadelphia.

Later May 1814: Wingfield back to Cheshire.

June 1, 1814: Wingfield advised he is to be returned to Canada.

June 13, 1814: Wingfield started for Canada on foot.

June 20, 1814: Discharged to British ship at Lake Champlain.

June 23, 1814: Wingfield arrived at Montreal.

July 15, 1814: Arrived at Kingston.

August 12, 1814: Wingfield returned to active duty.

August 1814 (no date supplied): Wingfield and companions captured two United States vessels off Grenadier Island.

Late August 1814: Captured Lieutenant Francis Gregory, USN and "Deal built gig" in Bay of Quinte.

October 14, 1814: HMS *St. Lawrence* made maiden voyage to Niagara River.

October 19, 1814: British ship, HMS *St. Lawrence* struck by lightning. Wingfield, who was on board, claimed the date was October 25.

December 24, 1814: Treaty of Ghent signed after four months of negotiations in Belgium.

February 16, 1815: United States Senate ratified Treaty of Ghent unanimously.

February 20, 1815: David is appointed acting lieutenant.

Late February 1815: News that peace had been declared reached the Great Lakes.

February 26, 1815: Wingfield left Kingston for Wasaga to take command of *Surprise*.

April 5, 1815: Arrived at Wasaga.

May 16, 1815: The vessel *Huron* arrived at Mackinac with officials to explore and select alternate base to Fort Mackinac, possibly Drummond Island.

May 22, 1815: Explored Drummond Island.

May 14, 1815: Careened and re-caulked *Surprise* at Drummond Island.

November 3, 1815: Wingfield left Drummond Island for last time.

November 5, 1815: Returned to Wasaga.

Mid-December 1815: Wingfield and companions departed on foot for Newmarket.

December 25, 1815: Dates for "frolic in the snow" are not given, but it seems they were back at Wasaga for Christmas dinner with the captain.

Early January 1816: Left Wasaga to explore the Nottawasaga River upstream.

May 5, 1816: Fitted out the *Surprise* at Wasaga, for summer duties.

Late May 1816: Wingfield started back for Kingston.

June 15, 1816: Arrived at Kingston.

July 1816: Wingfield and companions sailed over to visit Sackets Harbor as tourists.

August 25, 1816: Sailed to Niagara River on *Beckwith*. Although he does not say, presumably, he was master of the ship.

September 30, 1816: Wingfield left Kingston to return to England, where, upon his arrival his commission as lieutenant was confirmed and backdated to March 20, 1815.

APPENDIX F

The Friends of Cabot Head

Submitted by Ina Toxopeus, Chair, Friends of Cabot Head, 2008

The Friends of Cabot Head, a not-for-profit organization, was formed in 1990 and incorporated in 1994, by a group of concerned area citizens to take over the restoration, maintenance, and management of historic 1896 Cabot Head Light Station. Lease agreements were arranged with the Canadian Coast Guard and then-Lindsay Township, now the Municipality of Northern Bruce Peninsula.

Beginning in 1991, major renovation work was started on the Lighthouse using limited grant money and volunteer labour and expertise. With the help of several local businesses, service clubs, the Bruce County Museum, the Township of Lindsay and local families contributing time, money, and historical articles, a museum was constructed in the lighthouse building. Most of the major work was completed in 1996. As well, the lighthouse tower was rebuilt and now functions as an observation tower.

Now the adjacent light keeper's cottage is occupied by a full time onsite manager who runs the day to day activities of the lighthouse, supervises the "Light Keeper's Locker," a gift shop located in the same building, and the "Shipwreck" Art Gallery located in the fog-horn building.

The Friends of Cabot Head also run an Assistant Lighthouse Keeper Program from mid-May to the Canadian Thanksgiving Day weekend. With this program, couples (two persons) pay to stay in the lighthouse itself for a week, giving them time to explore the area, and donate some time to help maintain or meet and greet the visitors. The assistant keepers have the use of a bedroom with two single beds, and a sitting room on the second floor of the lighthouse as well as their own private bathroom and summer kitchen on the main floor.

The Wingfield Basin is a haven for boaters, giving them a safe anchorage for the night or shelter from adverse weather conditions. In 2007, the Friends put in a floating dock in the Basin to make it easier for the boaters to come ashore. For those visiting the Wingfield Basin, the manager keeps a supply of ice in the deep freezer.

As a totally volunteer organization, all the funds for restoration, maintenance, and management comes from visitor donations, membership dues, the Assistant Lighthouse Keepers Program, sales from the gift shop and art studio, and any other donations. The Lightstation is open seven days a week from Victoria Day weekend to Thanksgiving. Admission is by donation only.

Cabot Head Light Station is honoured to be one of only a few Canadian Great Lakes lighthouses to be rated a full "4 stars" on the basis of its accessibility and its facilities for casual visitors, especially families.

When visiting the light station, one can swim in both Georgian Bay and/or the Wingfield Basin, have a picnic on the grounds, go on nature hikes, put in one's canoe or kayak, view spectacular sunsets, or just come and visit and enjoy the peace and quiet.

A History of the Light at Cabot Head[1]

Early Cabot Head Light Station. This documentary photograph of unknown origin shows the Cabot Head Light at the entrance to Wingfield Basin as it appeared about 1896. It is under ongoing restoration by the Friends of Cabot Head and now houses a museum. Under a special program, visitors can sometimes become residential guests to act as voluntary lightkeepers.

Courtesy Friends of Cabot Head.

Light Station

Although the hazardous nature of the east shore of the Bruce Peninsula was well-known (and emphasized in the public mind at least by the occasional shipwreck), it was not alarming enough to prompt government action. Except for a small light at Lion's Head village, no beacon marked the coast all the way from Cove Island, in the entrance to Georgian Bay, to Griffith Island, lying off the mouth of Colpoys Bay, a distance of sixty miles. By the 1890s, however, the volume of steamer traffic passing Cabot Head to and from the ports of Owen Sound, Collingwood, and Midland had increased to such an extent that the necessity for a major improvement was conceded. In July 1895, the Department of Marine and Fisheries called for tenders for the construction of a light and fog-alarm station at Cabot Head. The main building consisted of a wooden dwelling house and light tower combined, painted white. The fog-alarm plant was constructed on the shore below and east of the light. The lantern atop the tower contained several parabolic metallic reflectors utilizing light produced by kerosene lamps. Manufactured by the Chanteloup Company, of Montreal, this "catoptric" apparatus was fixed to a rotating frame, which, driven by a clockwork mechanism, cast a beam of white light, with three flashes twenty seconds apart, then an eclipse of forty seconds. The fog-alarm consisted of a steam-powered horn, the boilers, and machinery, which were manufactured by Canier, Laine & Company, of Levis, Quebec. The lighthouse was in operation by 1896.

General Location

Cabot Head is situated on the Bruce Peninsula, in the northeastern extremity of the former Lindsay Township (now part of the Municipality of Northern Bruce Peninsula), some five miles north of Dyer Bay, a cottage hamlet overlooking Georgian Bay. The name is used to collectively describe the promontories of Boulder Bluff, Middle Bluff, and West Bluff, and below them the foreshore flats and cobbled ridges surrounding Wingfield Basin.

Courtesy of the Canadian Coast Guard.

Old Cabot Head Light and Outbuildings. This image shows the Cabot Head Light Station and outbuildings at a busy time in the early 1950s. The adjacent timbering industry had died by that time and the Georgian Bay fisheries had just begun their decline. Photo from the collection by Ron Walker, Department of Fisheries and Oceans, Canadian Coast Guard, Parry Sound.

The Niagara Escarpment, here so evident, forms the spine of the Bruce Peninsula, trending north and northwest. At Cabot Head it turns abruptly west in which course the last veneer of forested talus gives way to a dramatic precipice, unbroken but for the ancient erosions of Georgian Bay. It was an inhospitable place, of interest only because Wingfield Basin held the possibility of being useful as a harbour of refuge. But even at mid-century W.H. Smith, in his *Canada, Past, Present & Future* (vol. II, 1851) commented that the value of the Basin was "much diminished by the existence of a shallow bar across its entrance, effectually preventing the admission of large vessels, and rendering it at times inaccessible to even boats and canoes, especially when the wind is from the northward and westward."[2] Cabot Head and the land around Wingfield Basin remained largely unknown and undisturbed, save for those events which occurred upon the waters of Georgian Bay or along the narrow beaches below the Escarpment.

APPENDIX G

Cover Art and Artist Peter Rindlisbacher

Peter Rindlisbacher was born in Windsor, Ontario. Son of a boat builder and a commercial artist, he developed an intense early passion for everything nautical, becoming a racing sailor, model builder, and historical naval re-enactor. In the midst of obtaining a Ph.D. in psychology in the 1980s, his marine art career developed into its present full-time status.

His paintings are primarily in oils and generally feature Great Lakes and War of 1812 subjects. Museums and historic sites in the United States and Canada have purchased many of his paintings, while print editions of his work are sold as fundraisers for historic groups. He enters few shows, preferring private commissions instead, largely to the American market. His images have appeared on book and magazine covers, and in video and public television productions for stations such as The History Channel and National Geographic Channel.

Mr. Rindlisbacher currently lives and works in Amherstburg, Ontario, near Lake Erie, with his wife and two children.

NOTES

INTRODUCTION

1. There are several birth dates offered for Wingfield. (See Biography for details.) The inconsistencies can most likely be attributed to the fact that census takers of the day were careless. They also collected age rather than the date of birth. If we knew the exact day and month of his birth, we could determine whether 1792 or 1793 is the correct year. His birth record in Windsor has not yet been found, but we do know that he was buried in the graveyard at Horsley Parish Church near Stroud — where unfortunately there is no "Grave Location Plan." The inscriptions from around 1864 have become illegible, meaning that we can no longer locate his grave through any on-site inspection.

2. Verified in dialogue with Library and Archives Canada officials, summer 2008.

3. See *Dalhousie Review* vol. 52, no. 3 (Autumn 1972): 407–13.

4. As communicated in several email messages between Jocelyn Wingfield and Paul Carroll during the spring and summer of 2008.

5. *Ibid.*

6. *Ibid.*

7. *Ibid.*

8. *Ibid.*

9. *Ibid.*

10. A phrase commonly used for retirement after naval service. Half pay was a retainer for the services of unemployed officers. Since there were no general schemes of retirement before the mid-1800s, half pay frequently operated as a type of superannuation and no test of actual fitness was applied. Thereafter, half pay declined in importance, becoming simply a means of filling short gaps in the career of serving officers. It was abolished in 1938.

Half-pay records are mainly lists of names and the sums payable to them, but they sometimes include addresses and other information. In conjunction with full pay registers, they can be used as they were in compiling certificates of service, to present an officer's full career. http://www.nationalarchives.gov.uk : Royal Navy: Pay and Pension Records: Commissioned Officers, accessed during the summer 2008.

11. William R. O'Byrne, *A Naval Biographical Dictionary* (London: John Murray, 1849): 1310.

12. The official archives record for Wingfield's service record found at the General Records office, Kew, U.K., ADM 9/60/4363.

13. Port Cities London web page: http://www.portcities.org.uk/london/server/ show/ConNarrative.148/chapterId/3045/The-Royal-Hospital-for-Seamen-Greenwich-A-Refuge-for-All.html, accessed several times during the summer and fall of 2008.

14. The website address in 2008 was www.nmm.ac.uk — the easiest way to review the whole story is to Google the name on the Internet.

15. Prinia Riordan, in a note on: http://archiver.rootsweb.ancestry.com/th/ read/Bristol_and_Somerset/1998–10/0907395633, accessed on May 23, 2008.

16. Library and Archives Canada. *Union Lists of Manuscripts in Canadian Repositories*. 1975: 1330.

17. It is worth noting that there was, in fact, no group or organization of the name "Lake Service" or "Lakes Service" in Canada. It was a term used only in Britain, as we see it used by Wingfield in his own notes. At the time of Wingfield's arrival it was called the "Provincial Marine." Within a few days of Yeo's arrival, the Provincial Marine had been changed into the Royal Navy.

18. Napoleon issued a decree in 1806 that disrupted trade between "Neutrals" and Britain, particularly the British Army in Europe, which constantly needed provisions and military supplies. Britain retaliated with Orders-in-Council that forbade trade between Neutrals and all other European countries. Britain could enforce its blockade with its strong naval forces and the

results fell heaviest on those countries that traded with the United States. The United States now introduced embargoes that forbade trade with both European belligerents. This, too, hurt American traders more than either of the other two actions did. Especially hurt was New England, and many residents took up the profession of smuggling, which was profitable and an easy solution to overcome the trade blockades.

19. A white flag inscribed "Free Trade and Sailors Rights" in blue flew aboard the USS *Chesapeake* when it fought and was captured by the HMS *Shannon* on June 1, 1813, and aboard the USS *Essex* on March 28, 1814, when it was captured by the HMS *Phoebe* and the HMS *Cherub* off the coast of Chile.

20. Phraseology often used to described a temporary resident, derived originally from the Book of Genesis, 35–4: "I am a stranger and a sojourner with you: give me a possession of a burying place with you, that I may bury my dead out of my sight."

21. The concept of Manifest Destiny, as used in the Revolutionary War in 1776, along with the declaration of the Monroe Doctrine in 1823, provided precedent and support for United States expansion on the American continent. In the late 1800s, the American economic and military power enabled it to enforce the Monroe Doctrine. The doctrine's greatest extension came with Theodore Roosevelt's Corollary, which inverted the original meaning of the doctrine and came to justify unilateral United States intervention in Latin America. Even today, the original concepts seem to play an important role in the American involvement and intervention in other countries around the world.

22. *The Annals of Congress*: 11th Congress, vol. 1: 519. Henry Clay later became the speaker of the house, and in 1814, an American peace commissioner for the Treaty of Ghent negotiations.

23. Some writers call his story "The Wingfield Diary." Library and Archives Canada refers to the papers as "Com. David Wingfield Papers." Wingfield calls it his "journal." The material was written around 1828, perhaps from notes he made in the field, but we do not know for certain. It seems "Memoirs" may best describe the collection. See Library and Archives Canada, MG24 F18.

24. For more information on the art of building warships in the wilderness see

Don Bamford, *Freshwater Heritage: A History of Sail on the Great Lakes, 1670–1918* (Toronto: Natural Heritage Books, 2007) Chapter 15: 131–60.

25. The American intent to attack Montreal via Plattsburgh led to major land and marine battles. Prevost oversaw a British attack at Plattsburg on Lake Champlain in September 1814, and ordered an untimely withdrawal that led to defeat. He was roundly criticized for this action. Recent writers, specifically Patrick A. Wilder and Howard G. Coombs, confirm the opinion that the British were on the verge of successfully completing the attack and taking the forts, shipyard, and town, before the signal to retreat was given. Not only did Yeo "have words" with Prevost, but Major William Drummond objected vigorously to the retreat. As for Prevost, it is generally agreed that he was a good administrator and governor general, but he lacked military experience.

26. For more information on the Canada Company, see Robert C. Lee, *The Canada Company and the Huron Tract. 1826–1853: Personalities, Profits and Politics.* Toronto: Natural Heritage Books, 2004.

27. A provincial heritage plaque, located near the present-day site of Dundurn Castle, Hamilton, reads as follows:

> The Burlington Races 1813 — On the morning of September 28, 1813, a powerfully-armed United States fleet comprising ten ships under the command of Commodore Isaac Chauncey appeared off York (Toronto). The smaller British fleet of six vessels, commanded by Commodore Sir James L. Yeo, was in the harbour, but on the approach of the enemy set sail to attack. After a sharp engagement, the British squadron was forced to withdraw toward Burlington Bay where it could take refuge under the batteries on the adjacent Heights. A close chase ensued, but by skilful seamanship, Yeo was able to bring his ships through the shallow channel in the sand-bar to the safety of the bay. *Erected by the Archaeological and Historic Sites Board, Ministry of Colleges and Universities.*

It is noteworthy that Wingfield's own account of his survey experience for Little Lake would prove that it was impossible to bring large ships into "the safety of the bay" as noted on the plaque.

28. For more information on the *Nancy*, see Barry Gough. *Through Water, Fire, & Ice: Schooner* Nancy *of the War of 1812*. Toronto: Dundurn, 2006.

29. Oliver Hazard Perry has been called captain, commodore, and master commandant by various authors. The Trip Atlas summary on the website http://tripatlas.com/Battle_of_Fort_George, accessed on February 3, 2009, calls him a lieutenant in 1813.

30. A numeral, following a ship's name, designates the number of guns carried. Hence, the *Ruby* carried 64 guns. This format is long-standing marine usage.

31. Midshipman is generally defined as a youth or young adult, usually well-educated in mathematics, leadership, and propriety. He was a young gentleman who could possibly be trained for advancement. Wingfield probably entered the navy as a second-class volunteer and served four years before he made the rank of midshipman. His service record indicates that his captain probably made him first-class volunteer almost immediately.

PART I: THE JOURNAL OF DAVID WINGFIELD

CHAPTER ONE:
Joining the Lake Service — *Arrival and Adventures on Lake Ontario*

1. Wingfield did not know how fortunate he was in being able to sail right up to Quebec City. Others had not gotten off so easily. The 104th Regiment came over from England and was based in New Brunswick and Prince Edward Island before war was declared. The Regiment was ordered to Upper Canada in the winter of 1812, when the St. Lawrence River was not navigable. The men were taken as far as Fredericton, New Brunswick, by ship, then had to walk from there all the way to Kingston, in the dead of winter. Snowshoes and toboggans were provided, but in many cases there was no shelter except what the soldiers could build themselves. In spite of the great difficulties, they arrived with only one casualty though nineteen died soon afterwards, probably as a result of the hardships and cold that all had experienced. The *Quebec Gazette* of March 19 reported as follows:

"The liberality of the people of New Brunswick, in the assistance they have afforded to the 2nd Battalion of the King's Regiment, and to the detachment of seamen, recently arrived at Quebec overland from that Province, deserve public thanks. The inhabitants of the City of St. John [*sic*], alone gave three hundred pounds for the hire of sleighs to carry the Seamen and Soldiers from that place to Frederickton; and the House of Assembly of the Province voted an equal sum (300) to convey them on their route from Frederickton as far as it was possible for sleighs to proceed."

Many Canadian writers of the War of 1812 make some mention, or even provide great detail about this "Great March." The best may be found in an excellent book by Donald E. Graves, titled *Merry Hearts Make Light Days*, published in 1994 by McClelland & Stewart. It is based completely on the diaries of John Le Couteur of the 104th Regiment who spent the entire war years in Canada and personally took part in the Great March. He was born the same year as Wingfield, but took the army route rather than the naval one and was very successful in his chosen career. He participated in the Battle of Sackets Harbor, along with Wingfield, though there is no indication they ever met. He also took part in the wars on the Niagara Peninsula; in fact, he served in four out of six major actions in 1814. Le Couteur returned to England in 1816. He resigned his commission in the 104th but continued to be active in the militia of his native Jersey, as well as to participate in civic and political responsibilities. At the age of seventy-five, he died in Jersey in 1875 with the rank of colonel, and with a knighthood conferred upon him.

2. Wingfield is referring here to the then-current policy of advancement among the officers, when an officer was killed or incapacitated. In this case the sick officer returned to England, the next in seniority, at the level below him, was advanced to his level. The excerpt from Donald Graves *Merry Hearts Make Light Days* explains it well:

> The promotion system of the British Army at this time was complicated and convoluted. There were three ways for a regimental officer to advance in rank: by seniority, by patronage or by purchase. Promotion by seniority depended on the amount of time an officer had been in the regiment at his current rank. By tradition, if not regulation, all vacancies caused by combat deaths were filled by seniority; if a captain was killed then the most senior lieutenant

in the regiment would be promoted, his position in
turn being filled by the most senior ensign.

At the time of the Napoleonic wars, there was a frequent toast in the
wardroom on board, "To bloody battles and quick advancement."

Patronage gave the right to the commander-in-chief to fill high-rank
vacancies when he felt special reward was merited. Although Graves wrote
about the army, a somewhat similar practice was employed in the British navy.

An example of such promotion was Sir James Lucas Yeo. He was born
in 1782, into a family with superb naval connections, resulting in patronage
promotions for him during much of his career. He joined as a gentleman
cadet at the age of ten. At fourteen he had advanced to acting lieutenant.
And so on. He made post captain at twenty-five and, as a result of a successful joint British-Portuguese attack at Cayenne, he was knighted, first by
Portugal, then later by Britain. His performance confirms that he deserved
all these promotions and honours and, at age thirty, he was made commodore of the British forces on the Lakes of Canada. Following his service in
Canada he continued in the navy and died in 1818 as commodore of Britain's fleet off the coast of Africa where he contracted a tropical fever.

3.   The citizens of Kingston had reason to fear an assault. The American plan,
approved in Washington in early 1813, put Kingston at the head of the list
of Canadian bases to be captured. Chauncey and Dearborn had other plans,
however, though they initially had agreed to the plan to attack Kingston
first. York seemed a safer place to start. At least it was lightly defended
and the large ship, the *Sir Isaac Brock*, under construction there, could be
destroyed.

While Kingstonians were shaking in their shoes, so were the residents
of Sackets Harbor when they learned of the huge build-up of forces at
Kingston, including the 104th Regiment and Yeo's group of five hundred
men. When Yeo's group arrived, the Kingston *Gazette* of May 18, 1813,
declared: "We are happy to announce the arrival at this place of several distinguished naval officers, together with 400 or 500 seamen, as fine looking
fellows as were ever beheld."

Yeo immediately took command of all armed ships of the Provincial
Marine. By June 24, they had been reorganized into the Royal Navy under
trained British officers.

4.   The governor general here was Sir George Prevost.

5. Wingfield was a participant for much of the time while the British were attacking Sackets Harbor on May 28 and 29, 1813. Perhaps he was involved in the assaults all of the time.

He did not have access to statistics nor did he participate in the Commanders' War Councils before, during, or after the battles. In spite of this, his memory of events is very much in agreement with the expert historians. He was unable to confirm that Sir George Prevost had initiated the recall of the British forces on the 29th. Recent writers, specifically Patrick Wilder and Howard Coombs, confirm the opinion that the British were on the verge of successfully completing the attack and taking the forts, shipyard, and town, before the signal to retreat was given.

Not only did Yeo "have words" with Prevost, but Major William Drummond objected vigorously to the retreat. He was told, "Obey orders and learn the first duty of a soldier." See Patrick A. Wilder. *The Battle of Sackett's Harbor 1813*. (Baltimore, MD: The Nautical and Aviation Publishing Company of America, Inc., 1994): 109.

As for Prevost, it is generally agreed that he was a good administrator and governor general, but he lacked military experience. Perhaps he should not have had authority over the military to veto their decisions nor to interfere with their operations. Hindsight has a high accuracy rate.

Dr. William "Tiger" Dunlop served throughout the war, both as medical doctor and as soldier. He had a very distinct opinion of Prevost, which he stated in his book, *Recollections of the War of 1812*, as published in 1908 by the Historical Publishing Co. of Toronto: "A more incompetent Viceroy could hardly have been selected for such trying times. Timid at all times, despairing of his resources, he was afraid to venture anything."

Although Wingfield does not mention this, many of the soldiers and seamen had to spend two nights and more, sometimes in heavy rain, in their bateaux, while being towed from Kingston and while waiting for Prevost to allow the attack. These bateaux were open boats with no protection whatsoever and had no berths. Such treatment was very hard on morale.

The British forces were 1,570 all ranks, including seven hundred seamen, according to Coombs, see *The Search for Certainty: Sackets Harbour — May 28/29, 1813*. (Kingston: Queen's University, 2003): 8. The Americans had approximately 1,450 men in action, according to Wilder, as cited on pages 79–81. The British casualties included forty-eight killed, 195 wounded, and sixteen missing in the army. Wilder notes (119–23) that 25 percent of those engaged were lost. The American losses included twenty-five killed and 114 wounded. One hundred and fifteen Americans were taken prisoner.

This information is documented in four reports by actual participants in the battles: Master James Richardson, as presented by Robert Malcomson in *Sailors of 1812, Memoirs and Letters of Naval Officers on Lake Ontario*: Lieutenant Wingfield; Le Couteur from the 104th; and Sergeant James Commins of the 8th Foot. The latter's report is cited in "The War on the Canadian Frontier, 1812–14: Letters Written by Sergeant James Commins, 8th Foot," edited by Norman C. Lord, in the *Journal of the Society for Army Historical Research*, vol. 18 (1939).

Commins, as cited in Coombs on page 24, summed up the sentiments and conclusions very well:

> The loss of Sacketts Harbor has been severely felt since, could we have succeeded in taking it would have made us masters of Lake Ontario and prevented the Americans from fortifying the posts at Niagara, Oswego, Buffalo and Blackrock that afterwards became so formidable and not to be taken from them without great loss of blood both on lake and land which might have been easily taken but for our imbecility at Sacketts Harbor.

6. The Battle of Lake Erie, September 10, 1813, at Put-in-Bay. Others have written in excellent manner on this subject; also, it does not directly concern Lieutenant Wingfield, and therefore only a brief account follows.

Commander Robert Heriot Barclay, RN, was put in charge by Commander Yeo on his arrival in Canada, of the fleet, forces, and facilities at Fort Malden, on the Detroit River. Barclay supervised the building and equipping of the British fleet, and he led the fleet into battle. The fleet, however, was ill-equipped. Shortages of cannon and trained officers and crew were particularly detrimental, but this cannot be blamed on Commander Barclay. Shortages were abundant in all theatres. Yeo kept all available extra cannon and other supplies on Lake Ontario because he, himself, needed them. The same applied with naval officers and men. Cannon intended for Barclay's use were captured by the Americans when they took York.

Captain Oliver Hazard Perry, USN, was in charge of the American fleet, largely built at Presque Isle, the harbour for Erie, Pennsylvania. He would have been pleased with this acquisition of weaponry, which further denied the enemy from accessing sufficient resources.

The battle was conclusive. The Americans captured or destroyed the entire British fleet. The only British vessel to survive was the *Nancy*. Owned by a reading company, she was away on her regular transport business when the battle took place. This was the only significant naval engagement on the Lakes during the War of 1812. (The army acquired the *Nancy* in 1813.)

7. This appears to be an error. Yeo's fleet left Kingston on June 8 to pick up the wounded men of General John Vincent's forces during the withdrawal from Fort George.

8. The *Sir Isaac Brock*, under construction at York at the time of the attack on April 27, 1813, was torched by the Americans.

9. On June 16, the British captured five American transports, three schooners, and two sloops. One transport was the *Lady Washington*, whose name was changed to the *Vincent*. Wingfield was placed in command as master's mate. He used the *Vincent* for his survey of Little Lake at Burlington, and was transferred to the *Wolfe* in early August.

10. An explanation is needed here. The large bay is now known as Hamilton Harbour. It was then called Little Lake, though in one place Wingfield refers to it as Burlington Bay. Burlington Bay was, in 1813, an anchorage in Lake Ontario. George Heriot, whose two-volume *Travelling Through the Canadas*, as published in 1807, uses the name Burlington Bay for Little Lake. He also uses the name Coot's Paradise for the small body of water west of Little Lake. That name is still used today.

    Historians have offered various opinions about Burlington Heights in this era. Where exactly was it located in 1813; what was it? Was it a fort, a supply depot, or just a camp and gun emplacement that was set up by the British Army? It seems to have developed into a village, and perhaps it was located on the site of present-day Burlington?

    Several naval reports mention anchoring under the guns of Burlington Heights. Others mention loading or unloading supplies, including cannon, at Burlington Heights. There are reports of an army being camped there. Was there more than one place that was known as Burlington Heights?

    An old Map of the Niagara Frontier, held at the West Point Museum Collection, United States Military Academy Library, West Point, New York, has the most logical placement of any suggested locations, (see number "3" on the sketch-map in the text). It also offers the most strategic site. It protects the road that separates Lake Ontario and Little Lake (now Hamilton

Harbour). It is near the direct route from York to the Niagara Peninsula. It is close to the main road from York to Fort Malden. Its guns could protect ships anchored in Lake Ontario near the shore during unloading and loading operations.

Wingfield mentions being sent to the Heights (Wingfield Journal, page 39, September 28, 1813) using a "boat," and apparently passing through the opening into Little Lake, though capsizing the boat, then proceeding to the Heights. Presumably he beached the boat at the northeast corner of Little Lake, and then climbed to the Heights (number 3). Any other explanation seems unreasonable.

Another clue comes from J. Fennimore Cooper, in his *Naval History of the United States of America*, published in 1846. On page 380, he states, "There being nothing but a roadstead (an anchorage), under Burlington Heights, which the wind that then blew swept. As the enemy was known to have a considerable land force at this point, all who were driven ashore would necessarily have fallen into his hands." This could have been only the location indicated on the sketch-map submitted here as number "3." Pierre Berton also shows this location in *Flames Across the Border*, on page 212. He also shows another location (sketch map, location "1") in the same book on page 73.

Another instance serves as an example: On November 13, 1813, the *Julia* was assisting Chauncey to transfer soldiers from Niagara to Sackets. She was hit by a gale and in Chauncey's report, "She anchored within a mile of the head of the Lake, with two anchors out and fortunately rode out the gale in sight of the enemy's camp at Burlington Bay." (Chauncey to Jones, November 24, 1813. Captain's letters, vol. 32 [M125 Reel 10], item 126, as cited in Malcomson, Robert, "The Capture of the Schooner *Julia/ Confiance*," in the *American Neptune*, vol. 51, no. 2 (Spring 1991): 83–90.

Captain Arthur Sinclair, USN, writing to his brother-in-law, John Cocke, from on board the *General Pike*, at Sackets Harbor on October 10, 1813, adds to our quest to confirm the actual location. He tells of the "Burlington Races" and of the British ships anchoring off Burlington Heights "as they were covered by their army with a quantity of artillery." He also describes the bursting of a gun during the battle. His letters have been reprinted in Malcomson's excellent book, *Sailors of 1812*; see listing in the bibliography.

It is noteworthy that General Vincent had a base camp near the top of the Niagara Escarpment, near or within present-day Stoney Creek. Several writers have incorrectly placed Burlington Heights here. The sketch map shows this as "1." Perhaps then, the site suggested as number "3" was an outpost of this base camp.

Wingfield's report on entering, leaving, and surveying the Little Lake puts to rest all ideas that large ships could enter the Little Lake in the early years. Most writers have recognized this limitation.

Wingfield writes that he stayed in the Little Lake "for about a month." It seems that he was not involved in other activities on Lake Ontario from early June until early August. He may have passed through the shallow passage more times than he relates. Where would he get provisions for his crew for two months around Little Lake? Perhaps he went to York, or perhaps there was a military storehouse at Burlington Heights.

Historical records indicate that there was a hospital located at "2" on the sketch map, referring to it as Burlington Heights Emigrant Hospital. This was built in the mid-1830s to take care of emigrants sick with typhus, smallpox, or cholera. It was built at the tip of the point of land separating Coot's Paradise from Little Lake. This location does not meet any of the requirements of the naval stories of Burlington Heights (www.thh. mcmaster.ca/health care history/places/burlington.html, as accessed March 26, 2008).

11. Autumn 1813: Wingfield has not been generous in furnishing us with his dates. The war was going on no matter what he did, but it helps to see how his story ties in with the history. In the early part of 1813, actually up to August, while he was surveying Little Lake, there was very little accomplished by either side on the Lakes, except for shipbuilding.

Yeo left Kingston on July 31, to seek out Chauncey and try to bring about the destruction of the American fleet. On the same day, Chauncey was busy attacking the town of York, for the second time. On August 7, the two fleets came in view, ten miles northwest of the mouth of the Niagara River. On the night of August 7, a sudden squall caught the American fleet unprepared. The *Hamilton* and the *Scourge* capsized and sank with great loss of life. Ned Meyers was on board the *Scourge* when it foundered, along with a few of his fellow seamen. He was picked up by the *Julia*. While Chauncey and Yeo were sparring, the British captured the *Julia* and the *Growler* on August 9/10. The battle broke off and Yeo took his fleet to anchorage just west of York on August 11. Chauncey returned to Sackets Harbor minus four of his schooners. He was severely criticized in the American media, including claims that he was too frightened to continue the battle and that his conduct was "highly censurable."

The *Julia* was renamed the *Confiance,* and the *Growler* became the *Hamilton.* The word "confiance" means "confidence," but Yeo soon lost confidence in the ability of the *Confiance* to manoeuvre and relegated her to transport duties for the army. On August 19 through the 24th, the two ships were both in Navy Bay having their armament changed.

Yeo was transferring a large quantity of supplies, including twelve 24-pounders needed by Barclay for the *Detroit*, between August 26 and noon the next day. The transfer was made at Burlington Heights. It appears that the provisions did not get to Barclay in time for fitting out the *Detroit* for the Battle of Lake Erie.

September 1 seems to be the correct date for the Durham boat incident, and on the same day, Wingfield was transferred to the *Wolfe*, but that posting only lasted a couple of weeks. While on the *Wolfe*, he participated in the battle off the mouth of the Genesee River on September 10. Then the fleet went to Kingston.

Wingfield was put in charge of the *Confiance* on approximately September 16. On September 18, he was taking dispatches back to Burlington Heights. On September 26, the *Confiance* was part of a transport fleet taking supplies to Burlington Heights for troops in the Niagara campaign. On September 27, he took on board an unidentified officer with dispatches for Yeo. On September 28, he was marginally involved in a battle known as the Burlington Races. On October 2, he set out for Kingston. On October 3, he took on soldiers at York to be transported to Kingston. On October 5, near the False Ducks, a set of islands on eastern Lake Ontario, the *Confiance* was captured by the American fleet and Wingfield became a prisoner of war.

12. Wingfield means Fort George at Newark, today's Niagara-on-the-Lake.

13. The action that Wingfield is referring to here is commonly known as the Burlington Races, described earlier. Loss of control over Lake Ontario by the British navy would give the American army free reign to invade the Niagara Peninsula in greater numbers, attack York, and then move on to attack Kingston. Should the British gain total control, the American army, already establishing strongholds in the Niagara Peninsula, would not be able to hold it and Upper Canada would be far more defensible.

Others have written excellent accounts of the battle. Here are some brief highlights. The battle was joined under "stiff topgallant winds" according to Wingfield. The winds were out of the northeast. Yeo in the *Wolfe*, and Chauncey in the *Pike*, were able to bring their ships close enough that Yeo's carronades caused great damage. The *Pike* lost her main topgallant mast and had been holed several times below the waterline. It was necessary to keep her pumps going continually. A gun had exploded, killing and wounding several crew members. There was so much structural damage to the foredeck that a replacement gun could not be fitted.

Yeo, in the *Wolfe*, had his main topmast hit and it came crashing down, followed by the main yard and the mizzen topmast. The *Wolfe* was left a shambles, still under the guns of the *Pike*. Quickly, Captain Sir William Rowe Mulcaster brought the *Royal George* between the two adversaries. Soon the *Pike* had sustained further damage to her bowsprit, and to both fore and main masts. The *Wolfe* was able to get away, out of range, and Chauncey quickly broke off the fight. For his act of bravery and quick thinking, Mulcaster was made a post captain in recognition of his outstanding bravery.

The British fleet high-tailed it for Burlington Heights in gale conditions and anchored there to effect repairs. The American fleet pursued them and possibly could have brought about a final and definitive victory. But, suddenly, without apparent reason, they turned about and headed for the open lake. Chauncey had suffered considerable damage to the *Pike*. The *Governor Tomkins* lost a mast and had to be taken in tow. Perhaps it is better to read Chauncey's report to the Secretary of the Navy, to learn why he did not try to finish off the *Wolfe*:

> ...At the time I gave up the chase this ship [*Pike*] was making so much water that it required all our pumps to keep her free, owing to our receiving several shot much below the water's edge that we could not plug the holes from the outside: the *Governor Tomkins* with her foremast gone, and the squadron within about six miles of the head of the lake, blowing a gale wind from the east and increasing with a heavy sea on and every appearance of the equinox. I considered that if I chased the enemy to his anchorage at the head of the lake I should be obliged to anchor also, and although we might succeed in driving him ashore the probability was that we would go ashore also, he amongst his friends and we amongst our enemies, and after the gale abated if he could succeed in getting one or two vessels out of the two fleets it would give him as complete command of the lake as if he had twenty vessels. Moreover, he was covered at his anchorage by part of his army and several small batteries thrown up for the purpose. Therefore if we could have rode out the gale we should have been cut

up by their shot from the shore. Under all these circumstances, and taking into view the consequences
resulting from the loss of our squadron on the lake
at this time, I, without hesitation, relinquished the
opportunity of acquiring individual reputation at
the expense of my country.

Information from Tom Malcomson, "Engagements Between Chauncey
and Yeo" in *Inland Seas,* vol. 47 (1997): 297-313.

14. Wilkinson's Fiasco: In August 1813, John Armstrong, the American secretary of war, started plans to assault Kingston. It was October before
the plans were executed. Major General James Wilkinson, elderly and in
poor health, was placed in charge. On October 17, the expedition set out
from Sackets Harbor in wintry weather, with a force consisting of eight
thousand soldiers and officers in three hundred bateaux with twelve of
Chauncey's fleet of gunboats to defend them. Before the fleet had even
reached Grenadier Island, only eighteen miles from Sackets, a severe
storm with driving wind and heavy rain, hammered the fleet. Many boats
were driven ashore and wrecked. Military supplies and provisions were
soaked and destroyed, and a third of the rations were lost. "The morning disclosed a scene of desolation truly distressing," wrote Franklin B.
Hough. "The shores of the island and mainland were strewn with broken
and sunken boats." See Franklin B. Hough. *History of Jefferson County in
the State of New York from the Earliest Period to the Present Time.* Albany,
NY: Joel Munsell, and also Watertown, NY: Sterling & Riddell, 1854. No
page number available.

Many of the soldiers became sick and had to be sent back to Sackets. It
was October 28 before they could depart from Grenadier Island.

Even though they were close to Kingston, Wilkinson changed his mind
and decided to proceed down the St. Lawrence and to attack Montreal. The
fleet of bateaux, carrying some six thousand soldiers, stretched out some
five miles. Not far behind them was a fleet of British gunboats under the
command of Captain William Howe Mulcaster, RN, who had set out from
Kingston on a search and destroy mission. The British caught up with the
American forces by November 10, near Chrysler's farm in Upper Canada.
Wilkinson, quite ill by this time, decided to take a stand here. His campaign was doomed from the start. At Chrysler's farm, on November 11,
they met in pitched battle. The straggling American forces were defeated
by eight hundred British regulars and the Canadian militia, with the help

of Mulcaster's gunboats. This was one of the major land battles in the Great Lakes area during this war.

Wilkinson retreated to Fort Covington (currently Covington, New York, across the river from Cornwall, Ontario), with the remnants of his troops, his career over. Pierre Berton recounted the disaster well in his book *Flames Across the Border*. Wilkinson was to be court-martialled but died before the trial could take place.

As a matter of general interest, the well-known Warden of the Forest, Dr. William "Tiger" Dunlop, of Huron Tract fame, was assistant surgeon in the 89th at the time. He helped attend the wounded of both sides during this memorable battle.

CHAPTER TWO:
Capture and Experiences as a Prisoner of War

1. Army bills: Even before war was declared, merchants and army commissariats were hoarding supplies such as flour. Inflation quickly set in. Sir George Prevost, at Quebec in July 1812, initiated the issuing of paper currency to compensate for the deficiency of hard currency. This was the start of the extensive use of army bills. Before the war ended, bills to the value of some £1,249,000 had been issued in the two provinces. They paid a nominal interest to those who bought and held them.

    These bills were used to pay the seamen and soldiers, to pay for supplies, contracts, and all military expenses. Just like paper money today, they were intended to be used for general commerce, but because of the shortages, sometimes merchants could not (or would not) give coins to make change. Inflation increased.

2. This American lieutenant would have been Lieutenant Francis Gregory, USN.

3. The term *parole* is from the old French word *parole*, meaning "a word of promise or honour." Rather than be responsible for the care and feeding of captured prisoners, warring nations had long before developed a system whereby prisoners could be given partial or conditional freedom. In return, the captive offered his *parole d'honneur* or "word of honour" that he would not bear arms against his captors. Over the years the meaning had changed somewhat and by the time war was declared between the United States and Great Britain, prisoners usually spoke of acquiring a "parole"

from their captors, rather than of giving their "parole of honour" to the victorious enemy.

George Sheppard shows a parole, which contains this word, dated November 9, 1814, at Long Point, Upper Canada, and entirely handwritten. "This is to certify that Noah Fairchild, Sergeant in the Canadian Militia has this day been paroled not to bear arms against nor to do anything [prejudicial] to the interests of the U. States during the present war until regularly exchanged. C.S. Todd, Act Adj General."

The authors have inserted the word "prejudicial" as the word in the original image was illegible.

4. As Wingfield begins his travels as a prisoner of war, it might help to provide a brief summary of the points visited on his journey. The journal is not always clear about his whereabouts and sometimes he retraces his steps to return to places earlier visited or taken. As briefly as possible, the general route was as follows: He and others were captured by the Americans some thirty miles southwest of Kingston on Lake Ontario, and taken to Sackets Harbor. From there they travelled by wagon and carriage to Watertown and on to Utica, and continued on by barge on the Mohawk River, passing through several primitive locks along the way, then to German Flats and Schenectady to the City of Albany. At the army base here, known as Greenbush (where his baggage was left behind), he and others were sent by the Governor to Pittsfield. They crossed the Hudson River by barge to Massachusetts, then travelled by carriage to Pittsfield. From there he travelled to Cheshire, some nine miles off, seeking luggage left behind at Greenbush [near Albany], thence to Worcester, Salem, and Boston. From nearby Charleston (Massachusetts) he marvelled at Bunker Hill, the site of one of the first major battles of the American Revolutionary War, June 17, 1775, and then travelled to Cambridge, Concord, and Lennox. Returning to Pittsfield, he was then removed to Philadelphia to be imprisoned briefly, and released on his "parole" again to Cheshire and once again to Pittsfield. Finally, he was removed to Whitehall at the southern tip of Lake Champlain, after which he returned to Montreal and then moved on to Kingston where he rejoined the British forces. In all, David was held as a POW for a total of nine months.

5. This way of obtaining cash is difficult to explain. It stretches the imagination. Of the several bank managers consulted, none could explain it. In brief, a Commodore of the United States Navy was willing to provide $100 (a large

sum in those days) if the borrower, a master's mate of the Royal Navy and a prisoner of war, would "draw a private bill on a person" of known resources in Kingston.

Apparently, such a transaction of international finance originated in the 1600s in Europe. In modern banking, with its instant communication between computers, it has completely gone out of practice, even out of memory. In 1813, there was no such thing as instant communication and there was no bank at Kingston.

In effect, Commander Chauncey provided the cash on the say-so of a lieutenant of the Royal Navy, who claimed to have a brother in Kingston who had the resources and would pay back the hundred dollars when presented with a slip of paper, the "bill demanding payment" to Commander Chauncey.

Whether Chauncey ever got the money we shall never know. The most amazing feature of this transaction was the trust put in officers of the British navy by an officer of the United States Navy. Or perhaps it was Uncle Sam's money anyway! The resource for this information was mainly Webster's *Third New World Dictionary* with additional assistance from the London, Ontario, Public Library staff.

Prisoners of War: As you read the Wingfield account of his experiences as a prisoner of war, think of it as a peek at the experiences and thoughts of a member of an old and well-established, class-based society. Wingfield was not near the top of the hierarchy, and certainly he was not positioned near the bottom. He was dropped into the free and easy, liberal society of 1813–14 America — an America that was just getting used to its freedom and equality, and was feeling its oats.

The roadside tavern in 1813 has its modern equivalent in today's full service motel. It provided meals and drinks, beds, and a social centre in a greater or lesser degree of quality. Wingfield's experience indicates that the majority of those with which he dealt were acceptable or even better.

The 1813 equivalent of the bed and breakfast of today also existed in the form of a farm family that was known for its hospitality. Possibly family members (at least juniors) had to give up their beds and double up with siblings. Wingfield's experience with these was at least as good as with the taverns. In one case, he and his companions lodged with the United States officer in charge of the prisoners of war. In another instance, they chose to stay with a Canadian widow and her family.

The subject of the treatment of prisoners throughout history cannot be covered in detail here. The object of taking and keeping prisoners of war was solely to deprive the enemy of their fighting efficiency. Throughout history, it was generally expected that prisoners would be executed, sold into slavery, or ransomed. By 1800, it was recognized that there was no reason why those who gave their word not to engage in further hostilities should not be allowed to live as free people, or with few restrictions, if they could pay for accommodations until an exchange could be arranged. This was applied originally only to officers, and somewhat later, included all ranks. The members of the militia were commonly excluded from any parole arrangement and more frequently released and sent back to their farms or trades.

Such was the custom at the beginning of the Napoleonic Wars, but as Napoleon did not adhere to them, in his treatment of prisoners, then, in retaliation, Great Britain put more French prisoners into hulks and such prisons as Dartmoor. Hulks were old and frequently derelict naval ships, which were withdrawn from fighting service and converted to floating prisons. There was no international agreement on prisoner treatment until the Hague Convention of 1907.

According to Wingfield in 1813, Uncle Sam was expected to pay for transportation expenses plus accommodation, meals, and drinks for officers and their servants, until exchanged. He was returned to the Canadas as a prisoner of war and rejoined his ship, but was not permitted to resume his duties as a Royal Navy officer until officially exchanged, that is, until the paperwork caught up with him.

His incarceration may have been inconvenient, but it was generally a pleasant interval in his life with parties or balls every night, long walks, socializing, horseback riding — all contributed to passing the time enjoyably.

Did the British offer the same amenities to its prisoners? Diaries of American prisoners of war are rare and hard to find. British North America was not developed anywhere to the extent that New England had developed. It is therefore difficult to reach any conclusions. Ned Meyers was such a prisoner, but he was not an officer. He was captured in November 1813, was transported to Quebec, to Halifax, and next to a prisoner of war camp on Melville Island in Halifax Harbour. Others, less fortunate, were assigned into hulks or sent to prisons in England. Meyers considered that he was well treated and reasonably fed, though not as well as a British seaman held in American hands.

6. In the early days in America, the first ways of transportation involved the use of canoes and woodland pathways. This was followed by the construction of rough roads through the wilderness, and then came the canals, and

eventually the railways. Wingfield is writing about the first canal in New York State, which began at Lake Oneida and followed the Mohawk River Valley until it joined the Hudson River. It was begun by a private company in 1791, and completed in 1795, using wooden-walled locks and wooden gates held in place by wooden hinges fashioned from the Lignum vitae tree. The canal was rebuilt in 1802 using stone for more substantial walls.

It wasn't until 1817 that Governor DeWitt Clinton started a state plan for the canals of New York State. The improved canal ran from Troy on the Hudson River to Buffalo on Lake Erie, and was forty feet (12.5 metres) wide, four feet (1.2 metres) deep, and 340 miles (544 kilometres) long. There were also various side canals in his plans. The canal could accommodate floating barges carrying thirty tons (27.2 tonnes) of freight. These barges were pulled by teams of horses, along the towpaths that can still be seen today in some places.

The Erie Barge Canal has gone through many changes and improvements through the years and has become a major tourist attraction for the State. Today, in season, one will see many private yachts, power and sail (the latter with their masts down), passing through the canal in both directions. Some of the early canal walls have been left as memorials for the process of widening and deepening over the years.

The small part of the canal that Wingfield travelled goes through country that is very beautiful, and it still has five locks at Waterford with a combined lift of 169 feet (52 metres). The locks at Little Falls have been replaced by one lock with a lift of 40½ feet (12.5 metres).

Information was taken from Finch, Roy G., *The Story of the New York State Canals*. Albany, NY: J.B. Lyon Co., 1925. This and other helpful material was acquired from The Great Lakes Cruising Club of Port Huron, Michigan. Carmella R. Mantello, the director of The New York State Canal Corporation of Albany, New York, was also most helpful.

7. *Webster's New World Dictionary* shows the meaning of *cartel* as a written agreement between nations at war, especially as to the exchange of prisoners. Wingfield refers to the "cartel" as being the ship used to carry such released British prisoners.

8. It is not clear whether this is a spelling error or whether in fact the ship was designed by M. Dupay de Loine, the builder of the celebrated *Napoleon*.

9. Does Wingfield mean *sine qua non* … an essential action or condition; in this case, not to be taken lightly or unquestionable?

10. The term "fever and ague" has middle English origins, the standard dictionary definition being related to malarial fever marked by paroxysms of chills,
fever, and sweating that recur at regular intervals.

CHAPTER THREE:
Return to Active Duty on Lake Ontario

1. Cognawaga, or Kahnawaga in present-day spelling, is in New York State,
immediately south of Montreal.

2. *Cashiering* is a term used to describe the dishonourable discharge of military officers, sometimes accompanied by the public degradation of strip-
ping off one's epaulets or other forms of regalia. Wilkinson's ill-conceived
attack was a fiasco. His sentence was commuted to cashiering instead of
execution after his court martial.

3. Deal is a town on the English Channel coast of England, near Ramsgate.
Apparently one or more boat builders here had earned a reputation for their
boats being exceptionally fast. A "gig" is a light boat especially made for
speed and frequently used for delivering messages and/or officers between
ships or ship to shore.

4. This officer would have been Lieutenant Francis Gregory, USN.

5. The arrival of the *St. Lawrence*, now the largest ship on the Great Lakes,
so alarmed the Americans that they withdrew their blocking vessels to the
safety of their own harbours.

6. The word *orlop* comes from the Dutch *overloop* meaning "to cover," so
called because it covers the hold. It is the lowest deck, beneath water level,
and does not run the full length of the ship.
   It is easy to speculate what could have happened should this quantity
of ammunition have exploded. Certainly the *St. Lawrence* would have been
instantly disabled at minimum, or perhaps even totally destroyed. Some six
hundred seamen were on board and possibly as many soldiers. The loss of life
could have been much greater than that of any campaign in the entire war.
   Had this happened, and the Americans been sufficiently alert and
taken advantage of their sudden and unexpected complete control of the

Lake, and invaded at Detroit, Kingston, Montreal or Niagara, it could have completely changed the outcome of the war.

The negotiations for peace, under way at the time at Ghent would have been gravely influenced. It is most likely that the sought-after status quo "ante bellum" would never be gained. Fortunately for the British and the Canadians, the destruction of the mighty *St. Lawrence* did not occur.

7. "Exercising the men at the guns" is the activity of training the men to load, aim, fire, recall, clean, and reload. Not only accuracy, but also the speed of handling the new guns was extremely important. The men would be taught to fire "as you bear," that is, when they had a proper aim on their target, or to fire together, in other words, fire a broadside. Occasionally a wooden cask would be thrown overboard for use as a target.

CHAPTER FOUR:
Ordered to Lake Huron and Georgian Bay — Commanding the *Surprise*

1. The word *impressments* is little used today. It was common in the era of "wooden walls." The word *impressment* means to take something or someone to serve the government, against the owner's will or against the person's will, but not without payment. The word *expropriation* would be our nearest word for it in contemporary vocabulary. Many sailors in the Royal Navy were "pressed" into service with absolutely no warning. Most of these men never got home again, or, if they did, it was many years later. The chance of advancement or promotion for a pressed man was very slim. The term "wooden walls" was commonly used to describe the great wooden battleships of the Royal Navy. The phrase, "era of the wooden walls," referred to times when a protective barrier of vessels were scattered in the seas around England, moving around, keeping watch, to protect her from invasion by foreign naval forces.

2. "What is a Yankee? To a citizen of the world, a Yankee is an American. To an American, a Yankee is a Northerner. To a Northerner, a Yankee is a New Englander. To a New Englander, a Yankee is a Vermonter. To a Vermonter, a Yankee is a person who eats pie for breakfast." The origin of this quote is unknown, but believed to have been printed in *Outdoor Life* magazine, circa 1968, according to information from The Yankee Candle Company, Deerfield, Massachusetts.

Here, Wingfield is surely referring to extreme republican principles such as to refuse the seemingly unreasonable requests of government officials, in this case where commandeering private property is seen to be an offence to the supremacy of individual rights. Most likely, the citizens he encountered were recent immigrants from America who had more sympathy for the president than for the king.

3.   Kempenfeldt (or Kempenfelt) to Wasaga, The Nine Mile Portage Road: The route from York to Lake Huron was very important in the early history of the country. Briefly, the traveller either walked or travelled by sleigh or wagon, by road, if the route could be called that, from York to Holland Landing, a distance of some thirty miles. From there he would go by boat, in summer, down the Holland River, across part of Lake Simcoe, and up to the head of Kempenfeldt Bay, at the site of present-day Barrie. In winter, once the ice had become sufficiently strong, the route was the same, but travel was either on foot or by sleigh.

From Kempenfeldt, there had been an Indian trail for centuries, heading almost directly west to Willow Creek, a tributary of the Nottawasaga River. La Salle and Monsieur de Tonty used this passage in 1680 on their expedition to the Illinois River. In 1814, it was still an Indian trail, unfit for any kind of vehicle. Being nine miles long, it took the name of "the nine mile portage."

Once Willow Creek was reached, in summer, the Native people with their canoes, or soldiers with their bateaux, could travel, with little difficulty, to the Nottawasaga River, and from there, down the river to Lake Huron. This was considered the best way to get to Lake Huron at this time, and was used by several men famous in our history, including Rene Robert La Salle, Sir John Franklin, and Lieutenant-Governor Simcoe.

Once winter had settled in and the streams well-frozen, the same route was fairly easy for those equipped with proper winter clothing and familiar with the use of snowshoes. The creek and river were approximately 36 miles (58 kilometres) in length. They twisted and turned, had shallow places and rapids, and in winter featured many unsafe areas due to hot springs that prevented the water from freezing into ice strong enough to prevent a man from breaking through.

The land in the immediate vicinity included hardwood forests and conifer forests, rocks and hills, but most importantly, extensive marshes, through which it was impossible to travel in summer. These swampy areas were unsafe in winter until the water was frozen solid. A soldier who broke through the ice could find himself up to his waist in water and stuck in place with considerable soft mud restraining his feet.

Thus, the route was quite easy in summer for the well-equipped traveller. The same goes for the winter after the water was frozen solid. But in the late spring and early winter, it was virtually impassable or worse.

Wingfield and his group hit one of the worst possible conditions, freezing rain followed by heavy snow. He was caught unaware and totally unprepared: no snowshoes, inadequate winter garb, overburdened with a boat he could not use, and tending a herd of animals on the hoof. He must be commended for his leadership and for saving his entire group but one, and even arriving at his destination with almost everything he started out to get. It was a harrowing and edifying experience.

William Dunlop, a medical doctor and officer in the army, tells of a frightening experience when he was put in charge of building the Penetanguishene road, quite nearby, in 1816. He was out on a survey alone, properly dressed for the weather and equipped with snowshoes. He got lost in a heavy snowstorm and could not find his way back to base. Very tired, he knew that if he were simply to lie down to sleep it would be fatal. He dug a hole in the snow, lay down to rest, called his dog to his side and had it lie down on top of him.

It worked. He barely lived through it, with severe frostbite and several weeks of illness that followed. But the dog did not survive. Dunlop continued his army career in India then became associated with the Canada Company, which was instrumental in settling much of southwestern Ontario, the most well-known portion, in the region from Galt through Stratford to Goderich, in an area that was called the Huron Tract.

Initially, of course, there were no shelters along the route except for a rudimentary storehouse for provisions, and several crude huts near the junction of Willow Creek and the Nottawasaga River in 1815. These were never intended to be habitable, merely places for temporary protection from animals, intruders, and the absolute worst of the weather. This location became known as Glengarry Landing.

Later, a hut was built at the junction of nine-mile portage and Willow Creek. It was known colloquially as Fort Willow but was never really a fort. Over the years a small settlement grew up there. As settlers moved into the area after the war, many travelled and brought their possessions, supplies, and furnishing over the portage. Even then it could hardly be called a road. Opportunists settled at Fort Willow, taking advantage of the needs of these settlers, and transporting them and their possessions by sleigh or ox-cart over the portage and then down the river. In this way, they augmented their meagre income from farming and timbering.

4. A Brief History of Fort Mackinac: The reader should note that here we are concerned with the third site of Fort Mackinac. The early name was Missilimackinac, then Michilimackinac. The first fort was established in 1670 by the French at the site of the present Point St. Ignace. The second was at present-day Mackinaw City. It was also French at one time, established in 1712. The British captured it in 1760 and occupied it until 1781 when they decided to replace it with a new fort on Mackinac Island. They then held this fort, naturally much more easily defended, until 1796. In fact, it was known as the Gibraltar of the North. The British withdrew in 1796 and the Americans took possession, as one of the terms required in the 1796 Treaty of Paris.

When the American Congress declared war on Great Britain and Canada, on June 18, 1812, the news did not seem to travel as fast by military means as it did by commercial traders. While forces at the post at St. Joseph Island had been informed about the outbreak of hostilities, those at the American fort at Mackinac was still unaware that war had been declared. Captain Charles Roberts was in charge of British military forces at St. Joseph, namely forty-seven soldiers of the Royal Veteran Battalion, with two six-pound cannon and two gunners to man them. He had also collected together 180 volunteers, mostly settlers and traders, and four hundred Natives.

They landed in the dark and by dawn the whole force was drawn up in a position to attack Fort Mackinac from a nearby height of land. The American forces, under Lieutenant Porter Hanks of the United States Regiment of Artillery, were greatly outnumbered as well as surprised. They had no alternative but to surrender, which they did before noon, without a shot being fired. John Askin commanded the Native warriors in this affair, and they all were reported to have behaved admirably.

The British held the island and the fort until after peace was declared, and did not withdraw until July 18, 1815, when they moved to Drummond Island. However, the occupation was not all peaceful. The Americans, having taken control of the Upper Lakes at the Battle of Lake Erie, on September 10, 1813, were determined to regain control of Fort Mackinac. Captain Arthur Sinclair, USN, set out on July 3, 1814, for an attack on the fort with the brigs, *Niagara* and *Lawrence*, and six smaller gunboats with five hundred seamen and marines. They reached St. Joseph Island on July 16, and destroyed the trading post along with most of the traders' buildings, and then headed for Mackinac, which they reached on July 26. Attempts at bombardment and plans for a landing and assault on the fort were unsuccessful.

The defenders, under Colonel Robert McDouall, the British commander, were greatly outnumbered, though there were some 350 Natives on the island, which he felt he could count on. His trained force consisted of only 140 men of the Royal Newfoundland Regiment and the Michigan Fencibles. The Americans affected a landing on the morning of August 4, but by mid-afternoon they were in retreat. No further attempt to take the island was made.

The British gave up control of the island the following year, in accordance with the terms of the peace treaty. Barry Gough has written an excellent book, with much more detail than given here. See *Fighting Sail on Lake Huron and Georgian Bay*. Indianapolis, MD: Naval Institute Press, 2002.

McDouall's story merits relating briefly, for it, too, is heroic. In 1813, the British at Fort Mackinac were very much concerned by rumours that the Americans were preparing for an attack as they were desperately short of supplies.

The Relief Expedition: Lieutenant Colonel Robert McDouall, of the Glengarry Light Infantry, was ordered to take a relief expedition from Kingston to the fort, a journey of some six hundred miles. The force was made up of ten officers, two companies of the Royal Newfoundland Regiment, shipwrights, seamen and boatmen, and eleven field artillery men with four field guns, altogether some two hundred men. They left Kingston in February 1814, and in severe wintry weather they travelled to York, up Yonge Street to Holland Landing, and crossed the frozen lake to the head of Kempenfeldt Bay.

The force did not have time to clear the trail and turn it into a military road, but they did widen it somewhat, and managed to get all their supplies and even the field guns through. It took three weeks to pass over a mere nine miles on the portage. Near where Willow Creek joined the Nottawasaga, they made a small clearing, erected a storehouse and constructed several huts to live in. More amazingly, they cut down trees, trimmed them into planks and built thirty boats, probably bateaux, large and heavy enough to carry the artillery, two hundred men and the great quantity of supplies. This spot took on the name of Glengarry Landing. In late April they descended the river, breaking the ice as they went, then manoeuvring among the floes on Lake Huron, they travelled for some three hundred miles to Mackinac, arriving on May 18. When the Americans attacked on August 4, they were repulsed.

Captain Bulger, who was part of the British expedition, wrote a journal and his recounting of the trip is most interesting: "We embarked on the 22nd of April, having previously loaded the flotilla with provisions and stores, descending the Nottawasaga River — the ice in the upper part of which being still firm, we opened a channel through it — encamped on the night of the 24th of April in a dismal spot upon the north-eastern shore of Lake Huron [today's Georgian Bay — also called Manitoolin Lake by some of that day] and on the following morning entered upon the attempt to cross the lake, covered as it was, as far as the eye could reach, by fields of ice, through which, in almost constant, and, at times, terrific storms, we succeeded with the loss of only one boat in effecting a passage of nearly three hundred miles, arriving at Michilimackinac on the 18th of May. The expedition had occupied upwards of one hundred days, including our passage over the lake."

David Wingfield would have been very well acquainted with the Nottawasaga Passage. He must have travelled it many times.

The Michigan Fencibles, mentioned above were "a corps enrolled from the voyageurs and hangers-on at Mackinac, when the war and its disarrangement of the fur trade had left them stranded." This quote is from Louise Phelps Kellogg, in *The British Regime in Wisconsin and the Northwest*, (Madison: WI: 1935): 308, as cited in Fred Landon, *Lake Huron*. New York: The Bobbs Merrill Company, 1944.

5. The story of the *Nancy* is worth reporting briefly here. The *Nancy* was built at the shipyard near Detroit in 1789 for the Forsyth, Richardson and Co., fur traders of Montreal. She served as a transport, taking people and supplies to the settlers as far away as Michilimackinac, and all around Lake Huron, and bringing back furs, sugar, and farm produce to her base at Sandwich, Upper Canada, later part of Windsor, Ontario. She served the British forces in the war until the spring of 1814 when she was taken over by the Royal Navy and used as an armed transport.

Captain Arthur Sinclair, USN, having taken over the command of the American navy on the Upper Lakes in the spring of 1814, made the capture of Michilimackinac his highest priority. He set off with a fleet consisting of the *Lawrence* (20), the *Niagara* (20), the *Caledonia* (8), and two armed schooners, the *Tigress* and the *Scorpion*. The total force at his disposal was about nine hundred soldiers and five hundred seamen. On August 4, they disembarked the nine hundred soldiers and attempted to capture Fort Michilimackinac, but were driven back by Lieutenant Colonel Robert McDouall's 140 men of the Royal Newfoundland Regiment and the Michigan Fencibles, aided by about 150 Native soldiers. Failing in his attack on Michilimackinac, Sinclair decided to try to cut its supply route by capturing or destroying the *Nancy*. He had learned she was apt to be in the Nottawasaga area and headed the fleet for there.

McDouall, the commander at Michilimackinac, sent Robert Livingston of the Indian Department, in a canoe to warn the *Nancy* of the American search for her. At that time, Lieutenant Miller Worsley, RN, had been appointed to take command of the *Nancy*. With a small detachment of seamen he arrived at the mouth of the Nottawasaga about the middle of July, and when she arrived, he took command, replacing Lieutenant Newdigate Poyntz. He immediately proceeded to "load her to the gunnels" with provisions for the fort and headed there on August 1. Before they had gone many miles, Livingston, who had been sent to warn them of the American forces in the area, intercepted them. They immediately returned to the Nottawasaga and towed the vessel up the river about two miles to conceal her. They started to build a blockhouse and took the guns off the *Nancy* to help defend her in her hiding place.

Livingston immediately headed to York to get help. The British Army was busy fighting in the Niagara Peninsula, so a messenger was sent to Fort Erie and Livingston returned to the *Nancy*. Reinforcements were sent but did not arrive in time.

On August 13, the American fleet arrived and anchored offshore in Georgian Bay. They did not know exactly where the *Nancy* was located for she was hidden from view offshore by the cover of trees and underbrush, but soon learned her location when they put troops ashore. After bombarding the area for several hours, they gave that up and strategically positioned two howitzers on the spit of land. Soon they were doing real damage to the British forces. Worsley, realizing he could not win the fray, prepared to set the *Nancy* ablaze. This action was not necessary as a chance shot hit the blockhouse and started a fire on her decks. She burned to the waterline and sank with the load of provisions on board.

Worsley and his men retreated into the woods while Sinclair investigated the burned hulk of the *Nancy*, took the guns from the blockhouse and felled trees across the mouth of the river to impede its further use by the British. He also left the *Tigress* and the *Scorpion* to maintain a blockade of the Nottawasaga River while he returned to Lake Erie with the balance of the fleet. He also instructed the two vessels to seek out and capture any loads of furs coming from St. Marys to the French River, or loads of supplies coming the other way; however, they couldn't be in both places at once. After a few days, they left the open anchorage at Nottawasaga for the St. Marys River via the north shore of the lake, now called the North Channel.

Worsley immediately loaded all the provisions he could into two bateaux and one large canoe, and with twenty-three men, he set out for Michilimackinac. They made good time on the 360-mile voyage and almost reached the western end of the North Channel on August 29 when they spotted the two American vessels monitoring the De Tour Passage, found near the mouth of the St. Marys River where it empties into Lake Huron.

Worsley pulled his fleet into a cove, out of sight, and waited for darkness. Leaving the two bateaux behind, he put all the men into Livingston's canoe, and in the darkness they were able to pass the two American schooners within about one hundred yards without being detected. The next day, about sunset, they arrived at Michilimackinac.

Worsley quickly arranged with McDouall to lend him one hundred soldiers and boats, and promised the two American vessels in return. On September 1, they set out in four bateaux, accompanied by nineteen canoes containing some two hundred Native warriors under the direction of officers of the Indian Department. On September 2, they arrived at the De Tour, put the men ashore on an island and hid the boats in a secluded bay. Early next morning Worsley and Livingston set out in a canoe to reconnoitre. They found one of the American vessels anchored some six miles away. They proceeded with their full force after dark, but before they approached, the Native men were instructed to wait until they received further orders. However, three of the chiefs were taken along, making a total of ninety-two of all ranks in the British attack. They boarded from both sides and within five minutes the battle was over and the *Tigress* fell into British hands. The prisoners were sent away under guard.

During the night, the *Scorpion* anchored within two miles from the *Tigress*. At dawn next morning, Worsley ran silently down toward her, with most of the soldiers and seamen hidden. He was able to run right alongside and grapple with her. Again the battle was over in a few minutes.

Worsley now had two schooners to his credit. He had regained control over all of Lake Huron and could transport all the supplies desperately needed by Michilimackinac. The schooners were renamed the *Surprise* and the *Confiance*.

Wingfield later became commander of the *Surprise* and made many trips back and forth to Nottawasaga, and to other parts of the Lake. There is a little harbour of refuge at the North East tip of the Bruce Peninsula. It bears the name Wingfield Basin, for he had assisted William Fitz William Owen in surveying it in the summer of 1815.

This is only a brief summary of events. Lieutenant Colonel E. Cruikshank's article, "An Episode in the War of 1812: The Story of the Schooner, *Nancy*" in *Papers and Records of The Ontario Historical Society*, vol. 9, 1910, and Barry Gough's book tell the story much more completely and provide a plethora of interesting additional detail.

The remains of the *Nancy* lay on the bottom of the Nottawasaga from 1814. The lesser-known travellers like David Wingfield, and Miller Worsley, along with the more famous in Canada's history, passed over her charred remains. John Franklin RN, Arctic explorer, came this way in 1825, on his way to the icy northern climes. Many adventurers passed by, or over, her bones without knowing it, as did many settlers over the years, and later, even pleasure-seeking boaters. C.H.J. Snider, the publisher, historian and nautical story spinner, searched for the *Nancy* in 1911 and finally found the remains. In 1927, as the result of the efforts of Dr. J.F. Conboy, the artifacts were salvaged. The keel and parts of the ribs and stem were raised, and are now on display in a museum built in her memory. A visit to the *Nancy* Museum, in Wasaga Beach Provincial Park, Wasaga Beach, Ontario, is a very rewarding experience.

6. Native people had discovered maple syrup and how to refine the sap of the hard maple into sugar. They traded this much-sought-after commodity with the Europeans. In fact, it was probably the first manufactured product they used in trade.

    Susanna Moodie, an English lady, who emigrated in 1830 with her husband and settled on uncleared farmland in the Kawarthas, tells of her experience making sugar, with Indian help, in her classic book *Roughing It in the Bush: or, Life in Canada*. Troughs of tree bark were used to carry the sap from tree to kettle. After straining the final product through cloth, "a sugar as white and as sweet as any" was the result.

CHAPTER FIVE:
Arrival on Georgian Bay — Service on Lake Huron

1. See Notes for Journal — Part I, Chapter 4, Note 3, for the full story.

2. Very little is known about the construction of the bateau, probably because they were made by individuals to that person's ideas of what a bateau should be. The design varied somewhat from place to place, partly for this reason and partly by the choices of materials available in the vicinity. From the reports of early travellers such as George Heriot, and from the work of researchers and model builders such as Rear Admiral H.F. Pullen, R.C.N., we can come up with a typical version.

> The transport of merchandise, and other articles, from the island of Montreal to Kingston in Upper Canada, is conducted by means of bateaux; or flat-bottomed boats, narrow at each extremity, and constructed of planks. Each of these being about forty feet in length, and six feet across at the widest part, generally contains twenty-five barrels, or a proportionate number of bales of blankets, cloths or linens, and is capable of conveying nine thousand pounds weight. Four men and a guide, compose the number of hands allotted for working a bateau. They are supplied with provisions, and with rum, and are allowed from eight to eleven dollars each, for the voyage to Kingston, and from thence down again to La Chine, the time of performing which, is from ten to twelve days. The wages of the pilot or guide, amount to twelve or fourteen dollars. Each bateau is supplied with a mast and sail, a grappling iron, with ropes, setting poles, and utensils for cooking. The bateaux when loaded, take their departure from La Chine, in number, or from four to eight or ten together that the crews may be able to afford aid to each other, amid the difficulties and laborious exertions required in effecting this voyage. About fifty bateaux are employed on this route, and bring down for the objects of commerce which are conveyed up, wheat, flour, salted provisions, peltry and potash.

From George Heriot, *Travels Through the Canadas,* London, 1807, as cited in *Heritage Kingston*, by J. Douglas Stewart and Ian E. Wilson. Kingston, ON: Queen's University Press, 1973.

The usual way of propulsion was by oars, not by paddles or poles.

3. Wingfield tells us very briefly about what must have been a very hair-raising experience. There are many navigation circumstances on a sailing skipper's hate list. The lieutenant encountered a few of them on this trip. These include the following situations: Calm is hated more than gales. Fog is despised, especially when it is encountered among islands and shoals. A defective compass is worse than having none at all. An ignorant pilot, the same; having no pilot is to be preferred. Rain and snow can be tolerated, but freezing rain turns the vessel into an out-of-control prison. It is impossible to move on deck safely. The sails become unmanageable. Such icy conditions present the most-feared weather of all on the Great Lakes.

    We all know from personal experience what freezing rain can do to our cars. Most of us will have fallen, at least once, on ice-covered driveways. And we have seen what freezing rain does to branches, even toppling trees, breaking down electrical wires, poles and even high-tension towers. A sailboat, especially one with considerable top-hamper, or even a larger vessel, can be so loaded with ice that it will turn over and sink.

    But, back to Wingfield's account. The *Surprise* and *Confiance* left together but became separated. The *Confiance* apparently took the more protected route through the North Channel. The vessel *Surprise*, on the other hand, seems to have taken the route through the north of Lake Huron, open water generally, and usually safer, even in fog, as long as the vessel carries a good compass and a good chart, which the *Surprise* did not. Possibly, the pilot knew his way in the North Channel but had never taken the open route before.

    Wingfield showed good judgment to "hove to" as he headed for open water, but he relied on an incompetent pilot to tell him where the open water was. "Hoving to" is a standard sailboat manoeuvre when in a storm, or even when the skipper and crew are in need of a rest, or unable to sail the intended course because of wind direction, or other reasons. The rudder is set to turn the boat into the wind, the headsail is backed, and the mainsail tightened so that the boat is balanced in the wind, staying essentially in the same place (though drifting slowly downwind) in the most comfortable position achievable in such circumstances. We can presume that Wingfield set watches while he "hoved to."

4. "The Mirror of Literature, Amusement, and Instruction," vol. 13, no. 371, of Saturday, May 23, 1829, included the following reference: "Monsieur Ude, who is, unquestionably, the prince of gastronomes, has just published the tenth edition of his *French Cook*, of which, line upon line, we may say, 'Decies repelita placebit'; and Jarrin, the celebrated 'artiste en sucre', has also revised his *Italian Confectioner*, in a fourth edition. We should think both these works must be the literary furniture of every good kitchen, or they ought to be; for there is just enough of the science in them to make them extremely useful, whilst all must allow them to be entertaining."

5. The original word was *sewed*. This is probably merely an error of omission as Wingfield scratched out his memories quickly. Adding a *p* creates the word *spewed*, meaning to vomit.

6. The "Island" is Michilimackinac.

7. John Askin Jr. was a member of a well-known and successful family engaged in the fur trade and based at Sandwich, across the river from Detroit. When the war broke out, he was operating at the trading post on St. Joseph Island, and he took part in the capture of Mackinac Island in 1812. He was stationed there until the British were forced to give up the island in 1815 (following the Treaty of Ghent), serving as the Indian agent. Although he was well respected by Natives and the military alike, his views of the Native people seem to contrast with Wingfield's own opinions of the aboriginals living there. In one report of August 12, 1812, Askin writes of the Natives that they were in no condition to go anywhere, being "as drunk as Ten Thousand Devils." Wingfield's comments about the local Natives with whom he mingled at Mackinac Island are considerably more favourable than those of many writers of the time.

   Anyone wishing to learn more about the Native people of Simcoe County, Canada, might begin by reading the classic, by E.C. Drury, *All for a Beaver Hat*, published by The Ryerson Press of Toronto in 1959.

8. The ship arriving would, in all probability, be the *Huron*. She was built at Cleveland in 1810, and first named the *Ohio*. Later, she was purchased by the British for use as a transport. Her length was 54 feet, and she carried a beam of 17 feet, 3 inches. At this time, the *Huron* would have been based at the mouth of the Grand River in Lake Erie. Her captain would have been Lieutenant Thomas E. Vidal, RN, and among the passengers would

be Captain William Fitz William Owen, RN and Captain W.R. Payne, RE, who had recently made a plan for Penetanguishene Harbour, and finally, Captain Edward Collier.

Wingfield took the party on board the *Surprise* and delivered them to Drummond Island, which McDouall had decided would be the new British base, even though the final ownership of the island had not yet been settled. He participated marginally in the survey of the harbour, which was named Collier Harbour, but is now known as Sturgeon Bay. The *Surprise* went aground on rocks at the entrance and he soon found that she was taking in a serious amount of water. It was necessary to careen her and replace some of the oakum caulking. The Indian name for Drummond Island was Potagannissing.

While Wingfield made several more trips to Drummond, undoubtedly loaded with men and military supplies, he does not seem to have been a serious contributor to its development as a base for the military and a trading post. The *Confiance* wintered in Collier Harbour in 1815, frozen in the ice.

Captain Payne set about the major job of laying out a military town and overseeing construction of necessary houses, barracks, headquarters, plus a large trading post. Samuel F. Cook wrote an excellent little book, *Drummond Island, The Story of the British Occupation, 1815–1828*, which was self-published in Lansing, Michigan, in 1896, in which he describes what he saw of the remains of the British settlement: "Some of the houses were of large size, and were warmed during the long and severe winters by means of enormous stone chimneys having huge fireplaces on two of their sides. Some were two stories high." He describes "a lime kiln and open quarry close at hand." The number of soldiers and their dependents who were moved in was around 375. In addition, a large number of Natives settled in the new town "in order to share in their food." Payne had to make arrangements to shelter this large number of inhabitants before the approaching winter.

The British made an agreement with the Chippawa chief, Newbawgnaine, to purchase the island, should the Boundary Commission decide that Britain should hold it. To bind the agreement, the Native people were given "the freedom of the city, and a keg of rum." (While there are many definitions regarding the size of a keg, we believe the amount here was three gallons or about twelve litres.) The latter gift was repeated annually as long as the British stayed. Cook's book contains much more of interest to anyone studying this period, but we must get back to Wingfield. Yet, before doing that, a final story:

The British left Drummond Island in 1828 and most of the military transferred to Penetanguishene. Some settlers also went there, but many scattered around southwestern Ontario. The schooner *Alice Hackett* was one of the vessels used in the transfer. Captain Hackett had already made one trip, and this time, in addition to soldiers and supplies, he carried a man named Lepine with his wife and child, a tavern keeper named Frazer with thirteen barrels of whisky, along with considerable livestock and household furniture. No sooner had the little schooner got well underway from Drummond Island than Frazer opened shop with his supply of liquor. Before long the crew was in various stages of drunkenness. During the night, a storm blew up, but those in the vessel were in no condition to cope. They grounded on Fitzwilliam Island.

The crew and most of the passengers made it ashore. They lost much of the cargo, but, of course, they saved what was left of the whisky. Lepine's wife and child were left on the wreck, forgotten in the confusion. The woman fastened the baby to her back and tied herself to the mast where she remained throughout the storm. Next morning the people on shore became sober enough to realize the woman and child were missing. They went out to the schooner in the yawl boat, which had been saved, and rescued them. Both had survived the perils of the storm. The schooner was a total loss. Frazer, and what was left of his barrels of whisky eventually made it to Penetang, where he soon established another tavern.

For preserving this anecdote we are indebted, to C.H.J. Snider, a writer of many popular, and occasionally very imaginative stories of sail on the Great Lakes. He published this tale in one of his many columns called "Schooner Days" in the *Toronto Evening Telegram* between 1931 and 1957.

9. Drummond Island. Today this site is well-known to recreational boaters making a passage at the west end of the Manitoulin North Channel to cross the international border between the United States and Canada. It also is the location of a U.S. customs agent.

10. "… although it may appear *to be an exaggeration.*" Freiderich Munchausen (1707–97) was the name of a German raconteur, a Baron, who told preposterous stories about his adventures as a soldier and hunter. His name is now associated with any telling of exaggerated stories.

11. We have tried to research this reference to "cherries," but have failed to identify the fruit. At first we thought they might be sand cherries, high bush cranberries, or even elderberries, but none of these match Wingfield's comparison to English black cherries.

12. In this next section Wingfield seems to move between Drummond Island and his station at Wasaga, but his account is not always given in logical order. He has also omitted some events completely.

13. The Frolic in the Snow: This is the story of a simple expedition to secure provisions, on the hoof, and to give some of the men a break in the little village of Newmarket. It suddenly changed into a near tragedy due entirely to a sudden change in the weather. Only Wingfield's leadership abilities saved the men from death in the snow on a frozen river.

    This wasn't the first time weather had affected the outcome of a campaign, nor will it be the last. When Napoleon and the French Army met Wellington and the British Army at Waterloo, the weather was given much of the credit for the victory going to the British, thus affecting the history of all Europe and even the Canadas and the Americas.

    Wingfield was lax in not telling us enough details, for example the specific dates, and the number of men involved.

    In mid-December, he "and a Lieut. of Marines with a party of men" set out. They spent three days at Newmarket. Returning, he was delayed two days at Kempenfeldt. At Glengarry Landing he meets and presumably adds to his group, "a Mid. with a party of men and a bateau." The rain sets in "in torrents" changing to "snow, which fell in large flakes freezing hard at the same time."

    Now we have two lieutenants, a midshipman, and two parties of men, probably from twelve to fifteen in total. That number is only speculation. They have two bateaux, one large and one smaller, plus "four sheep, two large hogs and nine or ten small pigs."

    He keeps the lot disciplined, working together and as comfortable as possible. They persist for four or five days and nights in deep frost and heavy snowfall. Eventually, they reach the supply base known as the Establishment. The provisions, no longer on the hoof, are finally secured. Only one man loses his life, presumably from hypothermia. They arrive in time for Christmas dinner. The round trip was about ninety miles.

    We do not know how they were clothed, but it is reasonable to believe that they had winter issue and great coats. Possibly they had knitted hats and mitts, but this is speculation. They had no snowshoes!

14. This supply base was likely Schooner Town. An historic plaque can be found in the park at the southwest corner of River Road West and Oxbow Park Drive, Wasaga Beach, Ontario. The text reads:

The Nottawasaga River formed part of a transporta-tion link between Lake Ontario and the Upper Great Lakes which became a vitally important supply route to British Western posts during the War of 1812. The base of operations for the Royal Navy's vessels on Lake Huron was located here at the foot of naviga-tion on the River from 1815 to 1817. Buildings to house the base were erected in October 1815 by the ship's company of H.M. Schooner *Confiance*. Within two years orders were issued transferring the naval establishment to Penetanguishene, where superior anchorage was available and in late 1817 the naval base at Schooner Town was abandoned. In 1976 management of the site became the responsibility of Wasaga Beach Provincial Park.

15. Malgre: The direct translation from the French is "despite."

16. Ennui: The direct translation is "boredom."

17. The term *mould* is most often used in this context to describe a rich, organic type of soil.

18. Wingfield surely means May.

CHAPTER SIX:
Return to Kingston as Master of the *Beckwith* — And Home

1. These ships would have been the *New Orleans* and the *Chippewa*, which were never launched.

2. The matter of the "curious pistol": Wingfield recounts, "We were shown a curiosity by Captain Wolsey in the shape of a pistol barrel which dis-charged seven bullets successively." This device whetted our curiosity as well. Guns are not normally of interest to these authors, but we decided to try to find out more about this, and what, if anything developed from it. Wingfield gives us two clues: "pistol barrel" and "discharged seven bul-lets at the interval of a few seconds." But he was well-educated on the

subject and would not have deemed it a curiosity if he had seen the like previously.

A search through many library books on antique guns revealed, with some surprise, that there were many different kinds of weapons that had been developed down through the ages, using multiple barrels or with some sort of rotating cylinder mechanism. Multi-barrelled guns were old hat in 1816. They had been tested and used for centuries, but rarely by the military, basically because they were too heavy at the barrel end for convenience in loading or shooting. They were uncommon, yet not unknown, and both officers in Wingfield's account would likely have been up-to-date on developments in the weapons' field.

A seven-barrelled, revolving flintlock pistol made by John Twigg, London, in 1785, is described and illustrated in *Early Firearms of Great Britain and Ireland*, published by the Metropolitan Museum of Art, 1971. The same gun is addressed in *Handguns from Matchlock to Laser-sighted Weapon* by John Walter and John Carpenter. Newton Abbott, Devon, U.K: David and Charles Publishing, 1988.

It is unclear whether the cluster of barrels rotated automatically, as does the cartridge holder in a six-gun, or whether the barrels were fired in sequence and in situ. In some early models, the barrel cluster had to be rotated by hand between each shot. Although this style was manufactured in several European countries, no record of any American manufacturer was found.

The specimen mentioned may have been an earlier model, which later developed into the Colt revolver. As Samuel Colt of Connecticut was born in 1814, he had no hand in this gun, but neither was he the inventor of the common cowboy or police revolver with the rotating cylinder for projectiles. Although he is often given credit for the discovery, he improved the early designs, mass produced them, and popularized them. Thus, he is associated with the six-gun both in literature and in practice. Once the Colt revolver was accepted and cartridges came into use, multiple barrels were of little further interest, except in various machine guns. The cluster of multiple barrels, when viewed from the muzzle end, resembled a peppershaker, and took the name, common in early days, of "pepperbox."

Another book with illustrative details of a seven-barrelled pepperbox is *Small Arms* by A.J.R. Cormack, published by Profile Publications Ltd. of Windsor, Berkshire, England, in 1982. It also illustrates a single barrel pistol with a cartridge turret, but the book gives no maker, date, or history of this example.

Cormack does, however, give us a good explanation of the purpose of "arming the top." In his book he writes, "The British fighting on men-of-war at sea had the problem of dealing with the snipers in the fighting tops [a platform with safety rails around it, built onto the spars at the base of the topmast] of the enemy ships who were positioned to kill the enemy officers on deck. Lord Nelson was killed in this way. The problem of shooting one man with one shot from a swaying top position of a mast whilst he in turn swayed, called for the use of a spread of bullets. As the blunderbuss had not the range, a weapon invented by Captain John Wilson and manufactured by the famous gun-maker Henry Knock was adopted in 1780. This weapon is a magnificently constructed seven-barrelled flintlock, which although unwieldy, gave the marksman a chance of success if the flash of ignition did not set the rigging on fire." We have found no illustration, nor any further information regarding the Wilson invention. Our curiosity has not been appeased.

PART II: POSTSCRIPT TO THE JOURNAL

1. *Grunts* and *doughboys* are terms, apparently used in the Great War (1914–18), to describe the so-called dispensable, hard-working front line troops. The term *doughboys* may first have been associated with Horatio Nelson's sailors and Wellington's soldiers in Spain, who were both familiar with fried flour dumplings called doughboys.

PART III: THE BIOGRAPHY OF DAVID WINGFIELD

1. Cadet lines are those that are descended from other than the first-born; junior.

2. Many of the census records used or referred to in this section can be acquired online at www.GRO.gov.uk or through commercial sites such as www.Ancestry.com and similar sites.

3. From http://www.visionofbritain.org.uk, as posted by University of Portsmouth, United Kingdom, accessed on September 2, 2008.

4. The transcription of Moritz's work used by the University of Portsmouth was originally done by Project Gutenberg: http://www.gutenberg.org/wiki/Main_Page, accessed on September 2, 2008.

5. Information is taken from *A Naval Biographical Dictionary*, published in London by John Murray in 1849.

6. *Officers Services*, 4301 to 440, ADM 9/60/4363, GRO, at Kew, United Kingdom.

7. *Ibid.*

8. Wingfield Journal, original page 40.

9. See U.K. Department for Environment, Food and Rural Affairs. http://www.defra.gov.uk/wildlife-countryside/issues/landscap/aonbs.htm.

10. Information about the economy of the time, wages, and the cost of living has been extracted from the *Proceedings of the Old Bailey Criminal Court*, London; now listed online at www.oldbaileyonline.org.

11. Sourced from the *London Gazette,* gazettes-online.co.uk, Issue 20103 of May 27, 1842, Insolvent debtor, Dividend No. 44,202C.

12. *Ibid.*, Issue 21134 of September 10, 1850.

13. Sourced from: http://www.visionofbritain.org.uk created by the Great Britain Historical GIS Project (GIS stands for Geographical Information System), based in the Department of Geography of the University of Portsmouth.

14. *Ibid.*

15. *Ibid.*

16. *Ibid.*

17. J. Charles Cox's "Gloucestershire" (London, Methuen and Co., 1914): title page. Part of a series entitled "The Little Guides," one published per county.

18. *Ibid.* With additional information confirmed by Jocelyn Wingfield.

19. Church lore has been gleaned from a history pamphlet provided by Jocelyn Wingfield. It is excerpted from *Gloucestershire*, by J. Charles Cox. London: Methuen & Co. Ltd., 1914.

20. As noted in several places, much of the information about the early state of Gloucester has been gleaned from the prolific writings of John Marius Wilson, Imperial gazetteer of England and Wales (1870–72). His observations surely portray the character of the city, as David Wingfield would have seen it during his time in this area of the Shire. Sourced from: http://vision.edina.ac.uk created by the Great Britain Historical GIS Project (GIS stands for Geographical Information System), based in the Department of Geography of the University of Portsmouth, accessed on September 2, 2008.

21. For a comprehensive database of historical naval records, 1650–1850, the Internet site http:/www.sailingnavies.com is an excellent source. It contains dozens of links to outline lists and provides references to original source data. A valuable inventory included is P. Benyon's *Index of 19th Century Naval Vessels.*

22. Information is from Lyon, David and Rif Wingfield. *The Sail and Steam Navy List.* London: Chatham Publishing, 2004.

23. 1871 Census for Devon shows Henry E., single, age 21, as crew on the vessel *Tyrian*, as acting assistant engineer. The *Tyrian* was a sloop-rigged brig, in service of the coast guard at this time, following her use as a quarantine vessel. Previously, she was a 15-gun sloop-of-war fitted as a packet. For a comprehensive database of historical naval records, 1650–1850, the Internet site http://www.sailingnavies.com is an excellent source. It contains dozens of links to online lists and provides references to original source data. A valuable inventory included is P. Benyon's *Index of 19th Century Naval Vessels.*

    The 1881 Census for Devon shows Henry E. as a crewmember of the vessel *Audacious*. The ironclad battleship HMS *Audacious* was part of an experimental class of armoured battleships designed to expand on the success of HMS *Warrior*, built ten years before. The ships were intended to act as the frontline of the modern battle fleet, but being such a recent innovation, they were fraught with difficulties. *Audacious* was built at the Napier shipyards and cost £246,482 to complete. Launched in February 1869, she did not actually fire her guns in anger during her lengthy service life, which continued after her removal from frontline duties in 1902, by which time she was very obsolete. Information is from David Lyon and Rif Wingfield. *The Sail & Steam Navy List.* London: Chatham Publishing, 2004.

    Henry E. Wingfield's family is shown in the 1901 Census: Henry's age is corrected to read 51; wife is Jane, age 43; Gladys I., first daughter, age 12;

Edith M., second daughter, age 9; Dorothy S., third daughter, age 7. The family was prosperous enough to afford a servant, Ellen M. Norrish, age 36, listed as a cook and general domestic, from Plymouth, Devon.

24. Data from 1861 Census; probably spelled Arthur; possibly born Edward Arthur Wingfield, September 1851, Stroud, Gloucester; Records vol. 1: 455.

   It has been suggested that three additional birth certificates warrant further research: John Reinon Wingfield, b. Apr/June 1843, Stroud, Glos. [vol. 11:424]; James Wingfield, b. 09/1837, Gloucester. [vol. 11:233]; Edward Arthur Wingfield, b. 09/1851, Stroud, Glos. [vol. 11:455].

APPENDIX B: WINGFIELD FAMILY SOCIETY

1. The Wingfield Family Society provides access to DNA testing to confirm genetic family links.

2. The heraldic description is "Argent on a bend gules, cottised sable, three pairs of wings conjoined in lure of the field. Motto: Posse nolle nobile." The arms of this line were adopted since many United States members were descended from the line of Tickencote (Rutlandshire, near Stamford, Lincolnshire) — from Thomas Wingfield of York River (and of the Mattponi), Virginia (1664–1720).

   The arms of the Derbyshire Wingfields were: "Vert on a bend three crosses flory" (adorned with lilies of the valley). (British Library, *Ad. MS 6667*, p.605.) It is most intriguing that these arms are in the same format as those of the Wingfields of Suffolk — as indeed are the following:

   Wingfield of Corbridge, Northumberland: "Argent on a bend gules three pairs of wings argent between two bendulets sable."

   Wingfield (quartered by Rollestone of Watnoll or Watnoll Chaworth, Nottinghamshire): Vert on a bend argent three crosses patoncee sable. (*Visitation of Nottinghamshire, 1614).*

3. From Jocelyn Wingfield, *Virginia's True Founder, Edward Maria Wingfield and His Times* (Athens, GA: Wingfield Family Society, 1993. ISBN 0-937543-04-7; reprinted 2007 by Booksurge.com, LLC, North Charleston, SC: 2007, ISBN 1-419664-86-7 (hc) and ISBN-13: 978-1-419660-32-0 (pc).

4. From George E. Alexander, *Wingfield: Edwardian Gentleman.* Portsmouth, NH: Peter E. Randall, 13–21, 1986.

5. www.wingfieldfamilysociety.org; sub-section, Publications, "The Three Dozen Anecdotes" (a set of articles posted on the website by Jocelyn Wingfield) June 1993–May 1994.

APPENDIX D: GLOSSARY

1. From the *Doctrine of Naval Architecture*, Anthony Deane, 1670. Several modern transcriptions are available. This inventory is for a fourth-rate ship of the line.

2. *Officers Services*, 4301 to 4400, ADM/9/60/4363, GRO, Kew, U.K.

3. *Ibid.*

APPENDIX F: THE FRIENDS OF CABOT HEAD

1. From http://www.cabothead.ca/history/intro.html, accessed on October 13, 2008.

2. W.H. Smith, *Canada: Past, Present and Future, Being a Historical, Geographical, Geological and Statistical Account Of.* Vol. 1 (Toronto: Thomas Maclear, 1851): 56. The relevant passage reads:

> Along the coast from Cape Hurd, places of shelter are not so numerous as they are along the Manitoulin, and they are sometimes dangerous to approach. There are several good harbours at Cape Hurd, though it is to be apprehended, from the irregular and rocky character of the bottom, they can scarcely be called good anchorages; there is a harbour also, (called Wingfield's Basin, on Bayfield's Chart,) at Cabot's Head, but its value is much diminished by the existence of a shallow bar across its entrance, effectually preventing the admission of large vessels, and rendering it at times inaccessible to even boats and canoes, especially when the wind is from the northward and westward.

BIBLIOGRAPHY

Bamford, Don. *Freshwater Heritage: A History of Sail on the Great Lakes, 1670–1918.* Toronto: Natural Heritage Books, A Member of the Dundurn Group, 2007.

Barry, James. *The Battle of Lake Erie, September 1813: The Naval Battle That Decided a U.S. Boundary.* New York: Franklin Watts Inc., 1970.

Berton, Pierre. *Flames Across the Border, 1813–1814.* Toronto: McClelland & Stewart, 1981.

Bigsby, Dr. John J. *The Shoe and Canoe.* London: Chapman and Hall, 1850.

Cook, Samuel F. *Drummond Island: The Story of the British Occupation 1815–1828.* Lansing, MI: self-published, 1896.

Coombs, Howard G. *The Search for Certainty: Sackets Harbour: May 28/29, 1813.* Kingston, ON: Queen's University, 2003.

Cooper, J. Fennimore. *Ned Myers; or, A Life Before the Mast.* Annapolis, MD: Naval Institute Press, 1989.

Cruikshank, Lieutenant-Colonel E. "An Episode in the War of 1812: The Story of the Schooner, *Nancy.*" Ontario Historical Society, in *Papers and Records of the Ontario Historical Society.* vol. 9, 1910.

Douglas, W.A.B. "Worsley, Miller" in *Dictionary of Canadian Biography.* vol. 6, Toronto: University of Toronto Press, 1986.

Drury, E.C. *All for a Beaver Hat: A History of Early Simcoe County.* Toronto: The Ryerson Press, 1959.

Dunlop, William. *Recollections of the War of 1812.* Toronto: Historical Publishing Co., 1908.

Finch, Roy G. *The Story of the New York State Canals.* Albany, NY: J.B. Lyon Co., 1925.

Gough, Barry. *Through Water, Ice and Fire: Schooner* Nancy *in the War of 1812.* Toronto: The Dundurn Group, 2006.

_____. *Fighting Sail on Lake Huron and Georgian Bay: The War of 1812 and Its Aftermath.* Annapolis, MD: Naval Institute Press; St. Catharines, ON: Vanwell Publishing, 2002.

Graves, Donald. *Merry Hearts Make Light Days.* Ottawa, ON: Carleton University Press, 1994.

Hough, Franklin B. *History of Jefferson County in the State of New York from the Earliest Period to the Present Time.* Albany, NY: Joel Munsell, also Watertown, NY: Sterling & Riddell. 1854.

Hunter, Andrew F. *A History of Simcoe County.* Simcoe County, ON: Oro Township History Committee and Knox Presbyterian Church, 1986.

Laidler, George. "The Nottawasaga Passage. Simcoe County, Ontario." Ontario Historical Society, in *Papers and Records of the Ontario Historical Society*, vol. 35, 1943.

Landon, Fred. *Lake Huron*. New York: The Bobbs Merrill Company, 1944.

Malcomson, Robert. *Lords of the Lake: The Naval War on Lake Ontario, 1812–14*. Toronto: Robin Brass Studio. 1998.

_____. *Sailors of 1812: Memoirs and Letters of Naval Officers on Lake Ontario*. Youngstown, NY: Old Fort Niagara Association, Inc., 1997.

_____. *H.M.S. Detroit: The Battle for Lake Erie*. St. Catharines, ON: Vanwell Publishing, 1990.

_____. "What Really Happened? De-bunking the Burlington Bay Sandbar Legend." The War of 1812 website, http://www.warof1812.ca.

_____. "The Capture of the Schooner *Julia/Confiance*" in the *American Neptune*, vol. 51, no. 2 (Spring 1991): 83–90.

Malcomson, Tom. "September 1813: The Decidedly Indecisive Engagements Between Chauncey and Yeo." Vermilion, OH: The Great Lakes Historical Society, in *Inland Seas*, vol. 47 (1991): 299–313.

Moodie, Susanna. *Roughing It in the Bush: or, Life in Canada*. First edition edited by Carl Ballstadt. First published in 1852. Reprinted, Don Mills, ON: Oxford University Press, 1988.

Reid, Major Patrick and Maurice Michael. *Prisoner of War*. New York: Beaufort Book Publishers, 1984.

Rosenberg, Max. *The Building of Perry's Fleet on Lake Erie, 1812–1813*. Harrisburg, PA: Pennsylvania Historical and Museums Commission, 1950.

Sheppard, George. *Plunder, Profit and Paroles: A Social History of the War of 1812 in Upper Canada*. Montreal & Kingston: McGill-Queen's University Press, 1994.

Snider, C.H.J., Editor. *Leaves from the War Log of the Nancy, 1813*. Toronto: Rous and Mann Co. Ltd., 1936.

Suthern, Victor. *The War of 1812*. Toronto: McClelland & Stewart, 1999.

Twigg, John. *Early Firearms of Great Britain and Ireland*. New York: Metropolitan Museum of Art, 1971.

Walker, John and John Carpenter. *Handguns from Matchlock to Laser-sighted Weapon*. Newton Abbot, England: David and Charles Publishing, Devon, U.K., 1988.

Wilder, Patrick A. *The Battle of Sackett's Harbor 1813*. Baltimore, MD: The Nautical and Aviation Publishing Company of America, Inc., 1994.

LIST OF COLOUR PLATES

INDEX

ABOUT THE AUTHORS

DON BAMFORD graduated from the University of Toronto in 1942 as an electrical engineer and worked for several years in the field of electronic devices for the military, atomic energy, medical, and hospital applications. After a stint with the manufacture of small sailboats, he joined the Ontario government as an industrial consultant specializing in production efficiency and export marketing.

He retired in 1984 and immediately took up long-distance sailing. Don sailed his yacht, *Foudroyant*, into Lake Superior, which was the only one of the Great Lakes he had not previously sailed on, and then pointed his bow to Florida, the Bahamas, and other Caribbean Islands. In 1986, he sailed across the Atlantic from St. Petersburg, Florida, to the Hebrides and continued to sail European waters with his wife and friends. His wanderings took him from northern Norway, south to Tunisia, from Ireland to Cyprus — altogether covering about 25,000 miles, including every European country with a freshwater coastline except Albania. In 2000, family health problems brought an end to the sailing activities. Don sold his yacht in Devon, England, and returned to Canada.

In the early 1970s, when living and working in Chicago, Don took an interest in early sailing on the Great Lakes and researched the subject extensively, visiting many museums and historical societies in America and Europe. He collaborated with his current co-author to complete the 2007 publication of *Freshwater Heritage: A History of Sail on the Great Lakes, 1670–1918*, his third book. The current effort, to document an account of the life and travels of Lieutenant David Wingfield, has been in the works since 1972. Also, Don has had over a hundred articles on sailing and history published in magazines in Canada, the United States, and the United Kingdom. It is noteworthy that Don has sailed his own boat, the *Foudroyant*, into every harbour and waterway travelled by Wingfield, as mentioned in his diary, with the exception of the Nottawasaga River, where Bamford was born and raised during his early years.

Don currently lives in London, Ontario.

PAUL CARROLL, a lifelong teacher and former school board administrator, is a marine heritage enthusiast, amateur writer, and fledgling watercolour artist, who grew up as a "wharf rat." He had the privilege of gamming with the last of the "old salts" from Goderich Harbour. His first part-time job was working on the fishing tug *Larry John* operated by Ab Leonard and his wife Florence, who ran the Leonard Fisheries for a full generation. His interest in the waterfront has persisted. As a member of town council and reeve for the Town of Goderich in the early 1970s, he brought forward the first modern-day Waterfront Development Plan.

He has published a comprehensive set of historic notes dealing with marine heritage along the shores of Huron County for the Huron County Historical Society, where he is a life member. Paul has acted as editor for several annual editions of similar historic notes. He has published numerous articles on local history in Huron County and regional publications, and maintains a website www.shipwreck-wexford.ca that documents the history and loss of the packet freighter *Wexford* in the Great Storm of 1913. Paul was involved in the August 2000 sidescan sonar search for the long-missing shipwreck, the *Wexford*. He is also a member ex-officio of the Port of Goderich Marine Heritage Committee. His own book-in-the-works will comprise a detailed historical record of the *Wexford*, her history and travels, her captains and crew, and the infamous final voyage of November 1913.

Paul provided editorial and research support for Robert C. Lee for the 2004 publication of *The Canada Company and the Huron Tract, 1826–1853* and undertook the same type of support for Don Bamford in his preparation of the *Freshwater Heritage* volume mentioned above. His role in collaboration with Don Bamford on the David Wingfield memoirs has been more extensive, providing technical research and editing support, along with the preparation of several of the main components for the new book.

Paul currently lives south of Goderich with his wife, Mary, with whom he cruises on their sailboat *SolSean*, during the winter months in Florida, the Bahamas, the Yucatan Peninsula, Guatemala, and Honduras.

BY THE SAME AUTHOR

FRESHWATER HERITAGE
978-1-89704-520-6 $34.95

Freshwater Heritage: A History of Sail on the Great Lakes, 1670–1918
represents the culmination of a lifelong passion for sailing and for
the history of sail as it applies to Canada. Author, sailor, boat builder
Don Bamford takes us deep into the psyche of sailing as it applies to
historical events on the Great Lakes and to stories of the people and
places there at the time.

OF RELATED INTEREST

THE WAR OF 1812
The War that Both Sides Won
Wesley B. Turner
978-1-55002-336-7 $16.99

Tragedy and farce, bravery and cowardice, intelligence and foolishness,
sense and nonsense — all these contradictions and more characterized
the War of 1812. The real significance of the series of skirmishes that
collectively made up the war between 1812 and 1814 is the enormous
impact they have had on Canadian and American views of themselves
and of each other.

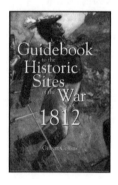

GUIDEBOOK TO THE HISTORIC SITES OF THE WAR OF 1812
Second Edition Revised and Updated
Gilbert Collins
978-1-55002-626-9 $24.99

There have been guidebooks to military sites before, but no other book
has covered the War of 1812 in its entirety. This well-illustrated updated
edition covers more than 400 historic sites of the War of 1812, both
well-known and obscure, in both Canada and the United States.

Available at your favourite bookseller.

www.dundurn.com